SCIENCE, TECHNOLOGY AND ENVIRONMENTAL MANAGEMENT

Science, Technology and Environmental Management

edited by
Richard D. HEY

and
Trevor D. DAVIES

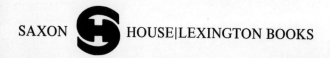

SAXON HOUSE|LEXINGTON BOOKS

Published by

SAXON HOUSE, D. C. Heath Ltd.
Westmead, Farnborough, Hants., England

Jointly with

LEXINGTON BOOKS, D. C. Heath & Co.
Lexington, Mass. USA

ISBN 0 347 01087 3
Library of Congress Catalog Card Number 75–3836

Printed in Great Britain
by Unwin Brothers Limited
The Gresham Press, Old Woking, Surrey
A member of the Staples Printing Group

Contents

List of Tables

List of figures

Foreword

In recent years the term "environment" has become the symbol of a 'cause' almost akin to the word "freedom". It has also come to signify a variety of different things. To some it means the protection of wild fauna and flora, to others the correction and prevention of pollution, to others again the need to obstruct any change in the landscape; it is also taken to imply the need to conserve countryside which is presumed to be natural, but which all too often has already been transformed by man. No word has caught on so fast. It has triggered useful public and governmental action at the same time as it has provoked well-intentioned, if sometimes ignorant, protests against the hard realities of a world in which none of us can avoid living. Some see the term as emphasising the possibility that man is fast exhausting the physical resources on which our survival depends. Others see death and destruction on our doorsteps if nuclear power stations are built in order to satisfy part of our need for the energy which binds together our social fabric, and a similar fate from the continued application of modern agricultural technologies. Environment is something for which the good will stand up and fight and to which the bad people who run our lives are always opposed.

If we exclude the emotive reactions which it evokes, environment implies the whole social and physical matrix of human existence, that is to say, the actual world in which we build our homes, buy our food, move around, look at television and plan our lives. It is therefore as much a political as a physical concept. It is in that sense that the term is the subject of this book which deals with some of the problems that relate to an environment which has to be managed as well as possible in order to accommodate our multiplying millions. That is where the academically trained person comes in. One cannot plan to use the resources at our disposal wisely unless we have a fair idea of their nature and quantity. We have to have a knowledge of developed and potential technologies which man can use within the constraints of a rational economic and political system. No single environmental specialist could deal with all the problems which are entailed in planning the use of the land, rivers and seas around us. No single authority could decree which way our resources should be used to best advantage. We do not know enough to be sure that the planning which is decreed for today will be right for tomorrow.

Research is wanted in any number of directions. The editors believe that this book indicates some of the issues in environmental management where scientists and technologists can usefully combine forces not only in research but also in helping those whose responsibility it is to reach wise decisions in the management of the real environment with which the planner has to deal.

S.Zuckerman,
March 1975

Preface

Public concern for the environment has, in recent years, focused attention on the protection and maintenance of environmental quality. This book, which is the outgrowth of a symposium on 'Applied Environmental Science' held at the 1974 Annual Conference of the Institute of British Geographers, is concerned with the contribution of scientists and technologists in environmental management and decision-making processes.

In the preparation of this volume the editors would like to acknowledge the co-operation received from the contributors, without which progress would have been impossible. For domestic facilities we should like to thank the staff of the School of Environmental Sciences, University of East Anglia, especially Miss Julie Riddock and Miss Erica Wathen for promptly and efficiently dealing with our typing requirements, and Mr David Mew and Mr Paul Willis for cartographic assistance. Last, but by no means least, we are indebted to the Council of the Institute of British Geographers for providing the forum for the original symposium.

On behalf of the authors the editors would like to thank the following individuals and bodies: Dr J. Tivy and the Countryside Commission for Scotland (Fig. 2.1), (Chapter 2); the Director of the Countryside Commission for permission to publish (although the views expressed are not necessarily those of the Commission), and Oliver Maurice of the National Trust for providing the information for Fig. 3.1, Chapter 3); Lymington Borough Council and the Department of the Environment for assistance in providing information (Chapter 5); Wye River Authority, Severn River Authority, Department of Agriculture, Fisheries and Food for Scotland, Tweed River Purification Board, and the Water Resources Board for the provision of data (Chapter 7); the Director of the Water Resources Board for permission to publish (Chapter 8); J.B. Thornes for data and King's College, University of London for support (Chapter 10); Ministry of Agriculture, Fisheries and Food, and Welland and Nene River Authority for data and the *Journal of Environmental Management* (Figs. 11.1, 11.3 to 11.5 and 11.9 to 11.11), (Chapter 11); the School of Botany, Cambridge for the provision of facilities (Chapter 12); R.C. Chadwick, M.J. Spiers, I.C. Cox for experimental help (Chapter 13); A. Bleasdale, M.C. Jackson, A.F. Jenkinson, J.F. Keers, R. Murray for helpful suggestions (Chapter 17); members of the East African Rainfall Project for contributions and the Transport and Road Research Laboratory for permission to publish (Chapter 19); Huntings Survey Ltd and Professor J. K. St Joseph for data and the Agricultural Development and Advisory Service, Cambridge for experimental help (Chapter 20); and M. McGovern and J.B. Williams for data (Chapter 21).

1 The Role of Science and Technology in Environmental Management

Dr T.D. DAVIES and Dr R.D. HEY

Recent years have witnessed a plethora of emotive publications about environmental issues. Some of these maintain the great Malthusian tradition by preaching environmental decay and doom. Others, particularly those emanating from the conservation lobby, indicate considerable concern for certain threatened biological species whilst apparently ignoring the claims of *Homo sapiens*.

The environmental issues which provoke such reactions are normally the by-products of economic growth. For example resource exploitation can result in spoliation and dereliction, waste disposal in pollution, and urban renewal in the destruction of established communities.[1] Inevitably such developments can have a deleterious effect on physical and mental health and sensory and participatory pleasures.

Conflicts between economic growth and environmental deterioration are difficult to rationalise because they both have a profound effect on our standard and quality of life.[2] Attempts to resolve them are made extremely difficult by the dichotomy which often exists between national and local interest; the former being predominantly concerned with increasing economic prosperity and the latter with the conservation of local environmental quality. Clearly fundamental decisions regarding the management of the environment should not be made on the basis of emotional feeling. Instead all the appropriate evidence should be carefully weighed so that the final decision has minimum possible impact on the environmental and sociopolitical system.

One of the earliest interpretations of the role of science, technology and social science in decision-making and management processes was made by Kates in 1969.[3] He recognised that there were three basic elements in comprehensive environmental planning: environmental science disciplines (public health, sanitary engineering, ecology and biomedical engineering): environmental design disciplines (architecture, planning): social and behavioural sciences (anthropology, economics, political science, geography, psychology and sociology). The behavioural and social sciences were considered to be the bridge linking environmental science and design because they are in the best position to assess public opinion and also test its reaction to management decisions. Whilst advocating the merits of behavioural and social scientists in this particular role he recognised their present failure to become significantly involved in this field. A new breed of 'super planner' was required, one who could appreciate all the scientific and technological evidence, relate this to the general public, assess reactions and produce acceptable management decisions.

This conceptual framework for analysing the interactions between man and his environments can be modified in the light of advances made within the last five years. In the United Kingdom environmental science is generally interpreted as the study of the natural physical environment and man's relation with it. Not only is it concerned with establishing the principles underlying natural processes and their interaction with man but also the application of these principles for the benefit of society. The body of information created in this manner enables the formulation and implementation of management policies and the design of political and legal institutions for the protection of the environment. Implicit in this definition is the need for a multidisciplinary approach embracing such traditional disciplines as chemistry, physics, biology, medicine, engineering, geology, geography, planning, economics, sociology and law. Each discipline has a traditional area of competence and approach to the environment and each has the ability to deal with single-purpose environmental problems. As soon as interaction and feedback loops begin to operate between different parts of the environmental system, decisions based on expertise from one particular discipline can at best be dangerous and at worst hazardous.

Unfortunately a tendency has developed over the last five years for planners, sociologists and economists to assume the mantle of environmental managers, and thereby they have relegated the role of science and technology to that of a service facility. This omission is undesirable because management decisions have repercussions and feedback on the physical environment as well as on society. To achieve acceptable management decisions it is imperative that all the necessary skills are integrated in the management unit.[4] Decisions would then by made by a competent team rather than by an individual 'super planner'. It is envisaged that such a team would include scientists and technologists as well as planners, sociologists and economists.

Some of the issues involved in the management of the environment, and

2

the role to be played by the scientist and technologist, are well illustrated in atmospheric management strategies.

Many scientists see atmospheric pollution as a socio-economic problem rather than a technological one. Strict control of many pollutants is technologically feasible, but at an unacceptable economic cost to the community. Developing technology not only creates new pollution problems, but also often reduces the economic cost of pollution control. Perception studies show that the section of the community experiencing the higher pollution concentrations is often less aware than other groups of the existence of any problem.[5] Such perception inequalities may present difficulties for the allocation of resources for atmospheric pollution control. Control priorities should be based on the most objective method of assessment possible.

The difficulties of atmospheric pollution control are often considerable. In the atmosphere the pollutant is not so spatially restricted as in a river, where man can make the decision to use the water as a pollution transportation medium and clean it up downstream as he requires the water. Dispersion rates in the oceans are slower than in the atmosphere, and although some severe local problems can exist, sea water has ample opportunity to render (some) pollutants less harmful.

The rash of pollution legislation over the last decade stems from the philosophy that the atmosphere fulfils two main functions for man. The main function is to sustain life. The secondary function is to sustain economic life in the role of effluent receptacle. Some groups felt that there was a real danger of the secondary function reducing the efficiency of the primary function. Most other animal species are more sensitive than man to atmospheric pollution. For them the atmosphere has one function only. In the event of pollution severely depleting a species, it will be hard to justify the subjective muddled thinking which has characterised many control strategies in the past. Scientific and objective assessments are required.

Atmospheric pollution legislation originated mainly as a reaction to 'disasters' where strong action was publicly demanded to prevent repetitions. The atmosphere is a relatively efficient waste disposal system; as such its management should be based on objective assessments, since it makes an important economic contribution to technological processes. Scientific investigation is needed to determine present atmospheric pollutant pathways and to assess the capacity of the atmosphere, on local and regional scales, to process pollutants. Ideally, an assessment of the evidence should be free of economic restrictions.

Another argument for the continuing participation of science in

3

atmospheric pollution control procedures, even where rigid control now exists, is that presently accepted standards may require modification. Further study may lead either to higher control or to a relaxation where scientific research reveals that controls were unrealistically severe because of the original public outcry. Many claims are exaggerated and are based on unreliable or circumstantial evidence in the absence of reliable data.

It has been suggested that the adoption of specific standards could lead to real economic differentials, since an industry in one country (or even in part of a country) could be more heavily penalised than the same industry in another country (or another part of the same country).[6] A reliable body of information from well-designed scientific investigations, and so acceptable to the international community, should preclude such difficulties. Sometimes there are very good reasons why standards should be different in different areas because of local topography and meteorology. It is difficult for laymen to understand why standards should vary; one of the responsibilities of scientists must be to provide intelligible and cogent reasons for such differences.

In countries where ambient air quality standards have been adopted, scientists and technologists are needed to monitor atmospheric pollutant concentrations in order to ensure implementation of control programmes, whatever the method of enforcement. The implemented standards should be determined with the fullest information, since polluters regard pollution concentrations up to the standard to be justified. Since scientists have (or are supposed to have) determined the standard in the first place, they will soon be discredited if they suggest changes.

In the UK some of the problems are avoided by the adoption of the 'best practicable means' concept. The fundamental rationale is that atmospheric pollution should be kept as low as possible, taking economic, social and technical factors into account. Implicit in the concept is the idea that revision of once-implemented standards will be difficult. The flexible nature of this control method means that continued scientific imput performs a valuable function. Control should not be modified on the basis of demand, technological advance or economic shift only. Increased scientific knowledge, in terms of dosage-response studies and dispersal mechanisms, should also be considered. Sulphur dioxide is a case where further investigation could lead to a revision of control policy. Most people have no 'perception' of this pollutant and so public opinion, except where it has been fostered by news media, cannot be regarded as one of the inputs into the decision-making process. It is economically undesirable to reduce sulphur dioxide emission considerably with present technology. High stacks have eliminated the local problems caused by sulphur dioxide pollution from large sources. Claims of damage in other countries from sulphur dioxide emitted in the UK highlight the need to examine the effects of high-level emission of the gas into the atmosphere. Researchers are examining the long-distance transport, the atmospheric chemistry and the life cycle of sulphur in the atmosphere. Such studies should show whether claims of remote damage can be sustained or refuted, and may conceivably lead to changes in the method of control in the UK.

Another method of control, regarded as a temporary measure only, is the implementation of pollution-forecasting systems. Many problems exist in the execution of action to be taken after the prediction of a pollution episode. But whatever is the nature of implementation problems, scientific imput is necessary to make the prediction in the first place.

Scientists have a real and valuable role to play in the management of the atmospheric environment both in terms of providing the original evidence for control programmes, and in the continuing process of implementation and possible modification. The contribution of the scientist and technologist is no less important in the management of other environmental resources. Too many management strategies have been stimulated by, and based on, emotional and irrational arguments in the absence of much of the necessary scientific framework. Scientists should not be satisfied to provide the basic data and leave the manipulation of the decision-making process to behavioural and environmental design scientists. Decision-makers sometimes experience difficulty in interpreting scientific information and understanding its implications. Scientists should be at hand to state their case and not rely on their data to do it for them.

In this book a number of problem areas in environmental management have been defined, and these are illustrative of the various roles scientists and technologists can play in the decision-making process.

Maintenance of acceptable environmental standards can only be achieved through an understanding of environmental and socio-economic processes and responses. Problems can then be identified, implications assessed and control strategies formulated.

Natural processes, such as floods and storm surges, are often responsible for catastrophic environmental modification, and it is normally a political expedient to provide some degree of protection against such hazards. Provided we have a basic understanding of these processes protection measures can be designed which are in harmony with the landscape and which offer more permanent protection. With respect to coast defence this could result in the use of sand injection techniques rather than sea walls, groynes and revetments (Part II). Equally for river channels the

5

appreciation of the factors controlling channel stability could obviate the need for expensive retraining works such as channel straightening (Part IV).

Man's influence can also have considerable impact on the environment although on occasions this is more difficult to detect. Indeed it is often the effects of change which help to establish causality, this being the approach that led to the banning of DDT. Constant vigilance and an appreciation of possible consequences is vital if such challenges are to be met. Original work of this nature, exemplified by the study of atmospheric pollution in rural areas (Part VII), may appear to be rather academic. However, this offers a classic opportunity to study the travel and deposition of pollutants; information which is fundamental for the formulation and modification of control strategies. Similarly study of the causes and consequences of long-term changes in water quality in rural areas is vital if public water supplies are to be protected (Part VI).

Once basic environmental processes have been established control strategies or solutions can be presented. In recreation site management both approaches are advocated; the former to prevent unacceptable deterioration through over-use and the later to regenerate areas which have previously suffered over-use (Part II). On occasions control or design decisions may have to be taken in the absence of basic information about environmental processes. For example, most urban drainage systems have been designed without prior investigation of urban storm rainfall. Current research will enable improved design techniques to be established (Part VIII).

Resource management has also a significant influence on environmental quality. Ineffective use of resources is not only economically undesirable but it may also give rise to unnecessary impact on the environment. Basic scientific research can often help to optimise resource development either through detailed work on physical processes, as in the case of soil water budgets and plant growth relationships (Part IX), or by the development of simulation techniques in the planning and control of water resource systems (Part V).

References

[1] Detwyler, T.R. (ed.), Man's impact on the environment, (McGraw-Hill, New York 1972).

[2] Barkley, P.W. and Seckler, D.W., Economic growth and environmental decay: the solution becomes the problem (Harcourt Brace Jovanovich, New York 1972).

[3] Kates, R., Comprehensive environmental planning in M.M. Hufschmidt (ed.), Regional planning: challenge and prospects (Praeger, New York 1969).

[4] Kneese, A.V. and Bower, B.T. (eds), Environmental quality analysis (Johns Hopkins Press, 1972).

[5] Burton, I., Billingsley, D., Blacksell, M., Chapman, V., Foster, L., Kirkby, A. and Wall, G., Behavioural correlates and policy implications of the perception of air pollution (International Geophysical Union, 22nd International Congress, July 1972).

[6] Scorer, R.S., Pollution in the air (Routledge and Kegan Paul, London 1973).

2 Carrying Capacity and Ecological Research

Dr J.P. BARKHAM

2.1 Introduction

Tivy[1] summarises in a succinct manner the work carried out in the United States on the concept and determination of the carrying capacity of recreational land. It is clear from her review and from other work on this side of the Atlantic[2, 3] that much space and intellectual energy has been given to defining the problem, to distinguishing between various sorts of carrying capacity, and to translating ideas, ideals and quantitative measurements into practical management strategies. In addition, Bayfield[4] has reviewed the problems and progress in site management research.

This chapter is primarily concerned with the contribution of the ecologist in this field but it is probably wise to repeat and consider briefly some basic definitions to which Tivy[1] has drawn attention. Wagar,[5] in a paper now regarded as an early classic, defined recreational carrying capacity as, 'the level of recreational use an area can withstand while providing a sustained quality of recreation'. Before a figure can be ascribed to this level further clarification is required. Firstly, it assumes some particular recreational activity as a constant and, unless management ensures that the latter is kept constant, any figure given to him will not prove very useful. Secondly, the definition requires some measure of the variable 'recreation use' which Chubb and Ashton[6] recommend should be expressed in terms of 'user-unit use-periods'. Thirdly, some measure must be made of what the area can withstand in terms of user-unit use-periods for the particular recreational activity concerned. It is in the latter sphere that the ecologist is probably most useful. Unfortunately we have often neglected the actions of pedological and geomorphological processes in recreational sites. Their influence can be significant in areas which are heavily used, have steep slopes, or a sandy substrate.

A further distinction has been made between 'spatial capacity' and 'carrying capacity' by Chubb and Ashton[6] (Fig. 2.1). However, this distinction is too fine to be useful, especially when we find 'daily spatial capacity' to be exactly equivalent to 'daily carrying capacity' according to the way in which these figures are derived. This perhaps exemplifies a trend, noticeable in this field, of an obsession with defining terms. It is obviously important for each of us to know what the other is talking about, but there is some danger of anarchy, and more of sterile directions developing from such work.

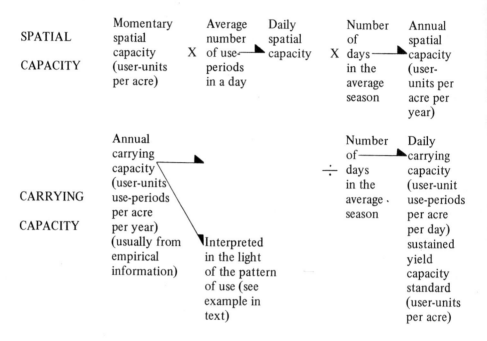

Fig. 2.1   Interrelationship between spatial and carrying capacity definitions (Chubb and Ashton[12] from Tivy[22])

The ecologist should first determine from the recreationist as clear a statement as possible of desirable aims including some idea of 'sustained quality of recreation'. Secondly, alongside other environmental scientists, the ecologist should seek to understand the patterns, processes and mechanisms which are characteristic of and operate in the natural environment of a recreation area. This may often, of necessity, include measurements of people,[7] especially where such information is not available from other sources. It will certainly include attempts to determine the exact relationship between people, including their artifacts, and their impact on plants, animals and the environment. In the case of walkers, for instance, measures of weight, horizontal and vertical pressures of feet, their variation in space and time, and their variation according to different forms of footwear are required.

2.2 Review of recent studies

The literature up to 1972 has been comprehensively reviewed by Speight,[8] so the need is only to highlight and comment upon certain of the major trends. Early studies were mostly concerned with primary and obviously necessary qualitative descriptions.[9] This is obviously a necessary first step and, indeed, later work has been hampered by the insufficiency of basic descriptive data in the literature upon which to base testable hypotheses. It is therefore hardly surprising that even in recent years workers in the field have had to devote considerable time and energy to basic descriptions. [10, 11]

The second necessary step is to relate effects quantitatively to recreational pressure in field sites, and over the last ten years there has been an increasing amount of work in this area. [12, 13] At the same time it has of course been increasingly necessary to separate the direct effects of recreational impact from the indirect effects and other unrelated factors causing ecological variation. The technique of partial correlation has been used successfully to distinguish between these different effects,[7] but the multivariate recreation ecology system is not easily subject to this type of analysis for several reasons. The most significant of these is the type of data, often obtained from interdisciplinary research, which can be incompatible due to the measurements being made on nominal, ordinal or interval scales. Coupled with this are the difficulties associated with spot or short-term measurements, and the difficulties experienced by any scientist who has to work outside his normal area of competence to obtain the data he requires. Thus, whereas soil variation, eutrophication and compaction have been quite well worked by ecologists, [11, 14, 15] slope processes in association with trampling and the mechanics of wear and tear have not. Similarly the field has been quick to attract plant ecologists, presumably due to the obvious visual impact of damage, but slow in attracting animal ecologists so that studies of disturbance of and changes in large animal [16] and invertebrate [11, 17] populations are few.

A further problem of field measurement is the inevitable time-lag between recreation and deterioration which, conversely, means that the situation observed today is the cumulative result of many years of pressure. The problem is analogous to that experienced in many other ecological field studies where attempts at elucidating present-day inter-relationships are not always successful.

There have been two responses to this problem: the setting up of long-term monitoring programmes, [18] and the development of field and laboratory experimentation. [14] The latter provides the third essential step

11

in the development of the subject. Experimental results can be used to erect hypotheses to be tested in field situations. Because of the power of experimental method it might reasonably be thought that this would have initially been the more profitable approach to an understanding of the subject rather than via a descriptive approach.

In all these essentially fundamental studies the role of sophisticated analytical procedures in analysing multivariate data is becoming increasingly evident. However, in most other ecological situations, relationships in this field are often non-linear and concern non-normal data with autocorrelation. Therefore the results of statistical manipulation must be regarded with caution. [19, 20, 21]

Statistical difficulties may delay the development of the fourth step — the production of a solid body of predictive data derived and presented in numerical form. Only the first very tentative steps have been taken in this direction. [12]

Lastly, work can be based on reinstatement, with observations being made on the recovery and recolonisation of damaged sites. Certain situations have already caused particular management concern such as new, unstable roadside embankments and cuttings, dunes and ski slopes, picnic sites and country parks. However, work giving details of reinstatement practices and their relative success is now being published.[18, 22, 23, 24]

2.3   Problems associated with ecological studies of carrying capacity

It is clear from this review that the notion of ecological carrying capacity has rarely, if ever, been explicit, although qualitative value judgments may have been implicit, in the minds of individual research workers. Ecologists obviously have not found the idea helpful in their research despite the apparent attractiveness of it to the countryside manager. As Brotherton[3] says, 'To argue the potential value of producing capacity figures for various situations is easy; actually to produce them is another matter altogether and one fraught with untold difficulties.' Why is this so?

Because we are not dealing with a genetically uniform human population all of the same age whose leisure time occurs on a flat plain at constant time intervals at the same density under the same weather conditions amongst homogeneous vegetation, it is extremely unlikely that 'ecological capacity' is anything other than a continuous variable, and as such is very difficult to measure. This suggests the ecological capacity is probably not an ecological problem at all. As Brotherton[3] suggests: 'In general terms we can say that acceptable ecological change on recreation areas is that which does not significantly detract from the visitors' enjoyment.' The converse of this statement is that ecological capacity can only be defined in terms of the perception of individual recreationists. The social scientist, or the manager, must be the one who attempts to describe the perception of the aggregate population of recreationists; and if he is bold he may attempt to calculate a mean value, an optimum 'aggregate satisfaction', as Brotherton[3] has suggested. Whether it is he or the ecologist who then applies ecological data to this figure in order to assist in future site management is not a matter of importance.

It is important that the scientific work of the ecologist should not be hamstrung by a concept which is the product of highly volatile value judgments. If the manager needs a figure for ecological capacity he must produce it himself or with the aid of an expert in perception. The question for the ecologist then becomes much clearer: how should this area be managed in terms of a specific recreation input and to prevent unacceptable ecological change which has already been defined?

A general model might usefully be constructed round a system that involves:

(a)   ecological responses — what are the results of recreational use?
(b)   mechanisms — how are these responses produced?
(c)   prediction — how will the system behave in the future?

2.4   Current research needs

The results of ecologists' work in prediction and reinstatement are of most interest to the recreation manager. Whereas qualitative judgments as to what is going to happen and how best to cope with it are fairly easily made by an observant layman, more useful quantitative information, precise in spatial and temporal terms, should be provided. There is undoubtedly a need in management for numerical prediction of future site quality, predictions expressed in terms of probabilities and presumably based on stochastic models in the first instance.

Work is perhaps most urgently needed under the heading of mechanisms because explanation and adequate numerical prediction are dependent upon understanding the causes of deterioration and the mechanics of the process. Explanation requires more than simple correlation of suspected causal factors with organism responses, measured in the field. To reach a satisfactory level of explanation experiments to test hypotheses are required in both laboratory and field situations.

It is clear that the range of responses likely in any given recreational situation is such that studies may continue more or less indefinitely. Such descriptive data are always useful, particularly now for management purposes in specific areas and for constructing predictive models in general. In some cases, particularly with regard to animal responses where observation and measurement may often be difficult, there is an urgent need for information. Perhaps a data bank would help to centralise the pool of unpublished material in this area.

This chapter embraces the implicit assumption that the ecologist is not the manager. In some cases he may be, for example in the case of the UK Nature Conservancy Council. The manager will have different priorities and these have been discussed by Bayfield[4] and will be amplified in the following chapter.

2.5   Conclusions

Carrying capacity is a notion of little direct use to the research ecologist and, in consequence, it has made little impact on the firm or direction of ecological research. However, it may help recreational land managers to ask ecologists specific and answerable questions in the future.

In contrast recreation ecology research holds much more promise. Although it is recognised that descriptive response data will always be of value the subject will only gain scientific acceptance provided it concentrates on the study of mechanisms and processes and the development of numerical prediction models.

References

[1] Tivy, J., The Concept and Determination of Carrying Capacity of Recreational Land in the USA: a Review (Countryside Commission for Scotland Occasional paper No. 3, Perth 1973).
[2] Barkham, J.P., Recreational carrying capacity: a problem of perception (Area 5 [3], 1973).
[3] Brotherton, D.I., The concept of carrying capacity of countryside recreation areas (Recreation News Supplement 9, 1973).
[4] Bayfield, N.G., A review of problems and progress in site management research (Recreation News Supplement 9, 1973).
[5] Wagar, J.A., The carrying capacity of wild land for recreation (Forest Science Monographs 7, 1964).

[6] Chubb, M. and Ashton, P.G., Park and Recreation Standards Research: the Creation of Environmental Quality Controls for Recreation (a report to the National Recreation and Parks Association, Parks and Recreation Administration, Department of Resources Development, Michigan State University 1969).

[7] Goldsmith, F.B., Munton, R.J.C. and Warren, A., The impact of recreation on the ecology and amenity of semi-natural areas: methods of investigation used in the Isles of Scilly (Biological Journal of the Linnean Society 2 [4], 1970).

[8] Speight, M.C.D., Outdoor recreation and its ecological effects: a bibliography and review (Discussion Papers in Conservation No. 4, University College, London 1973).

[9] Bates, G.H., The vegetation of footpaths (Journal of Ecology 23, 1935).

[10] Bayfield, N.G., Use and deterioration of some Scottish hillpaths (Journal of Applied Ecology 10 [2], 1973).

[11] Chappell, H.G., Ainsworth, J.F., Cameron, R.A.D. and Redferns, M., The effect of trampling on a chalk grassland ecosystem (Journal of Applied Ecology 8 [3], 1971).

[12] Burden, R.F. and Randerson, P.F., Quantitative studies of the effects of human trampling on vegetation as an aid to the management of semi-natural areas (Journal of Applied Ecology 9, 1972).

[13] La Page, W.F., Some observations on campground trampling and ground cover responses (US Forest Survey Research Paper, NE—68, 1967).

[14] Liddle, M.J., The effects of trampling and vehicles on natural vegetation, PhD thesis, University College of North Wales, Bangor 1973.

[15] Streeter, D.T., The effects of public pressure on the vegetation of chalk downlands at Box Hill, Surrey in E. Duffey and A.S. Watts (eds), The Scientific Management of Animal and Plant Communities for Conservation (Oxford 1971).

[16] Barrow, G.C., The Gairloch Conservation Unit, Wester Ross: a technique for monitoring recreational use in upland areas (Brathay Exploration Group Field Studies Reports, No. 19 [Ambleside], 1972).

[17] Duffey, E.A.G., An assessment of dune invertebrate faunas in habitats vulnerable to public disturbance in E. Duffey (ed.), The Biotic Effects of Public Pressures on the Environment (NERC, 1967).

[18] Barrow, G.C., Brotherton, D.I. and Maurice, O.C., Tarn Hows experimental restoration project (Recreational News Supplement 9, 1973).

[19] Austin, M.P., and Noy-Meir, I., The problems of non-linearity in

15

ordination: experiments with two gradient models (Journal of Ecology 59 [3], 1971).

[20] Mead, R., a note on the use and misuse of regression models in ecology (Journal of Ecology 59 [1], 1971).

[21] Yarranton, G.A., Mathematical representations and models in plant ecology: response to a note by R. Mead (Journal of Ecology 59 [1], 1971).

[22] Bayfield, N.G., Some effects of walking and skiing on vegetation at Cairngorm in E. Duffey and A.S. Watt (eds), The Scientific Management of Animal and Plant Communities for Conservation (Oxford 1971).

[23] Dunbar, G.A., The effectiveness of some herbaceous species for montane and subalpine re-vegetation (Proceedings of the New Zealand Ecological Society [18]. 1971).

[24] Lindsey County Council, Countryside Recreation: the Ecological Implications (1970).

3 Conservation and Recreation — the Challenge to Management

D.I. BROTHERTON

3.1 Introduction

Recent years have seen a considerable increase in the number of visitors to the countryside and, as a result, a parallel increase in damage to the resource. Enjoyment of the beauty of some of our finest stretches of countryside may be marred by the state of the ground which may be unpleasant to sit on, uninspiring to view, slippery when wet, or a miniature dust bowl when dry. Trampling destroys the vegetation cover, wind and surface water erode the soil and produce what is, perhaps, the most obvious ecological effect of visitors on the countryside.

As a means of developing and testing the measures which need to be taken, if the preferences of visitors and other interests are to be balanced against the value and sensitivity of the resource, the Countryside Commission is undertaking a series of experimental projects on sites suffering from overuse. The contribution of ecologists to these projects at Ilkley Moor (Yorkshire), Kynance Cove (Cornwall), Tarn Hows (Cumbria) and elsewhere is of considerable importance.

The role of the ecologist lies largely in three areas: (a) in assessing nature conservation interest; (b) in assessing the vulnerability of a site to different patterns and kinds of recreation use; (c) in advising on resource management techniques required to restore and maintain valued landscapes.

It is difficult to consider these aspects in total isolation and probably undesirable to do so. Many considerations affect management aims, and methods for achieving these are also numerous and varied. A brief look at the overall management framework, within which the ecologist operates and to which he contributes, therefore provides a convenient starting point.

3.2   The management framework

The aims of management are determined by the managing authority in the light of various people's perception of the resource and its value for different purposes. Visitors and potential visitors have viewpoints which are relevant. Equally the views of many of the diverse interest groups, which may include commoners with grazing rights, local residents and conservationists, have to be respected. The manager then has to reconcile these. views with the advice received from consultants and make a decision based on his organisation's aims, functions and budgetary limitations. Out of this complex of viewpoints and potential viewpoints must come some aims of management, synthesising a picture of what the site is to look like and the way it is to be used. These aims will define, amongst other things, optimal or acceptable resource states for different parts of the area. Various constraints may limit this vision. For example the ecologist's understanding of the resource's susceptibility to damage will be required to indicate a general pattern of use which, if exceeded, would result in unacceptable deterioration. Methods for achieving these aims, whereby the preferences and wishes of visitors and other interests are balanced against sensitivity and value of the resource, are many and varied and may influence the pattern of use, and the views of users and resource management.

The processes involved in determining the aims of management and criteria for acceptable ecological change are vitally important yet extremely complicated. We must also recognise that viewpoints change with time, sometimes extremely rapidly so that what is judged unacceptable now may not be in ten years' time. Management methods themselves may change attitudes. Notices explaining the reasons for temporary barriers, erected to permit recovery of vegetation, help to increase the visitors' awareness of management problems. Equally such control may affect perception of the site or favour one user group at the expense of another.

These difficulties are not underestimated. However, if we can leave them aside and accept the viewpoint that unacceptable change has resulted at our experimental sites, we can return to the role of the ecologist in restoring and maintaining their attractiveness and interest.

3.3   Site restoration

Britain has a climate remarkably equitable to plant growth and, in the great majority of situations, vegetation will re-establish itself provided the trampling pressure is removed and provided we are prepared to wait. Attempts to assist re-vegetation are largely aimed at shortening the time scale to prevent further soil erosion and encourage the development of an appropriate sward.

Techniques for reintroducing soil and stabilising it with netting, boarding or bitumen emulsion, for breaking up a compressed soil, and for effecting drainage, seeding, turfing, fertilising and watering are fairly well known.[1] Much information is available from bodies such as the Sports Turf Research Institute and from commercial seed breeders and wholesalers about establishing and maintaining swards with particular characteristics such as wear resistance, low maintenance and shade tolerance. It is however widely scattered, and the success and appropriateness of different measures in countryside situations requires further investigation. Restoration exercises offer opportunities for learning more about the quickest and cheapest ways of restoring different vegetation covers in different situations and for assessing the response of the established sward to the reintroduction of trampling pressure. If return to the indigenous vegetation is sought, it is necessary to know how quickly and effectively this is able to invade and replace the established nurse crop. Moreover it is imperative to ensure that no vigorous new species are introduced which are superior in competition and able to oust valued components of the 'natural' vegetation.

On many sites this agricultural approach to assisting vegetation recovery will probably prove satisfactory. There are however some situations in which it may be undesirable or indeed impossible to establish the readily available commercial varieties satisfactorily. Bayfield[2] has drawn attention to the commercial re-seeds established on the eroded slopes of Cairngorm. These form incongruous bright green patches against the darker indigenous vegetation or heather and deer sedge. Great care must be taken to guard against this possibility especially if recolonisation by the natural vegetation is particularly slow. Difficult site factors may also preclude establishment of readily available commercial seed even with intensive cultural treatments.

This is one of the problems faced at the National Trust's Kynance Cove property on the Lizard peninsula in Cornwall. Visitors' feet have destroyed *Erica vagans* heathland after first transforming it into a short grassy 'rock heath' dominated by *Festuca ovina* and *Calluna vulgaris*.[3] Subsequently sheet erosion and gullying have caused the loss of more than 100 tons of soil from the cliff top. Some features of the site, the long growing season and neutral soil reaction, favour vegetation recovery whilst others such as the soil salinity and thin soil cover discourage regeneration.[4] The impact of salt spray leading to high soil salinities is considered particularly serious and may preclude the use of commercial seed mixture, and possibly commercial turf, for restoration. In these circumstances small-scale experimental plots are being set up to identify the species and treatments which offer the best chance of re-establishing the turf cheaply, permanently and in an acceptable manner, before committing major resources to full-scale restoration.

Reseeding techniques are hampered by the limited range of species available commercially due to the difficulties of harvesting and storing seeds of wild species. Moreover, much of the fundamental research regarding the effect of dormancy mechanisms on germination is still in its infancy. This, coupled with our lack of knowledge about species characteristics, responses and competitive relations, combine to make the direct establishment of more natural swards a difficult task, but a challenging field for ecological research.

3.4   Assessing acceptable use patterns

Once the appropriate vegetation is restored, be it trample-resistant, species-rich or an unproductive, low-maintenance turf, the question then becomes one of how it can be maintained. Unless some restrictions are placed on the pattern of use and/or the number of visitors the site will once again degenerate.

It would be extremely helpful if at this point the ecologist was able to say just how many people each part of the site could accommodate without suffering unacceptable deterioration. Consideration of some of the factors which would affect his answer illustrates the extreme difficulty of doing this.

Deterioration will be affected by the nature of the resource, in particular the soil, slope, aspect, drainage pattern and microclimate, as well as the status of the vetetation cover, which these factors in part determine. It will also be affected by the type of use and the pattern of use as well as the way in which use is distributed in space and time. The pattern of use is itself affected by many factors, which may be difficult to predict. Some such as the weather are beyond control, whilst others, including the siting of facilities, are dependent on management decisions. At a detailed level there may be a dynamic interaction between the pattern of use and the resource. For example deterioration can affect the spatial distribution and behaviour of visitors which, in turn, affects future resource damage. Clearly this is a complex situation and it is not easy to predict the effect of a particular pattern of use, or the extent to which this is susceptible to modification by management.

This is however the problem we must attempt to solve, and there are two kinds of information available for guidance. Firstly, on a heavily used site, the present situation contains much relevant information. Determining the present pattern of use and relating this to the vegetation composition, cover and damage, allowing where necessary for the effects of other factors which determine these[5] enables assessment of the deterioration associated with different levels of use. In this way Drs F.B. O'Connor, F.B. Goldsmith and M. Macrae, consultants on the project at Kynance Cove, have established the approximate patterns of use at which heath deteriorates to grassland and then to bare ground on that site. This approach presumes a certain stability within the use/deterioration complex, which may not in fact be the case.[6] It does however provide a first approximation which, hopefully, is adequate for management purposes. Secondly, although the way in which vegetation type, topography and drainage affect resource vulnerability may not be known with any precision, there is an increasing understanding of the factors and situations which are conducive to rapid deterioration. Thus it is often possible to rank vegetation types of species in terms of their relative sensitivities and to appreciate the general way in which soil type and moisture content, water runoff, slopes, etc. affect deterioration.

The approach is therefore to look at the problems caused by the present use of the site, whilst recognising the likely conditions conducive to rapid deterioration and to take actions which either modify the pattern of use or increase the site's resilience.

3.5   Influencing the pattern of use

It is certainly worth a brief digression to consider some of the ways in which the pattern of use can be altered, as this will in general provide the most potent way of balancing preferences with resource vulnerability.

94 per cent of all visitors to the National Trust's Tarn Hows property in the Lake District arrive by car and the number of people leaving each of the three car parks (A, B and C) on an average day in 1972 is shown in Fig. 3.1. 45 per cent walked all the way round. Other visitors walk, picnic, play ball-games, swim or canoe from or around the southern end of the lake.[9]

As the two car parks A and B are roughly 50 m higher than the lake access to the latter is, in the absence of any other influences, via a relatively steep slope (Fig. 3.2). These areas (M and N in Fig. 3.1) have no particular conservation interest, but their steepness makes them particularly vulnerable to direct descents. Eroded sections within the area M have been restored. In order to prevent further soil erosion hardened surfaces could be introduced, but this was considered undesirable. Therefore modification to the pattern of use must be made before the temporary barriers are removed in the spring.

In 1973 one of the car parks (A) was closed and, although this decision was taken to reduce the intrusion of a skyline of cars, its closure is clearly helpful in solving erosion problems. Data extracted from Fig. 3.2 shows that the predicted number of crossings of slope M is reduced from 706 to 456 per day by the closure of car park A (Fig. 3.3).

Comparison of this new situation with the effects of 475 people per day on the lesser slopes of area N (Figs. 3.1, 3.2) suggests that the reduction in use of area M resulting from the closure of car park A will be insufficient to prevent the return of erosion problems. Further modifications to the pattern of use must therefore be made and an information board is being placed in car park B advertising two way-marked circular walks, in an attempt to encourage the distribution of use shown in Fig. 3.4. If wholly effective, this will reduce the number of crossings of area M by a further 40 per cent. Additional beneficial effects may be achieved by encouraging the visitors to ascend rather than descend the steeper slopes as this is probably less damaging. It has proved difficult to predict the exact return routes to car park B from stile E, the options ranging from a steep direct ascent to a longer, gentler-sloping return. This situation may be helpful in dispersing rather than concentrating use over the return slopes. Any development of new tracks across areas M and N must be watched carefully and further actions taken to affect the use pattern should this prove necessary. Increased use of the main tracks may also require a greater maintenance commitment.

This crude approach is necessitated by our inadequate understanding of the complex relationships between use and deterioration mentioned above. The soundness of the measures taken will be judged by determining the new pattern of use and assessing future deterioration. If we find that these measures are not sufficient, there are many others that could be invoked, although in considering these it is important to remember that some of them may be less acceptable than the damage they are designed to prevent. Before any are used, it would be necessary to ensure compatibility with management policies at the site.

Length of stay is an important variable and may affect deterioration.

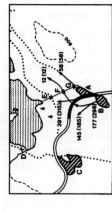

Fig. 3.2 Visitor flows on average day 1972, leaving and returning to car parks A and B

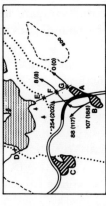

Fig. 3.3 Pattern of visitor flows on average day to be encouraged by providing information in car park B

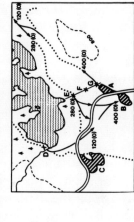

Fig. 3.4 Pattern of visitor flows on average day to be encouraged by providing information in car park B

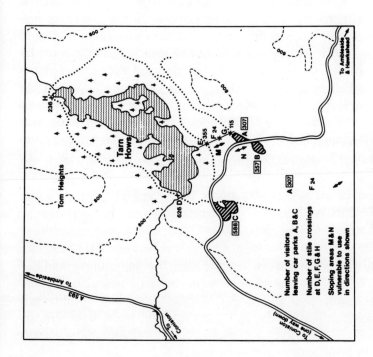

Fig. 3.1 Tarn Hows – site layout and pattern of use on an average day, March–November 1972

23

When car parks are well used, increasing the length of stay will reduce the total number of people visiting the site. In addition people who stay longer are likely to travel further, in which case use in the region of car parks, where deterioration is typically greatest, is likely to be reduced. Providing information or, possibly, charging, [10] may increase the length of stay and pattern of dispersion.

Use of Tarn Hows as a whole could be discouraged either by removing signposts in Hawkshead and neighbouring places, or by withdrawing the nature trail leaflets currently available from information centres within the region. Use of the top car park (B in Fig. 3.1) could be discouraged at the expense of the lower car park (C) which, although accepting a greater usage and having a capacity roughly five times that of B, is currently the source of less damaging impact, being roughly on the same level as the Tarn. This might be achieved by charging for car park B, but not for C, or by advertising the existence of car park C on the entrance road, south of car park B (Fig. 3.1). Some of these measures, such as signposting, may have the desired effect in the short term, but lose their impact as the proportion of visitors familiar with the site increases. Actions to modify the pattern of use in one area almost always have repercussions in others, and an overall view is required to guard against the danger of transferring problems within a site or to another one.

These are some of the measures which can be invoked to influence the pattern of use and, thereby, protect the site against unacceptable deterioration. It does not follow that all these methods would be acceptable at Tarn Hows, neither does it imply that they would all be successful. As yet we know very little about the short- and long-term effectiveness and acceptability of these various measures in different situations.

3.6 Site maintenance

3.6.1 *Footpaths*

The development and maintenance of footpaths in the countryside and the factors affecting deterioration such as the pattern of use, soil type, vegetation, slopes along and across the surface, present width, surface wetness and surface roughness on and off the path, have been studied previously. [7, 8, 11] These have shown the importance of maintaining a good walking surface on both natural and constructed paths if excessive surface deterioration, undue increases in width and soil erosion are to be avoided.

This will often require maintenance of suitable drainage and a comfortable walking surface over an adequate width. Drainage of bogs and other wet areas with friable soils may however facilitate erosion. In these cases, where the vegetation and soil structure are often extremely susceptible to pressure, sleeper paths and the like are often more appropriate. Excessive increases in path width, which often result when people choose to walk to the side of a badly maintained path, are also discouraged if the adjacent ground surface of vegetation is by contrast rough or scrubby.[7] Erosion often results on direct ascent or descent tracks [11] and there are occasions when it may be desirable to introduce stepping, or to harden surfaces in a way which harmonises with the character of an area. [12]

Subsequent management effort can help minimise damage by siting facilities and designing and encouraging the use of paths which avoid situations conducive to rapid deterioration.

3.6.2   *Areas subjected to intermediate pressures*

Near car parks and other facilities we often find areas of ground subjected to intermediate pressures or relatively heavy but intermittent ones where vegetation is present but cover is incomplete. These areas may be deteriorating or in balance with the trampling, or vehicular, pressure. In either case, there may be instances when it is desirable to affect the composition and vigour of the established sward as a means of increasing its tolerance to deterioration. In general the trampling pressure will itself lead to a relative increase in species which by virtue of their life cycle, growth form, morphology and responses to soil compaction and foliage damage are relatively tolerant to trampling pressures. [13, 14] Inadequate knowledge of species characteristics, requirements and responses may make the effect of cultural treatments difficult to predict. The autecological approach to these problems reviewed by Liddle [15] can be supplemented by experiments designed to assess the effectiveness of different treatments applied to small plots within trampled areas. The value of any treatment will be determined by the extent to which trampling resistance is increased and by its costs and acceptability.

3.6.3   *Landscapes not subjected to heavy recreation pressures*

The great majority of the countryside that we seek to enjoy is not in fact subjected to heavy recreation pressures, but management may none the less be necessary to retain or enhance attractiveness and interest and to increase the compatibility between different uses. Our aim now may be to arrest a succession in order to maintain an open grassy area. Alternatively it may be desired to increase species diversity or, more generally, favour certain interesting or attractive species or assemblages at the expense of others.

The complexities of managing plant and animal populations for these ends are great, although Harper[16] has drawn attention to the well-tried techniques which have enabled the agronomist to manipulate multi-species grasslands with considerable success. Management has usually been by modification of edaphic conditions (liming, fertiliser applications and cultivations) together with partial control of the biotic factors (grazing animals, pests, disease organisms and competitors).

The successful use of these methods for conservation ends will require a much greater understanding of the mechanisms by which wild plant populations are naturally regulated[17] and of the factors controlling species naturally regulated and of the factors controlling species diversity.[16, 18] Agricultural, economic and organisational problems may also have to be solved. For example it may prove desirable to reintroduce a form of grazing, presently uneconomic in agricultural terms, to maintain an area of grassland. On other occasions it may be necessary to exercise control over the grazing pressure or reconcile the conflicts between grazing and other activities.

3.7   Conclusions

Exercises involving natural resource management are, by their nature, slow to yield results. At this early stage in the restoration experiments, it has proved impossible to do more than outline the approach which is being taken and to indicate some of the methods which are being tested.

The approach to solving the problems of excessive wear and tear is designed to determine whether or not capacity is exceeded at each of the sites studied. Ecological capacity will be exceeded if the preferred pattern of use results in unacceptable deterioration.

Perceptual capacity is another matter altogether. Basically this depends on the reaction of individuals to the problem of overcrowding. Provided alternative areas are available and people are sufficiently aware of the problem to modify their visiting behaviour, both spatially and temporally, it will be possible for them to achieve the experience they seek.[19] Burton[20] provides some evidence that visitors do distribute themselves in this way. It is important that we move towards a better understanding of capacity values not only to safeguard sites for present and future enjoyment, but also to determine whether the present supply of sites will cope with predicted demands.

The extent to which it will be possible to solve the problems of excessive wear and tear by increased management effort within a site, without discouraging total usage, has yet to be determined. Management will need to be effective yet unobtrusive. There is a fascinating relationship between conservation and recreation, with one in part a justification for the other. They are not, however, always compatible, and greater understanding of the measures required to balance the two provides one of the most fundamental problems surrounding the present-day use of the countryside.

References

[1] Lovejoy, D. (ed.), Spon's Landscape Handbook, Specifications and Prices, (London 1972).

[2] Bayfield, N.G., A review of problems and progress in site management research (Recreation News Supplement 9, 1973).

[3] Coombe, D.E. and Frost, L.C., The heaths of the Cornish Serpentine (Journal of Ecology 44, 1956).

[4] Countryside Commission, Approaches to the experimental restoration of heavily visited areas of countryside: Kynance Cove (1974).

[5] Goldsmith, F.B., Munton, R.J.C. and Warren, A., The impact of recreation on the ecology and amenity of semi-natural areas: methods of investigation used in the Isles of Scilly (Biological Journal of the Linnean Society 2 [4], 1970).

[6] Burden, R.F. and Randerson, P.F., Quantitative studies of the effects of human trampling on vegetation as an aid to the management of semi-natural areas (Journal of Applied Ecology 9, 1972).

[7] Bayfield, N.G., Use and deterioration of some Scottish hill paths (Journal of Applied Ecology 10, 1973).

[8] Countryside Commission, Pennine Way Survey (1973).

[9] Barrow, G., Brotherton, D.I., and Maurice, O.C., Tarn Hows experimental restoration project (Recreation News Supplement 9, 1973).

[10] Van Lier, H.E., Determination of planning capacity and layout criteria of outdoor recreation projects (Centre for Agricultural Publishing and Documentation, Wageningen 1973).

[11] Huxley, T., Footpaths in the Countryside (Countryside Commission for Scotland, Perth 1970).

[12] Countryside Commission, Surfacing materials for use on footpaths, cycle tracks and bridleways (1973).

[13] Speight, M.C.D., Outdoor recreation and its ecological effects: a bibliography and review (Discussion Papers in Conservation No. 4, University College, London 1973).

[14] Streeter, D.T., The effects of public pressure on the vegetation of chalk downland at Box Hill, Surrey in E. Duffey and A.S. Watts (eds), The Scientific Management of Animal and Plant Communities for Conservation (Oxford 1971).

[15] Liddle, M.J., Outdoor recreation: a selective summary of pertinent ecological research (Biological Conservation, 1975).

[16] Harper, J.L., The role of predation in vegetational diversity in G.M. Woodwell and H.H. Smith (eds), Diversity and Stability in Ecological Systems (Brookhaven Symposia and Biology 22, 1969).

[17] Harper, J.L., Grazing, fertilisers and pesticides in the management of grasslands in E. Duffey and A.S. Watts (eds), The Scientific Management of Animal and Plant Communities for Conservation (Oxford 1971).

[18] Grime, J.P., Control of species density in herbaceous vegetation (Journal of Environmental Management 1 [2], 1973).

[19] Brotherton, D.I., The concept of carrying capacity of countryside recreation areas (Recreation News Supplement 9, 1973).

[20] Burton, R.J.C., A new approach to perceptual capacity — some results of the Cannock Chase research project (Recreation News Supplement 10, 1973).

4 Coast Protection by Sand Injection Techniques

Dr S.J. CRAIG-SMITH

4.1 Introduction

Much of the East Anglian coast between Weybourne in north Norfolk and Felixstowe on the Suffolk-Essex border affords a classic example of an actively eroding coastline. The cliffed section between Weybourne and Happisburgh has been retreating at approximately 1 m/yr over the last eighty years,[1] whilst south of Happisburgh the annual retreat has been slightly slower over the same period of time, ranging from 0·6 to 0·9 m/yr (Fig. 4.1).[2]

This rapid retreat is a result of a combination of factors. The coastline, according to Tanner's[3] classification of the littoral zone, based on annual mean breaker height, falls into the category of high energy. The geology of the area comprises loose unconsolidated Quaternary and Holocene deposits[4] which not only yield readily to marine attack but also suffer from wind erosion and slumping due to sub-aerial water action. With a world-wide rise in sea level of approximately 1 mm/yr and a local land subsidence of 0·5−1·0 mm/yr there is an annual rise in sea level relative to the land of between 1·5 and 2·0 mm/yr.[5]

During the period 1970−73 the School of Environmental Sciences at the University of East Anglia undertook an intensive study of a 40 km section of this coastline between Winterton in Norfolk and Benacre in Suffolk. This was sponsored by the three local authorities of Great Yarmouth, Lowestoft and Lothingland who during this period collectively spent over £970,000 on sea defence (approximately £8,000 km/yr). The limits of this study were purely arbitrary and the area under investigation differed little from the rest of the East Anglian coastline between north Norfolk and the Thames Estuary. Apart from establishing an extensive data acquisition programme the study was intended to assess the relative value of various sea defence methods and suggest possible alternatives.

29

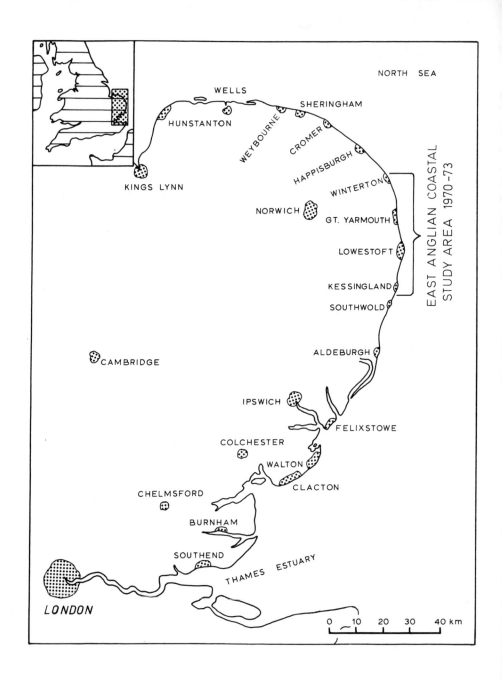

4.1 East Anglian coastal study area

30

4.2   Physical Environment

4.2.1   *Coastal change and sediment budget*

Although this is essentially an eroding coastline there are a limited number of areas where active accretion is taking place. Locally these are referred to as 'nesses' and within the study area they occur at Winterton, Yarmouth North Denes, and Benacre.[6-11] Figures relating to the sedimentary budget (Table 4.1) indicate that the rate of accretion has remained practically constant since 1883 although the rate of erosion has been more variable.

Whilst there is no significant difference between the annual volumes of sediment loss during the first two periods there has been a dramatic reduction in the amount eroded since 1953. This is due to the rapid development of coastal defence works following the 1953 storm surge.

Table 4.1

Sediment Budget Figures 1883−1970

Period	Loss (erosion) $\times 10^3 m^3 yr^{-1}$	Gain (accretion) $\times 10^3 m^3 yr^{-1}$	Net loss $\times 10^3 m^3 yr^{-1}$	Sediment interchange $\times 10^3 m^3 yr^{-1}$	Accretion: erosion
1883−1906	218	69	149	287	1 : 3·2
1907−52	208	74	134	282	1 : 2·8
1953−70	86	74	12	160	1 : 1·2

4.2.2   *Geology*

The study area comprises three cliff sections of almost equal length broken by Breydon Water at Yarmouth and Lake Lothing at Lowestoft. Footing the cliffs in all three sections is the Cromer Forest Bed Series but these are rarely exposed; only after exceptional storms when the beach is stripped of sediment are these deposits visible. The bulk of the cliffs above beach level is composed of two till layers separated by an intervening sand series.[12, 13] On average the cliffs consist of 4 per cent gravel, 62 per cent sand and 34 per cent mud as defined by the Wentworth classification.[14]

In contrast the beach sediments are much coarser in character and show a definite increase in size towards the south. On average they comprise 25 per cent gravel and 75 per cent sand with a mean grain size in the sand fraction of 0·3 mm or 1·43ϕ. The latter is simply an expression of the mean grain size in phi units, namely $\log_2$ of the particle diameter in mm.

Over 80 per cent of offshore sediment falls within the sand size class

31

with a mean grain size of 2·13ϕ. It is therefore finer than that within the beach zone. The remaining 20 per cent of offshore sediment is almost equally divided between the gravel (9 per cent) and mud (11 per cent) size classes. The gravel is exposed on the floor of the major offshore channels whilst the mud forms an almost continuous belt about 1 km wide which is never less than 1 km from mean low water mark. [15]

4.2.3 Wave climate

There is only a limited amount of information immediately available about the wave climate of this area. Data from Smith's Knoll light-ship (52° 43' N, 2° 18' E), 35 km east of Great Yarmouth in 50 m of water, [16, 17] suggest that the most common wave conditions are those with a height of about 0·8 m and a period of between 5·5 and 6·0 seconds, conditions typical of shallow coastal waters.

Supplementary information was obtained by twice-daily observations at Lowestoft Ness during the study period. [18] It revealed that a 1 m high wave is exceeded 30 per cent of the time in winter (October to March) and 30 per cent in summer (April to September). A 2 m high wave is only exceeded 10 per cent of the time in winter and 1 per cent in summer. The percentage exceedance for wave steepness of 0·0200, 0·0300, 0·0400 and 0·0500 is 65, 35, 15 and 5 per cent respectively [10]. This indicates that the most frequent wave type experienced at Lowestoft during the study period has a period of between 6·0 and 6·5 seconds and a height of 1·0 m.

Although the actual volumes of beach material in transit along the coast are unknown it is possible to quantify the longshore wave energy component from wind data records by the Vollbrecht method. [19] This has been computed for the ten-year period 1963–72 based on hourly wind readings collected at Gorleston Meteorological Station. This method of analysis has many limitations especially when applied to a water body the size of the North Sea. However, in the absence of any alternative technique it can be used to calculate the relative amounts of energy expended along this stretch of coast.

The number of energy units per year for the ten years is around 4,000 ± 500 with the exception of years 1963, 1967 and 1970 with approximately 1,500 ± 100 energy units (Fig. 4.2a). During these three years a greater percentage of the winds were westerlies. Marked seasonality is also revealed by the data. Summer is characterised by a monthly mean of 180 units and winter by a monthly mean of 370 units (Fig. 4.2b). When longshore wave energy is divided into northerly and southerly components it is revealed that there is little variability in the number of energy units

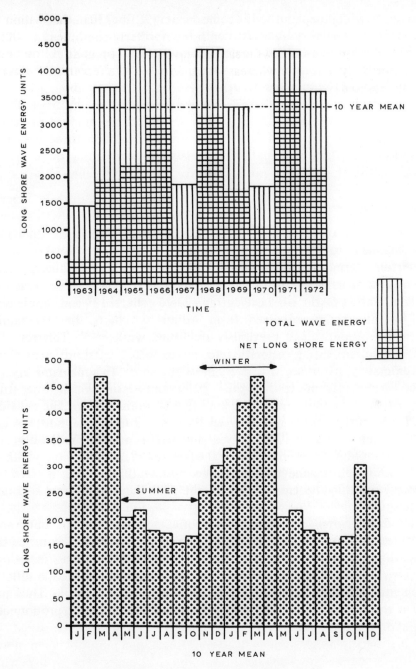

Fig. 4.2a   Annual long shore wave energy 1963–1972

Fig. 4.2b   Mean monthly long shore wave energy 1963–1972

associated with the southerly component (70 ± 250) whilst there is considerable variability associated with the northerly component (2,000 ± 1,100). The longer fetch to the north allows greater seas to develop under the influence of strong northerly winds, whereas to the south the fetch is too short to enable large seas to develop.

Every month and year revealed a net excess of energy towards the south. Only for periods shorter than a week did the amount of energy from the south exceed that from the north. Based on these data it is possible to conclude that material travels southwards along the coast for 70 per cent of the time and northwards for only 30 per cent.

4.2.4 *Tidal current action*

The study area offshore comprises a complicated network of sandbanks and channels roughly parallel with the coast. Exceptions occur at Winterton, Yarmouth North Denes and Benacre, where sandbanks trend towards the coast as a result of local sediment accretion in those areas.

Data relating to the offshore currents were collected [20] and supplemented by information obtained from Admiralty charts, the Hydraulics Research Station, [21] and previously published work. [22-24] This revealed that maximum spring velocities to be expected offshore vary from approximately 1·0 m/sec within 3 km of the shore, to approximately 1·6 m/sec further offshore (out to the −20 m contour line which varies from 4 km offshore in the south to 10 km offshore in the north). The net tidal residual is to the south, and between Bacton and Great Yarmouth it is 4 km/day, approximately 0·05 m/sec, and between Great Yarmouth and Orford 1 km/day or approximately 0·01 m/sec. [24] Although the width of the coastal belt characterised by the net southerly drift is affected seasonally, within the immediate offshore zone the tidal residual is always to the south.

The data above, although only a brief summary of the data now available as a result of this survey, are sufficient to emphasise some of the physical problems affecting this area. It is a high-energy coastline which has a strong northerly component of wave energy, and this results in beach and offshore sediment travelling from north to south. Thus not only is this a coastline in retreat but also it is a coastline with pronounced littoral drift to the south.

4.3 Previous defence policy

Sea walls and groynes can be seen at any of the seaside resorts —

Sheringham, Cromer, Mundesley, Great Yarmouth, Lowestoft, South-wold, Aldeburgh and Felixstowe. Because of their economic importance the majority of these towns have been defended since the middle of the last century. Although the rate of erosion at these defended areas has been considerably reduced it can never be completely halted over a period in excess of 30 years. At Lowestoft Ness for example the present sea wall is the third in fewer than 90 years (Fig. 4.3).

Although walls and groynes afford immediate, albeit temporary protection at a particular site, their construction can lead to several unfortunate side-effects.

4.3.1 Defended headland problems

If erosion continues at either side of a defended stretch of coast, then the protected zone will soon become a headland. Because wave attack is concentrated on headlands the problem of maintaining defences becomes even more acute. Overstrand in north-east Norfolk is a good example of this problem.

4.3.2 Terminal groyne effect

Once a groyne system has been created the longshore supply of beach material is cut off to the unprotected area immediately down drift. Erosion will occur at this site until all the groyne employments are infilled at the protected site and the longshore transport of material is restored. This process is often referred to as outflanking because erosion simply outflanks the protected area. Pakefield beach affords a good example of this problem (Fig. 4.3). During the latter half of the nineteenth century almost all the seafront at Lowestoft was protected by a sea wall and groyne system. Shortly afterwards very severe erosion occurred at Pakefield which is immediately down drift of Lowestoft. Over 150 m of coastal retreat were experienced before the groyne employments to the north became infilled and the natural longshore supply of material restored.

4.3.3 Beach scour

Groynes are only effective in maintaining the beach provided there is some longshore sediment movement. As soon as this source of supply ceases, due to natural causes or the development of a new groyne system further updrift, scouring can occur with the result that the groynes and sea wall become completely exposed. The beaches at Cromer, Mundesley,

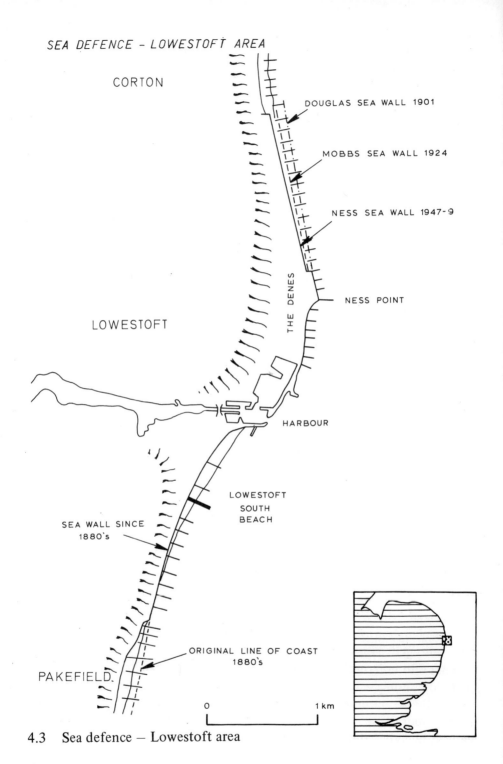

CORTON

DOUGLAS SEA WALL 1901

MOBBS SEA WALL 1924

NESS SEA WALL 1947-9

NESS POINT

THE DENES

LOWESTOFT

HARBOUR

LOWESTOFT
SOUTH
BEACH

SEA WALL SINCE
1880's

ORIGINAL LINE OF COAST
1880's

PAKEFIELD

0   1 km

4.3   Sea defence – Lowestoft area

36

Gorleston and Lowestoft are all deficient in sand and are covered by the sea from about half tide onwards. Problems of beach access then become important.

To avoid the problems of outflanking the entire coast can be defended, and long-term plans already exist to defend all the East Anglian coast. To date 75 per cent of the study area is affected by sea defence. However, by defending all the coast the natural supply of beach material from the cliffs is cut off and this, in turn (100 years) may result in the beaches being eroded and the groynes and sea walls undermined. Lowestoft South Beach affords an excellent example of this.

As part of the East Anglian Coastal Study the beaches were sampled twice yearly and, between Great Yarmouth and Lowestoft monthly. The sampling revealed that the beaches comprised about 75 per cent sand and 25 per cent gravel with one exception, Lowestoft South Beach. This comprised 100 per cent sand on each occasion it was sampled and the mean sand size ($2 \cdot 1 \, \phi$) was very much nearer the offshore mean grain size than the rest of the beach system. This beach has been isolated from the cliffs behind it for over 100 years and separated from the beaches to the north and south by sea walls and harbour works. Therefore this beach can only receive a very restricted longshore supply of beach material. As a result it is permanently in a poor condition and submerged from half tide onwards. This could be an environmental indicator of what could happen to all beaches if the natural sediment supply from the cliffs is terminated.

4.4   Sand injection

In spite of man's attempt to defend the coastline poor beaches persist in many places. Beaches with deficient sand supply render sea defences vulnerable, create problems of access because of the high walls and groynes, and are detrimental to the holiday industry. Under these circumstances replacement of lost sand is a logical solution to the problem especially when incorporated with a groyne system to stabilise the newly injected material.[25] This process may, in the long term, be cheaper than strengthening or repairing a sea wall behind an eroding beach. Thus, there are three important occasions when injection should be considered: (a) when the natural longshore drift of sand is interupted by the construction of a harbour, pier, sea wall, or system of groynes; (b) when the beach has a high amenity value for the local authority; and (c) when injection is a cheaper proposition than the construction and/or maintenance cost of other forms of sea defence. In some cases all three situations may apply to one beach.

4.4.1 *Economic considerations*

The cost of an injection programme is dominated by the location of the source for the injected sand. The borrow material can come from one of three areas.

(a) Inland quarries — this has the advantage that it can be carried out in all weathers, but this source can be expensive because of transport costs especially if implemented on a large scale; it can also cause environmental problems when there is poor road communication to the beach.

(b) Coastal sites: from the updrift side of a headland or large groyne or from an area of natural accummulation. This however can cause strong local opposition in areas of removal. Of greater significance it may, in some cases, upset the balance in an accreting environment.

(c) Offshore: where large quantities of sand exist. Sand size however can cause problems because offshore sand tends to be finer than that on the beach. This has already been shown to be the case off East Anglia.

On economic grounds almost every large-scale scheme must involve the use of offshore material, but it is not always possible, even with careful investigation, to choose a sediment source where material is of a suitable grain size and degree of sorting. Krumbein and James [26] have developed a method of estimating the amount of offshore material required to produce a given stable volume of sediment on the beach. Their model assumes that the offshore material is both finer and less well sorted than the beach sand and that the two sediment types are essentially log-normally distributed. Both these factors apply in the East Anglian example.

Table 4.2

List of Sediment Properties for Empirical Approach

Size grade in phl units	Beach sand (WT.%)	Offshore sand (WT.%)	Ratio WT.% beach to WT.% offshore
−1·0 − −0·5	1·6	0·4	4·0
−0·5 − 0·0	1·8	0·5	3·6
0·0 − 0·5	3·8	1·6	2·4
0·5 − 1·0	11.3	4·8	2·4
1·0 − 1·5	28·0	11·9	2·4
1·5 − 2·0	34·3	26·0	1·3
2·0 − 2·5	16·8	30·8	0·5
2·5 − 3·0	2·0	13·0	0·2
3·0 − 3·5	0·3	6·3	0·0
3·5 − 4·0	0·1	4·7	0·0

The empirical approach involves the construction of histograms for the offshore and beach material (Table 4.2). An estimate of the number of cubic metres of offshore sand required to produce a residual of one cubic metre on the beach after initial sorting is given by the maximum ratio of beach to offshore sand in any one size class. In this case the maximum ratio is 4·0 in the size class −1·0 to −0·5 ϕ.

When the particle size distributions of the beach and offshore material are known, or can be assumed, rather more rigorous calculations can be applied. For this analytical approach curves of beach and offshore sediment must be drawn on arithmetic probability paper and their distributions defined mathematically (Table 4.3). Krumbein and James'[26] equation for computing the phi ratio $R\phi_{crit}$ is as follows:

$$R\phi_{crit} = (S_{\phi 0}/S_{\phi b})e^{-(M_{\phi b} - M_{\phi 0})^2/2(S_{\phi b}^2 - S_{\phi 0}^2)}$$

By inserting the corresponding values in the above formula a value of nearly 3 is obtained. This is more reliable than the figure derived from the empirical approach because the analytical method is independent of the size classes used in the analysis. In effect, the maximum ratio is found analytically in terms of the continuous frequency distributions rather than by class increments. Thus, if offshore sand is utilised three times the actual required amount of sand will have to be injected. This value can only be reduced if there are areas in the offshore zone characterised by coarser sediments. Such areas do exist off East Anglia on the floors of the major flood and ebb channels.

Table 4.3

List of Sediment Properties for Analytical Approach

	Beach sand	Offshore sand
Mean grain size	$= 1.506\phi = M_{\phi b}$	$= 2.066\phi = M_{\phi 0}$
Standard deviation	$= 0.599\phi = S_{\phi b}$	$= 0.737\phi = S_{\phi 0}$
Phi variance	$= 0.359\phi = S_{\phi b}$	$= 0.543\phi = S_{\phi 0}^2$

If the beach to be injected is eroding rapidly it may be desirable to inject with coarser sand than that already comprising the beach. The coarser the material the greater the percolation into the beach and the less the backwash on the beach surface. Findings of the Coastal Engineering Research Centre[27] suggest that a material with a coarser mean grain size than that of the beach to be injected is desirable because 'beaches and near shore zones composed of coarse sediment are more stable than those beaches and nearshore zones composed of finer grained sediment for a given set of environmental conditions therefore producing a decrease in erosion rate, frequency of required nourishment, and increase in direct protective and recreational benefits'.

4.5   Gorleston Beach sand injection scheme

Gorleston Beach lies immediately south of Yarmouth Harbour entrance and extends southwards for approximately 1700 m to the borough boundary (Fig. 4.4). Its width today varies from about 80 m at its northern end to 50 m at its southern end (limits of low water spring tides) but this is less than half its width in the early 1960s. Backing the beach for its entire length is a concrete wall and behind that the artificially sloped and grassed Gorleston Cliffs.

Prior to 1962 Gorleston Beach showed little sign of erosion, beach levels dropped after severe storms but sand volumes readjusted themselves after a relatively short period. Since that date however there has arisen a serious problem of erosion which shows no sign of abating (Fig. 4.5). The annual net loss over the last eleven years has taken its toll on the sea wall backing the beach. Between 1964 and 1966 emergency schemes were undertaken to strengthen the northern part of the sea wall using toe piling and a concrete apron, but this was only a preventive measure and not a cure.

The deteriorating situation led the borough engineer to commission the Hydraulics Research Station to carry out a preliminary study. This commenced in 1966 and involved an analysis of beach profiles taken since 1964. The final report suggested two possible remedial measures; either to prevent reflected wave energy from arriving at the beach by introducing wave damping, or to inject sand on to the beach. Neither of these suggestions was taken up at the time.

Meanwhile erosion continued, reaching alarming proportions in February 1969 when a 100 m section of the sea wall collapsed near the borough boundary. This was hastily repaired thereby completing the strengthened sea wall begun in 1964. During the autumn of 1969 losses occurred of even greater severity than in the previous February so the second of the two measures suggested by the Hydraulics Research Station, namely sand injection, was implemented.

The operation to inject the sand commenced in December 1969 and

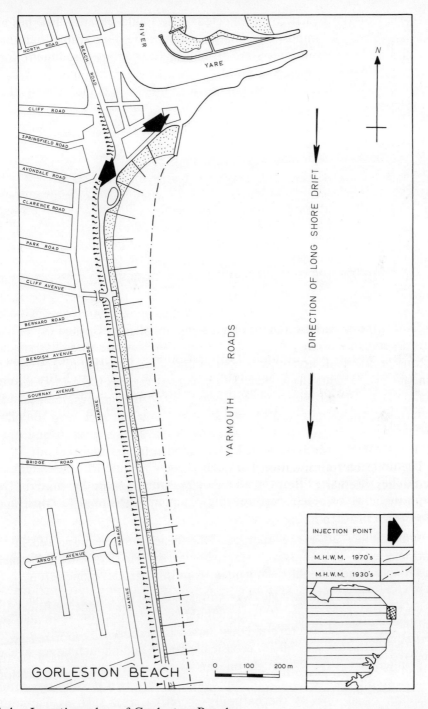

4.4   Location plan of Gorleston Beach

41

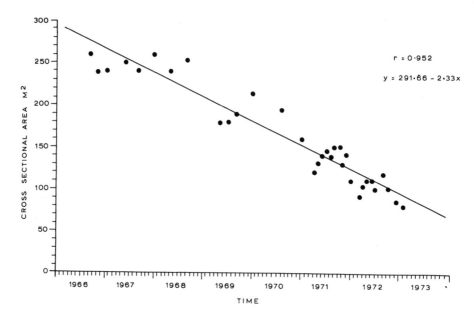

$r = 0.952$

$y = 291.66 - 2.33x$

4.5   Temporal variation in beach cross-sectional area: Gorleston

took five weeks. As Yarmouth Corporation viewed this as an experiment, it was restricted to the northern end of the beach, and tipping was confined to two points, one by the spur breakwater and the other by the yacht pond (Fig. 4.4). During this period 15,000 m³ of sand were injected. [28]

The material was transported from sand pits at Aldeby about 20 km from the beach. This source had been chosen because the excavated sand could be injected without grading or washing. Once the material was deposited on the beach, earthmoving equipment was used to construct a new beach profile.

Immediately after the operation the beach volume improved at the northern end. This improved state, however, lasted for only one season and no permanent benefit was gained from this particular operation.

In retrospect this scheme was too small to have a great chance of success, especially when it is remembered that injection took place in winter and groynes were not constructed to stabilise the newly injected sand. Nevertheless, the idea was basically sound and a much larger scheme is planned for 1975 although on this occasion it will be necessary to choose an alternative source of supply. There are two possibilities, either offshore, or at one of the naturally accreting areas such as Yarmouth North Denes which is only 6 km to the north.

42

4.6   Conclusions

Since the winter of 1969/70 two very much larger sand injection schemes have been implemented within the United Kingdom; one at Bournemouth involving 80,000 m^3 of sand in the summer of 1970 and the other involving 180,000 m^3 of sand at Portobello near Edinburgh during the summer of 1972. Both these schemes have been successful.

This case study illustrates how sand injection can be used as a form of sea defence in areas down drift of an impermeable structure. Although in this area injection has been confined to only one locality it could be applied to many similar areas along the East Anglian coast. The fact that all the sand did not remain on the beach does not mean that the experiment was a total failure. Sand injection should be viewed as a continuing rather than a unique process and may in the long run (30 years) be cheaper than other forms of sea defence. Even at the same cost, with none of the unfortunate side-effects caused by groynes and sea walls, this method of sea defence should be seriously considered in the future.

References

[1]   Cambers, G.M., The retreat of unconsolidated quaternary cliffs, unpublished PhD thesis, University of East Anglia 1973).

[2]   Craig-Smith, S.J., The East Anglian coast: the changing system (East Anglian Coastal Study, Report 3, School of Environmental Sciences, University of East Anglia, August 1972).

[3]   Tanner, W.F., Offshore shoals in areas of energy deficit (Journal of Sedimentary Petrology 31 [1], 1961).

[4]   Chatwin, C.P., British Regional Geology — East Anglia and adjoining regions (4th edition 1961).

[5]   Dunham, K.C., The evidence of submergence (Philosophical Transactions of the Royal Society of London 272A, 1972).

[6]   Hardy, J.R., An ebb—flood channel system and coastal changes near Winterton, Norfolk (East Midland Geographer 4 [1] 1966).

[7]   Robinson, A.H.W., Residual currents in relation to shoreline evolution of the East Anglian coast (Marine Geology 4, 1965).

[8]   Steers, J.A., The Coastline of England and Wales (2nd edition, London 1964).

[9]   Steers, J.A. and Jensen, H.A.P., Winterton Ness (Transactions of the Norwich and Norfolk Naturalists Society 17, 1952).

[10]   Williams, W.W., An East Coast Survey: some recent changes in the

coast of East Anglia (Geographical Journal 122, 1956).

[11] Williams, W.W. and Fryer, D.H., Benacre Ness: an east coast erosion problem (Royal Institute of Surveyors, Journal 32, 1953).

[12] Banham, P., Description of Barton cliff section (Quaternary Research Association Field Report, Norwich 1970).

[13] Blake, J.H., Explanation of horizontal sections (Sheet 128, Geological Survey of England and Wales, 1884).

[14] King, C.A.M., Techniques in Geomorphology (Edward Arnold, London 1966).

[15] Craig-Smith, S.J., The East Anglian coast: sedimentary characteristics of the coastal/offshore system (East Anglian Coastal Study Report 4, School of Environmental Sciences, University of East Anglia, January 1973).

[16] Darbyshire, M., Waves in the North Sea (Docks and Harbours Authority 41, 1960).

[17] Draper, L., Waves at Smith Knoll Light Vessel, North Sea (National Institute of Oceanography Internal Report A 33, September 1968).

[18] Craig-Smith, S.J., The East Anglian coast: inshore wave action (East Anglian Coastal Study Report 6, School of Environmental Sciences, University of East Anglia, March 1974).

[19] Vollbrecht, K., The relationship between wind records, energy of longshore drift, and energy balance off the coast of a restricted water body, as applied to the Baltic (Marine Geology 4 [2], 1966).

[20] Craig-Smith, S.J., The East Anglian coast: current action (East Anglian Coastal Study Report 7, School of Environmental Sciences, University of East Anglia, April 1974).

[21] Hydraulics Research Station, An investigation into movement of Lowestoft sand bank (Report E.X. 214, July 1963).

[22] Jolliffe, I.P., A study of sand movement on the Lowestoft sandbank using fluorescent tracers (Geographical Journal 129, 1963).

[23] Reid, W.J., Coastal experiments with radioactive tracers; recent work on the coast of Norfolk (Dock and Harbour Authority 39, 1958).

[24] Riley, J.D. and Ramster, J.W., The pattern of bottom currents along the coast of East Anglia, unpublished paper read to the International Council for the Exploration of the Sea, C.M. 1969/C:15.

[25] Craig-Smith, S.J., Sand injection in the United Kingdom: the position in 1973 (East Anglian Coastal Study Report 5, School of Environmental Sciences, University of East Anglia, January 1973).

[26] Krumbein, W.C. and James, W.R., A lognormal size distribution model for estimating the stability of beach fill material (Coastal Engineering Research Centre, Technical Memorandum 16, 1965).

[27] Berg, D.W. and Duane, D.B., Effect of particle size and distribution on stability of artificially filled beach, Presque Isle Peninsula, Pennsylvania (Coastal Engineering Research Centre, Reprint R1–69, 1968).

[28] Craig-Smith, S.J., Gorleston Beach; littoral drift problems (East Anglian Coastal Study Report 2, School of Environmental Sciences, University of East Anglia, August 1971).

5 An Analysis of Decision Making in Coast Protection

Dr P.H. PHILLIPS

5.1 Introduction

The coastal zone represents one of the most dynamic geomorphological systems, responding to variations in energy inputs from the earth, ocean and atmosphere. The system is characterised by a number of conservative feedbacks which tend to maintain it in a state of dynamic equilibrium. In certain circumstances, however, the system may pass through a critical threshold, or be inherently unstable and consequently subject to continuous change. Coastal erosion may be generated by either situation and represents a progressive degradation of the land which will continue until an equilibrium condition is established.

Since Victorian times there has been a growing tendency for people to locate at the coast. This has exposed an increasing number of people to the vagaries of the natural system and has resulted in certain areas in a growing conflict between the nature of the operations of the physical processes and the character of land occupance. A traditional response to erosion problems, which dates from the legislation in Henry VI's Bill of Sewers of 1427,[1] has been a technological solution rather than an environmental one based on a positive intervention in the biophysical system.

A major innovation of the Coast Protection Act of 1949[2] which now regulates coast protection in Great Britain was the acceptance of a substantial element of central government responsibility for finance. Until the passage of this Act, coast protection was seen, as can be ably demonstrated by the Coleridge judgement,[3] as a particular type of private demand − one which an individual could be compelled to demand through royal prerogative. Coast protection was recognised by the new legislation as an appropriate sphere for collective action. With this changed perspective, however, comes the responsibility to monitor the efficiency of the allocation of public resources, the impact of actions on the coastal system, and the effectiveness of current management strategies.

5.2   A model of coast protection decision-making

This analysis of the decision-making process in coast protection employs a model which has a more general application in environmental management. Strongly emphasising the biophysical setting, the model is characterised by the potential for the continuous flow of information concerning the state of trajectory of the physical system. A comprehensive range of factors which impinge on decision-making and their structural interrelationships are incorporated. The degree of abstraction of the model is enhanced by the inclusion of a number of elements which in practice receive no or only cursory consideration.

The orientation of the model reflects the role of the deleterious effects of the operations of biophysical processes in initiating problem definition. The model can, however, be employed in situations where it is the interventions in the biophysical system which generate the problem and which are only manifested in such phenomena as water and air pollution. Information concerning the operations of biophysical processes and their effects may generate action on the part of the general public, their elected representatives, or the professional staff of the relevant statutory authority. At the decision-making stage there should theoretically be a thorough analysis of all alternative strategies in the light of the full range of operative social, political, technical, financial and environmental constraints. The actions taken on the basis of the decision may have an impact not only on the biophysical system but also, through the feedback of confirmatory or contradictory information, on social attitudes and the socio-economic system.

The model as applied to coast protection is illustrated in Fig. 5.1. The generalised level of presentation restricts the detailed specification of the relevant factors in the socio-economic system. Although all of the elements can be elaborated it is this area in particular which requires the most attention as the groupings are more comprehensive. This imbalance in presentation reflects, in part, the sectoral nature of environmental management. It is significant to note, however, that whilst the environmental aspects are stressed, the management decision involves the same range of factors which would be incorporated in a comprehensive planning approach. The difference is one of emphasis rather than coverage.

For the purposes of the analysis the coastal system is considered to be a process-response system[4] undergoing progressive change. The interface is defined as the zone subject to the influence of the tidal range. In elaborating the model the first area in the socio-economic system to which attention is paid is that of the legislation.

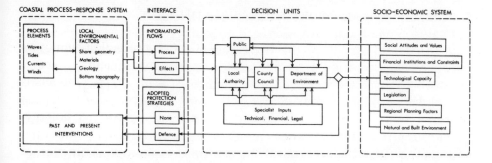

| COASTAL PROCESS-RESPONSE SYSTEM | INTERFACE | DECISION UNITS | SOCIO-ECONOMIC SYSTEM |

5.1 Model of coast protection decision-making

5.2.1 *Legislation*

Under the terms of the 1949 Act, each maritime county borough and district was constituted as coast protection authority for its own area. Subject to certain constraints imposed by the Act, coast protection authorities were empowered under section 4 to carry out such protection work, whether within or outside their administrative area, as might appear necessary to them for the protection of the land within their area. Coast protection work was defined in section 49 to include any work of construction, alteration, improvement, repair, maintenance or removal for the protection of the land including the sowing and planting of vegetation. The authorities were also empowered to serve notice on the owner or occupier of any land which had coast protection works in need of maintenance and to undertake the repairs at the owner/occupier's expense if they were not completed in a reasonable time. The power to regulate the private construction of sea defence works was vested in the authorities under section 17, and under section 14 the minister could authorise them to acquire land by compulsory purchase according to the procedures laid down in the Acquisition of Land (Authorisation Procedure) Act of 1946.

The purpose of the Act as stated in the Preamble was the regulation of the protection of the land of Great Britain from erosion and encroachment by the sea. The legislation was directed explicitly to an 'engineered solution' to erosion and flooding problems and established the constitution, powers and operating procedures of local bodies to undertake the work.

5.2.2 *Finance*

The financial provisions of the Act went some way towards satisfying the

49

representations made by the National Sea Defence League to the Royal Commission on Coastal Erosion and Flooding which was appointed in 1906. Under the terms of the Department of the Environment Circular 66/71 coast protection is a 'key sector' activity. Financial control is exercised by central government in a number of ways. Exchequer grants ranging between 20 and 80 per cent of the total capital costs are made for approved schemes. (These are supplemented by County Council grants which often range up to 50 per cent of the difference between the total cost and the Exchequer grant.) In addition, capital expenditures are controlled by the central sanction on loan raising which is necessary for schemes of any significance.

The recovery of coast protection charges from individuals or groups of property owners was an original provision of the Act which was designed to recoup some contribution to expenses from the most direct beneficiaries. This follows the traditional principle in coast protection that the beneficiaries should be financially responsible for the works which they were instructed to undertake by the Crown. The recovery of the coast protection charge was abandoned in 1962 following the Ministry of Housing and Local Government Circular 41/62.

The question of central government contributions to revenue expenditures on scheme maintenance has been the subject of a great deal of discussion – reference can be made to the adjournment debate on 2 June 1965 in Hansard for the most recent government statement. At this time the then Joint Parliamentary Secretary to the Minister of Housing and Local Government, Mr R. Mellish, indicated that the government considered revenue expenditures to be a solely local affair. In practice, however, certain works which have been essentially of a repair nature have been classified as capital costs and grant-aided. Through the control on the public purse, central government exercises the powers previously vested in the royal prerogative. The assessment of the merits of a scheme and the decision to provide a grant-in-aid does not, however, include a social cost-benefit analysis. This might be considered desirable in the light of the expenditure of public funds.

5.2.3 Social attitudes and values

In the determination of social attitudes and values to coast protection there are two major levels of interest – the general public, and those directly involved in a coastal erosion situation. It might be suggested that the law may be considered representative of the group attitude, but it must be recognised that to the vast majority the topic will have little or no meaning and that the law essentially reflects informed opinion and the activities of pressure groups. The limited relevance of the problem of coastal erosion to the general populace provides the basis for the lack of a public attitude to the problem, and it seems reasonable to suggest that no coherent public attitude exists outside the legislation.

A limited study of public information and attitudes to coastal erosion and protection undertaken in Christchurch Bay, Hampshire[5] suggests that whilst the public may (and almost certainly will) lack information concerning the nature of coastal processes, if a problem is perceived then coast protection, financed by central government, is seen as virtually a right. Certainly the overwhelming majority are unaware of the allocation of responsibility, source of finance or the extent of expenditure on coast protection. Yet the demand for positive intervention in the physical processes through the construction of sea defence works is a frequent occurrence. It is significant to consider to what extent the legislation facilitates the success of the efforts of uninformed pressure groups who will bear little of the direct costs of protection measures and yet who may derive a considerable amount of benefit.

5.2.4   *Technological capacity*

The technological capacity to undertake successful sea defence measures depends on a limited number of conventional engineering designs upon which there are innumerable variations. Most tend to be aimed at treating symptoms rather than causes and to be essentially reactive in character and operation. Groynes, in a variety of materials and designs, are used primarily in the stabilisation of beaches, temporary reduction of the rate of littoral drift, and the provision of upland protection through the creation of an effective buffer to wave action in the form of a beach. Enhanced erosion on the downdrift side (terminal scour) of the groyne is an inevitable consequence of the mode of operation. A veritable panoply of designs of sea walls, bulkheads and revetments have been employed in situations where a static delineation of the sea—land interface has been required. Whilst the stabilisation of the coastline fronted by the works may be achieved, no protection is afforded to areas flanking the structure. Erosion may in fact be accelerated, again especially at the downdrift end, and any predisposition to sediment loss from the beaches exacerbated. Breakwaters are used mainly to protect harbour entrances although their use in coast protection has occurred. Whilst the creation of a calm area of deposition landward of the breakwater is more process-orientated than the purely reactive operation of land-based walls, breakwaters have similar side-effects to those of groynes through the common abstraction of the littoral drift. Beach feeding with sediments represents a major divergence from the other, rather negative, techniques. In that a deficiency of sediments in the system is often a root cause of erosion problems it represents a rather more meaningful approach. In general, however, coast protection engineering tends to operate on a limited acknowledgement of the scale of the operation of environmental processes with the consequent generation of unforeseen or unstated externalities.

5.2.5 *Regional planning and environmental factors*

The regional planning factors associated with an area represent an extremely significant element in the appraisal of a coastal erosion or flooding problem. Unfortunately coast protection planning has no specific integration with the normal town and country planning process. The alternative strategies available in coast protection are therefore restricted to the preparation of a coast protection scheme comprising 'work' as defined in the Act, or the rejection of the problem and the adoption of a policy of inaction. The natural and built environmental factors which are incorporated in the model are site-specific and incorporate some evaluation of land capability, past and present investment, and associated variables.

5.2.6 *Decision units*

As indicated in the model, the formal decision-making process in coast protection takes place at three levels within the hierarchy of local government. The process may be initiated by problem recognition by a member of the public, or the technical or elected members of the local council. Within the council responsibility is often delegated to a special-purpose committee. It is often this group which brings forward to the council its assessment of a problem and its suggestions for action. Acceptance of the existence of a problem leads to the preparation by the Borough Engineer or a consulting engineer of a coast protection scheme. Subject to the approval of the committee and the full council, the scheme is forwarded to the County Council and the Department of the Environment for vetting.

At the local level the critical decision 'milestones' occur at problem specification, strategy analysis and project analysis. When the proposed scheme is evaluated by the full council, technical advice is available from the engineer responsible for its preparation, the Borough Treasurer and the Town Clerk. Information is presented concerning the technical feasibility of the scheme, the ability of the Borough to accept the additional rate burden and the legal implications of the proposals. The primary decision is the acceptance or rejection of the proposed scheme since the analysis of alternative strategies involves, as noted above, a simple choice between engineering works and inaction.

The application of the model in monitoring present coast protection policy may be demonstrated by the examination of coast protection measures undertaken at Barton-on-Sea, Hampshire.

5.3 Barton-on-Sea, Hampshire: a case study

Opening in a spiral from the relatively resistant point of Hengistbury Head, the coastline of Christchurch Bay, Hampshire (Fig. 5.2) reflects the action of relatively high energy, predominantly south-westerly waves on inherently unstable and readily erodible materials. The tertiary sands, gravels and clays, which form cliffs up to 36 m in height in the Barton-on-Sea area, have at times retreated at rates in excess of 1 m/yr. A marked reduction in the quantities of material in the net easterly-flowing littoral drift is probably the major consequence of the extensive coast protection measures in the Bay, which date from attempts in 1660 to stabilise the entrance to Christchurch Harbour.

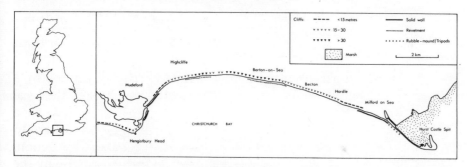

5.2   Coast of Christchurch Bay, Hampshire

Barton-on-Sea is the site of the largest sea defence scheme undertaken in the Bay to date. The condition of the cliff prior to stabilisation works, a complex of landslips, reflected its inherent hydrological and geological character. Below the free face, which was associated with the easterly dipping strata (Fig. 5.3) and increased in height eastwards, there was a sediment mass lying on a friction surface above the impermeable Barton Clays. Energised in part by the hydraulic gradient, this became semi-plastic and mobile in wet phases. When it dried out it became converted to broken, hummocky ground. The general nature of cliff retreat is summarised in Fig. 5.4. Over the hundred year period of the map record for the area, cliff retreat averaged one metre per year.

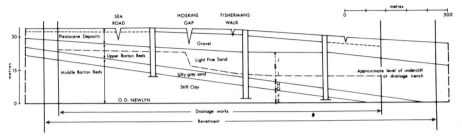

Fig. 5.3   Longitudinal geological section of cliff

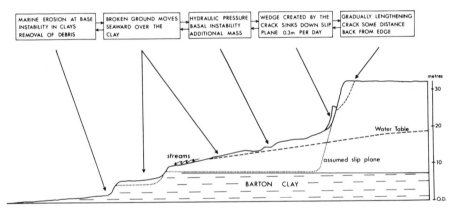

Fig. 5.4   General nature of cliff retreat prior to stabilisation

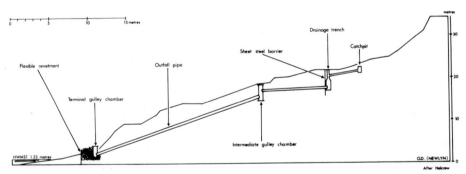

Fig. 5.5   Cross-section of protection works

To combat the dual sources of instability in the cliff of percolating water and wave attack at the cliff base, the protection measures combine a

54

longitudinal filter in the main body of the cliff and a flexible wooden revetment at the cliff foot (Fig. 5.5). Set in a suitable granular filter and faced with a sheet-steel piled curtain, the drain transfers the trapped water to the beach through a system of outfalls at about 100 m centres. The revetment of greenheart oak (*Ocotea rodiaei*) incorporates a backfilling of large stone as a medium for absorbing wave energy. Groynes were installed at a spacing of approximately 130 m along the 2,000 m length of the revetment and the works were completed by cliff shaping.

The final cost of the works which were undertaken over the period 1964 to 1968 was £617,000, of which £450,000 was derived from an Exchequer grant and £89,810 from a grant from Hampshire County Council. Lymington Borough Council was therefore responsible for £77,190 or approximately 12·5 per cent of the capital costs.

The Barton-on-Sea scheme may be examined from the economic, social and environmental standpoints. A cost-benefit analysis of the scheme indicates that it produced a net present value of benefits of *minus* £1,564,715 at 1971 prices. Combining the benefits of property protection, recreation benefits calculated by the consumer surplus technique, a variety of 'saved costs' and miscellaneous incomes, the scheme yielded benefits of £132,871. Set against this figure is the aggregate of the capital, maintenance and joint costs of £1,697,586, resulting in a costs to benefits ratio of over 12:1. Excluded from this analysis because an adequate methodology does not exist for their evaluation, were the costs of visual intrusion, construction period 'disbenefits' (e.g. noise pollution), and the costs of the destruction of wildlife habitats and a Site of Scientific Special Interest. The costs of the reduction of the littoral drift along this section of coast were also omitted as they may be internalised by Lymington Borough Council through works at Milford-on-Sea. The inclusion of such elements in the analysis would naturally only further raise the net social cost.

In this instance the major beneficiaries of the scheme would appear to be the frontagers since the total recreation benefits (which would probably be the most widely distributed benefit in coast protection) which can reasonably be attributed to the scheme over its fifty year operating life were assessed as £66,696 at 1971 prices. In this case of a predominantly retired population (32·2 per cent being over 65 years of age compared with the national figure of 12·3 per cent) with a marked concentration in social classes 1 and 2 (38·1 compared with 17·5 per cent) there appears to be the possibility of social redistribution occurring which is in the opposite direction to the normally accepted concepts of social equity.

The defence scheme has worked efficiently in its early years although there have been a number of problems with a section of the revetment overturning, some beach depletion necessitating the placement of a quantity of large stone on the foreshore to protect the revetment, a certain amount of leakage through the sheet-steel curtain which has required further drainage and cliff blanketing works and the collapse of a groyne. The design naturally suffers, however, from all the classic problems of a linear sea defence structure and there has been a certain risk of outflanking and rapid terminal scour despite an elaborate terminal groyne arrangement. The sealing off of a 2,000 m section of the cliffs which had previously been eroding rapidly, thereby reducing the supply of sediments to the littoral drift, and the modification of the condition of the beach through an increase in sediment size, steepening of the beach face angle, and the consequent reduction in usable beach area, represent the most significant environmental impacts of the scheme.

5.4 Conclusions – basic issues in coast protection planning

It is very easy to say with hindsight that according to some or other criterion a particular action should not have been undertaken. The very existence of the product of such action negates in part the value of such an analysis. The principal lessons to be drawn from such an evaluation are those at the general level of policy formation. The appraisal on an individual action can be unrepresentative but it can also indicate the potential of the decision-making system. Grouped into environmental, social and regional planning areas, the observations and issues raised by the case study and the examination of other coast protection projects may be considered the primary results of the monitoring activity.

The principal issues raised relating to the biophysical environment are the product of the decision-makers' ignorance of the nature of environmental processes or a choice to reject them. A major consideration is the fact that conventional sea defence measures, through an emphasis on the imposition of an artificial delineation of the sea–land interface, are preoccupied with the symptoms of the problem rather than the causes. This is the case even when the perspective is limited to the environmental aspects and it is presumed that environmental processes rather than perhaps inappropriate location decisions are the basic cause of the problem. The negative nature of the approach is exacerbated by the difference in time scale on which environmental and social processes operate. At the end of the lifetime of a sea defence scheme it is extremely

56

likely that the initial problem will remain and highly probable that the situation will have been made worse by the effects of the sea defence works on the coastal process-response system.

A further important characteristic of the coastal system is the considerable interdependence of areas and processes within the physiographic unit. Actions at one point in a coastal unit are likely to generate spillover effects (principally in the downdrift direction) creating external costs which are almost invariably uncompensated. This situation creates problems through the frequent non-correspondence of administrative and physiographic units. Whilst provision is made in the legislation for the establishment of joint boards, this has been implemented only once. There also appears to be a certain reluctance on the part of local authorities to fund work outside their administrative area. Management on the basis of the physiographic unit, as in catchment-based river control, would seem to be the most logical in coast protection in particular and environmental management in general.

The social issues relating to coast protection are derived essentially from the distribution of benefits and the identity of the beneficiaries. In the case of protection from flooding the number of direct beneficiaries is likely to be quite high. This, as illustrated by the Barton-on-Sea example, is much less likely to be the situation where the problem is one of erosion of cliffed lands. The narrow distribution of direct benefits must be accompanied by a widespread incidence of secondary benefits if coast protection by collective action is to be justified on more than an altruistic basis.

As suggested in the Barton-on-Sea case, there is a potential in the incidence of direct benefits for the contravention of the normally accepted principles of social distribution. The character of the coast as a high-amenity location mitigates against equal opportunity in the housing market. The support of an affluent minority through general taxation would appear to be an undesirable form of social redistribution. This is compounded by the fact that the housing-location decision is positive in character, and it would not seem unreasonable that individuals should appraise themselves of any potentially hazardous characteristics of the area in which they are choosing to reside. This would appear to be particularly appropriate in areas where there is coastal erosion as there is usually a long history of the problem.

The exposure of the decision-making system to the activities of self-interested pressure groups may be considered to be of some concern. With the abolition of the coast protection charge the contribution of direct beneficiaries to coast protection costs is minimal. Even at the local authority level, through the system of Exchequer and County Council grants, the financial burden of expensive schemes may not be great. In some ways the system is predisposed to permit individuals to promote considerable social costs through a private location decision whilst deriving major personal benefits. There would appear to be the potential for development at the local level of an undue lack of concern for the scale of coast protection expenditures compared with the benefits derived and the promotion of socially costly schemes.

Perhaps the most important single issue concerning present coast protection policy is the unidimensionality of the analysis. There is in the lack of integration with the regional planning process an undesirable lack of a holistic perspective. The two alternative strategies which are available to the decision-maker reflect a monistic preoccupation with the environmental aspects of the problem. If coast protection planning were viewed in its regional context a much wider range of alternative strategies, including zoning, loss-bearing, compensation and property insurance would be available and a less socially costly pattern of coastal land utilisation might ensue.

References

[1] Bill of Sewers, 6 Henry VI, c. 5 (1427).

[2] Coast Protection Act, 12 and 12 George VI, c. 74 (1949).

[3] Hudson v. Tabor, QBD 2 (1877), 290; Law Journal, QBD 46 (1877). 463; Law Times 36 (1877), 492.

[4] Krumbein, W.C., A Geological Process – Response Model for Analysis of Beach Phenomena (Annual Bulletin of the Beach Erosion Board 17, 1963).

[5] Phillips, P.H., Public Information on Coastal Erosion and Attitudes to Coast Protection: a Case Study. (Forthcoming.)

6 Design of Meandering Alluvial Channels

F.G. CHARLTON

6.1 Introduction

The study of the uniform flow of water in channels with rigid beds and banks goes back many centuries, and has resulted in the equations of Chezy, Darcy, Ganguillet-Kutter, Manning and others. These permit the engineer to compute one dependent variable, often depth, once the independent variables discharge, slope, breadth, channel roughness, etc. have been established. The application of this single equation to the design of channels with erodible banks where the breadth may change, and movable beds where the slope may change, often resulted in channels which scoured or accreted. It was not until towards the end of the nineteenth century that attempts were made to establish additional equations for the computation of the other dependent variables, with the concept of the non-scouring non-silting velocity of Kennedy. With the great effort in the construction of irrigation schemes in the twentieth century went an increased interest in the laws governing the behaviour of alluvial channels. Two independent approaches emerged; one, empirical, using the data from existing canals, and the other attempting to establish the physcial basis for the movement of the material on the bed and banks of a channel. Both the empirical and the quasi-rational approaches have failed to produce a universally acceptable set of equations for the determination of the hydraulic geometry of alluvial channels with their differing compositions of bed and bank material and range of discharges. Research is however continuing; our understanding of the behaviour of canals, and more recently rivers in alluvium, is improving and methods for the solution of some problems are well established.

6.2 Factors affecting channel geometry

The geometrical properties of an alluvial channel are generated by several independent quantities which include the discharge, physical properties of water, and the size, shape, grading and density of the material of the bed and banks of the channel. Many papers have been written on the choice of these independent variables and the derivation of dimensionless groups of variables for the examination of data.[1-3] For a dynamically stable channel with a uniform flow, the dependent quantities often assumed to be adequate to describe its geometry, are breadth, depth, slope, amplitude and wavelength of bed forms, meander length and meander breadth.

The design of irrigation and drainage channels usually assumes that the three important dependent variables are breadth, depth and slope. For such straight channels many sets of three basic equations have been developed.[4-8] In design problems related to natural rivers, however, it is often more useful to assume that the slope is an independent variable and the three most important dependent variables become breadth, depth and sediment transport rate.

6.3 Methods of computing channel geometry

There are three different methods of approach to the design of channels. They have either been developed from the correlation of field data, as in the regime-type equations, or have been deduced from equations describing the roughness of the channel, the sediment transport rate and the stability of the banks. The three basic approaches to the problems are as follows.

6.3.1 *Regime equations*

These are empirical equations deduced from field measurements and are generally applicable to channels with beds of fine to medium sand, smooth silty banks and negligible bed load. However, attempts have been made to extend these equations to cover channels with appreciable sediment loads and channels with gravel beds but negligible bed load. The best-known equations of this type are those of Lacey,[6] Blench,[4] and Simons and Albertson.[8] For rivers with gravel beds the relations of Kellerhals[5] are available.

6.3.2 *Tractive force methods*

These equations are based on research into the initiation of movement of bed materials[9] and, when used in conjunction with the roughness formulae of Strickler or Manning, they enable the designer to compute the geometry of channels with inactive, plane coarse beds, with limitations on the range of depth to grain size. Lane's method is the best known.[7]

6.3.3 *Sediment transport formulae*

Numerous equations deduced from theoretical considerations, and adjusted in the light of observations largely from laboratory studies, have been developed for the computation of sediment transport rates. These may be used to develop sets of equations for the computation of channel geometry, provided that relations for roughness in the active bed phase are available, and assumptions regarding bank stability are made. The absence of reliable roughness equations for the active plane bed, and active duned bed phases, have hindered progress in this field. The sediment transport equations are numerous, and they also are limited in their application.[10]

6.4   Channel patterns

While artificial channels are usually straight the natural channel is rarely so for any appreciable distance for a variety of reasons. The basic patterns adopted by natural channels are straight, meandered and braided. Although many reasons for the development of the different channel patterns have been put forward, the explanation is still in dispute; however, some of the factors conducive to their formation are known.

Channels of low hydraulic gradient are associated with low sediment transport rates. They do not develop large shoals,[11, 12] and the secondary currents are probably fairly weak due to the narrowness of the channel and the energy available. These channels, therefore, tend to be straight or have only minor irregularities of the bank line.

Channels of a steeper hydraulic gradient are associated with higher sediment transport rates. Such channels develop shoals causing the flow to describe a marked sinuous path, attacking the bank more strongly. The secondary currents may also be stronger and the net result is that the forces attacking the channel exceed the resistance of the bank; erosion and embayments occur, resulting in a meander pattern. Because of the strong dependence of channel geometry on discharge it has been found possible to deduce empirical equations defining the values of slope at which different channel patterns begin to develop.[11] For small discharges, the following equations apply (Fig. 6.1):

(a)   Straight channels without prominent shoals:

$$S_s < S_b \qquad (6.1)$$

where S_s is the water-surface slope of a straight channel or the straight-line slope of a meandered channel, and S_b the water-surface slope of a straight channel at the threshold of shoaling.

(b) Straight channels with prominent shoals:

$$S_b < S_s < S_m \tag{6.2}$$

where S_m is the water-surface slope of a straight channel at the threshold of meandering.

(c) Meandering channels:

$$S_s > S_m \tag{6.3}$$

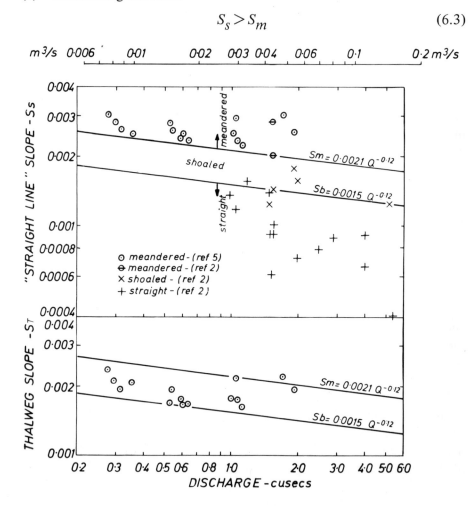

Fig. 6.1 Limiting slopes for small channels

The equations defining these threshold values of slope are given by:

$$S_b = 0{\cdot}0015Q^{-0{\cdot}12} \qquad (6.4f)$$

$$= 0{\cdot}00098Q^{-0{\cdot}12} \qquad (6.4m)$$

$$S_m = 0{\cdot}0021Q^{-0{\cdot}12} \qquad (6.5f)$$

$$= 0{\cdot}0014Q^{-0{\cdot}12} \qquad (6.5m)$$

where Q is the steady sustained discharge of a channel or the dominant discharge of a channel with a variable flow. The equation letters 'f' and 'm' refer to dimensional equations in feet-second or metre-second units respectively.

For channels with larger flows the following equations apply (Fig. 6.2):

$$S_m = 0{\cdot}00018Q^{-0{\cdot}21} \qquad (6.6f)$$

$$= 0{\cdot}00085Q^{-0{\cdot}21} \qquad (6.6m)$$

Thus, for a given discharge, there are threshold values of slope which offer an approximate method of establishing which is the natural pattern for a channel. Since sediment transport rate is an alternative independent variable there should also be a threshold value of sediment transport rate below which a channel will naturally remain straight and above which it will naturally meander. [12]

6.5 Meander Geometry

The meander geometry is strongly dependent on discharge and thus simple empirical equations have been developed relating meander length and discharge. Such relations, while valuable for most practical purposes, only take into account explicitly one independent variable, and the value of the coefficient and exponent are dependent on the range of data from which they were derived. More complete analyses have been attempted [1] but simple relationships are sufficient for most practical purposes and have been widely used. [12, 13]

Thus:

$$\lambda = 36Q^{0{\cdot}5} \qquad (6.7f)$$

$$\lambda = 65Q^{0{\cdot}5} \qquad (6.7m)$$

where λ is the meander length.

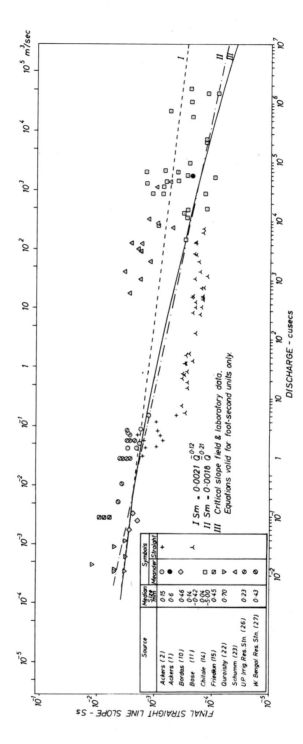

Fig. 6.2 Limiting straight-line slopes for large channels

64

In natural channels with varying discharge hydrographs it is important to be able to select a value of discharge which may be used in the computation of meander length. Studies of the relation between meander length and varying discharge [13-15] suggest that the bankfull flow, or the mean discharge during the month of maximum flow, are suitable values for use in equation 6.7.

Alluvial rivers with sandy beds do not all have the same slope or carry the same sediment charge. Each of these factors can modify the meander geometry. Increasing slope tends to increase the meander breadth and decrease the meander length. If steeper slopes are associated with higher sediment charges than an increase in sediment load should cause a decrease in the meander length. Multiple correlation supports this, [12] although present available data indicate a poor dependence of meander length on sediment transport rate.

Meander patterns have normally been defined using the two parameters meander length and meander breadth, and thus a second equation to define the latter is required. Meander breadths have been related to discharge alone and also to channel width alone, [12, 13] and a variety of relations has emerged. The ratio of meander breadth to meander length may vary between 2·86 for rivers with flood plains to 2·2 for incised rivers. [13] Laboratory channels seldom develop ratios greater than about 0·6 and river data [16] (mainly for Indian rivers) give a ratio varying between about 0·3 and 0·8. It is obvious that while the meander length may be computed with reasonable confidence for most practical purposes, the same is not true for the calculation of meander breadth.

6.6 Effect of non-linearity of rivers

Meandering affects the width, depth and slope of channels; hence the basic regime equations deduced for straight prismatic channels are not applicable without modification. Before examining this further the term slope must be defined, as it has several meanings. Rivers with sinuous patterns have a slope which may be measured along the curved path of flow; this may be called the thalweg water-surface slope or simply the thalweg slope. The slope may also be measured along the axis of the valley through which the river flows; this is termed the straight-line water-surface slope, or more simply the straight-line slope.

The quantitative effect of meandering on the mean width and depth of channels is little known. On meandering the cross sectional shape changes; it ceases to be approximately prismatic and a trench forms within the channel, which varies in depth as it alternates between one side and the other. These changes in cross-sectional shape, coupled with changes in direction of flow caused by the sinuous pattern, increase the rate of loss of energy. The effective roughness of a straight prismatic channel is dependent on the size of the particles on the bed and the shape and size of the bed forms only. On the other hand the non-straight, non-prismatic channel has a different slope, width and depth, while the greater sediment loads associated with such channels further affect the geometry.

Coefficients are quoted[4] for computing the slope of a meandering channel knowing the slope of a straight channel carrying the same liquid discharge, or vice versa. The slope of a straight channel, however, is not unique but depends upon the sediment load as well as on the liquid discharge; increasing sediment loads demand steeper slopes and, once meandering occurs, slope may continue to depend in part on the sediment load. Thus, to define the ratio of the slope of a meandering channel to that of a straight channel, it is necessary to specify the sediment transport rates of the two channels for which the coefficient is applicable.

Two ways of defining the effect of meandering on channel slope emerge. There is the meander correction factor K of Blench.[4] First the slope S_s of a straight channel is computed for a given discharge, sediment discharge and type of bed and bank material (equation 6.8f).

$$S_s = F_{b0}^{0.83} F_s^{0.083} k^{-1} Q^{-0.17} (1 + 0.12C)^{0.83} (1 + \frac{c}{233})^{-1} \qquad (6.8f)$$

where F_{b0} is the Blench bed factor for a channel with negligible load, F_s is the Blench side factor, Q the discharge, C the bed sediment transport rate in parts per hundred thousand, and $k = 3.63\ gv$ where g is the acceleration due to gravity in feet-second units and v the kinematic viscosity in the same units. Secondly the water surface slope of the meandering channel S_T is obtained simply by multiplying S_s by Blench's meander correction factor K (equation 6.9).

$$S_T = K S_s \qquad (6.9)$$

There is also the meander slope ratio M which is the ratio of the slopes of meandering channel S_T and a straight-line channel at the same discharge but with negligible bed load S_0 (equation 6.10).

$$S_T = M S_0 \qquad (6.10)$$

Fig. 6.1 shows plots of straight-line slopes S_s and thalweg slopes S_T against discharge for channels carrying a discharge of about 1 ft³/s, and with a median bed particle size of 0.15 mm. From the plotted points for

66

straight channels with active beds in Fig. 6.1 the minimum slope S_0 must be less than S_m and S_b given by equations 6.5 and 6.4 respectively. Assuming that the exponent of Q is -0.12, the value of S_0 could not exceed

$$S_0 = 0.00065Q^{-0.12} \qquad (6.11\text{f})$$

$$S_0 = 0.00032Q^{-0.12} \qquad (6.11\text{m})$$

if it is to be below all the plotted points. Thus at the threshold of meandering from equations 6.5 and 6.11

$$M \doteq \frac{S_m}{S_0} = \frac{0.0021Q^{-0.12}}{0.00065Q^{-0.12}}$$

$$= 3.2$$

At this stage the sinuosity of the channel, or the ratio of the sinuous path of the channel to a straight line, is of course unity.

In the laboratory studies the thalweg slopes S_T of meandered channels were not observed to fall below a value given by S_b in equation (6.4), (Fig. 6.1), at which the sinuosity had increased to a maximum of

$$\frac{0.0021Q^{-0.12}}{0.0015Q^{-0.12}} = 1.4$$

and the minimum meander slope ratio from equations (6.4) and (6.11) becomes

$$M = \frac{S_b}{S_0} = \frac{0.0015Q^{-0.12}}{0.00065Q^{-0.12}}$$

$$= 2.3$$

Thus, small meandering channels with sinuosities ranging between 1.0 and 1.4, have meander slope ratios M which range between 3.2 and 2.3. Both these values may be greater if the value of S_0 given by equation 6.11 is less, which it probably is.

The ability of these small meandering channels to adopt a thalweg slope flatter than the greatest slope of a straight channel at the threshold of meandering S_m suggests that, under some conditions, the sediment-transporting capacity of meandering channels may be greater than that of straight channels carrying the same discharge.

67

For channels carrying larger discharges the minimum slope of a straight channel with negligible bed load may be given by equation 6.8f where $C = 0$, i.e.

$$S_0 = F_{b0}{}^{0.83} F_s{}^{0.083} k^{-1} Q^{-0.17} \qquad (6.12f)$$

Fig. 6.3 shows a plot of thalweg slopes against discharge. Since for unit sinuosity thalweg and straight-line slopes are the same, a plot of equation (6.6) and two lines representing equation (6.12) for different values of bed and side factor have been added. From equations (6.6) and (6.12) it may be deduced that at the threshold of meandering the meander slope ratio M may lie between values of about 3 and 6, depending on the magnitude of the bed and side factors. Comparison of the plotted thalweg slopes and the straight channel slopes for similar discharges and bed gradings gives a range of values of M from 0.94 to 17.7, the majority of the points lying between about 2 and 6. Lack of information about the sediment transport rates of these channels prevents more detailed examination or the incorporation of factors to account for the sediment charge and sinuosity.

Blench[4] recommends a meander correction factor of $K = 2$ for use with equation (6.8f) and (6.9) to account for the effect of meandering. From equations (6.9), (6.8f) and (6.12f) it may be deduced that

$$M = \frac{S_T}{S_0} = \frac{K\,(1 + 0.12\,C)^{0.83}}{1 + \dfrac{C}{233}} \qquad (6.13f)$$

For values of $C = 10$ and 100 parts per hundred thousand, and with $K = 2$, the value of M varies between 3.7 and 11.9 respectively.

While the absence of data on sediment transport prevents checking the reliability of these values, the calculated range of M (3.7 − 11.9) is above the majority of observed values (2 − 6). It was concluded earlier that the sediment-carrying capacity of meandering channels might, under some circumstances, be higher than that of straight channels. If this is true, then equations for calculating channel slope which include the effect of sediment transport rate might require a meander correction factor K equal to or possibly even less than unity under these conditions, or a meander slope ratio M of between 2 and 6. It must be concluded that at present insufficient is known, and more data and analyses are required to obtain a comprehensive understanding of the subject.

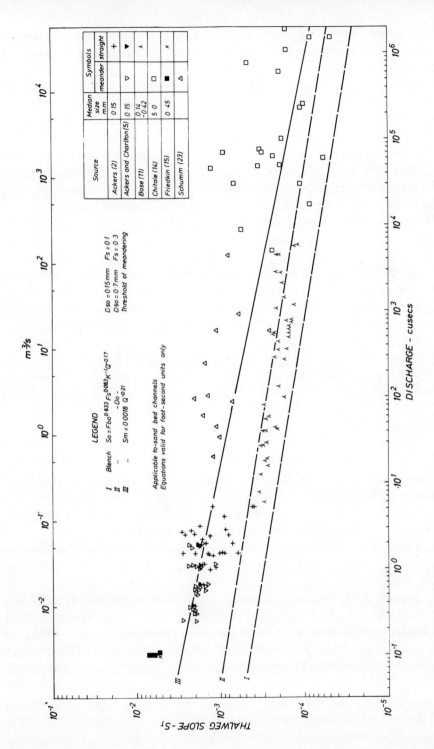

Fig. 6.3 Comparison of thalweg slopes for meandering and straight channels

6.7   Conclusions

Although there is no satisfactory explanation of meandering enough is known about the necessary and sufficient conditions for their development that allowance can be made for this phenomenon in channel design.

Experiments have shown that straight dynamically stable channels are associated with low slopes or low bed-sediment-transport rates, whilst meandering channels are dynamically stable on steeper slopes or where bed load transport rates are higher. In contrast braided channels are inherently unstable and develop when the straight line water surface slope is insufficient to transmit the discharge and input sediment load.

Whilst simple empirical equations suitable for the estimation of meander wavelength for design purposes have been developed, relations for the prediction of meander breadth are less reliable. Alternative approaches based on the ratio of thalweg slope of meandering channels to the slope of straight channels are available but care should be exercised in the use of these methods because the ratio is dependent on bed load transport rates. Under some circumstances the sediment-carrying capacity of meadering channels may be greater than that for straight channels, in which case the meander correction factors, which treat the effect of sediment load on slope explicitly, may be less than unity.

References

[1] Ackers, P. and Charlton, F.G., Dimensional analysis of alluvial channels with special reference to meander length (Journal of Hydraulic Research 8 [3], 1970).

[2] Barr, D.I.H. and Herbertson, J.G., A similitude framework of regime theory (Proceedings of the Institution of Civil Engineers 41, 1968).

[3] Yalin, S.M., A theoretical study of stable alluvial systems (Central Water and Power Research Station, Poona, Golden Jubilee Symposia vol. 2, 1966).

[4] Blench, T., Mobile bed fluviology (University of Alberta Press 1969).

[5] Kellerhals, R., Stable channels with gravel paved beds (Proceedings of the American Society of Civil Engineers 237, 1953).

[6] Lacey, G., Uniform flow in alluvial channels and canals (Proceedings of the Institution of Civil Engineers 237, 1953).

[7] Lane, E.W., Design of stable channels (Transactions of the American Society of Civil Engineers 120, 1955).

[8] Simons, D.B. and Albertson, M.L., Uniform water conveyance

channels in alluvial materials (Proceedings of the American Society of Civil Engineers, Journal of Hydraulics Division 86 [HY5], 1960).

[9] Shields, A., Anwendung der Ähnlichkeitsmechanik und der Turbulenzforschung auf die Geschiebebewegung (Mitteilungen der Preussischen Versuchsanstalt für Wasser- und Schiffbau, Heft 26, 1936).

[10] American Society of Civil Engineers Task Committee, Sedimentation transportation mechanics, sediment discharge formulas, (Proceedings of the American Society of Civil Engineers, Journal of Hydraulics Division 97 [HY4], 1971).

[11] Ackers, P. and Charlton, F.G., The slope and resistance of small meandering channels (Proceedings of the Institution of Civil Engineers Supplement XV, 1970); Paper 7362 S and Supplement IX, 1971; discussion on paper 7362 S).

[12] Ackers, P. and Charlton, F.G., The geometry of small meandering streams (Proceedings of the Institution of Civil Engineers Supplement XII, 1970); Paper 7328 S and supplement IX, 1971; discussion on paper 7328 S).

[13] Inglis, Sir Claude C., Meanders and their bearing on river training (Maritime and Waterways Paper No. 7, Institution of Civil Engineers, January 1947).

[14] Ackers, P. and Charlton, F.G., Meander geometry arising from varying flows (Journal of Hydrology XI [3], 1970).

[15] Carlson, C.W., The relation of free meander geometry to stream discharge and its geomorphic applications (American Journal of Science 263, 1965).

[16] Chitale, S.V., River Channel Patterns (Proceedings of the American Society of Civil Engineers, Journal of Hydraulics Division 96 [HY1], 1970; 96 [HY10], 1970; 97 [HY1], 1971; and 97 [HY5], 1971).

7 Design Discharge for Natural Channels

Dr R.D. HEY

7.1 Introduction

It is universally recognised that discharge is the most important independent variable that governs the shape and size of alluvial channels. Indeed this particular variable has featured in every stable channel design equation, either directly or indirectly, since the turn of the century. For artificial channels the discharge value used in the design equations is the constant transmission discharge. Natural channels, however, experience a range of flows and the choice of a single design discharge is not obvious. This chapter attempts to rationalise this problem.

7.2 Dominant discharge

Before stable channel design equations can be applied to natural channels it is necessary to decide which constant discharge is the equivalent of the variable river flow. It has been argued that the steady discharge which produces the same gross shapes and dimensions as the natural sequences of discharges could be used for design purposes and this was referred to as the dominant discharge.[1-3] More recently, however, it has been suggested that different aspects of the hydraulic geometry have different dominant discharges.[4-6]

One definition of dominant discharge was obtained after observations of natural channels indicated that the wavelength of river meanders was associated with flows at or about bankfull stage.[4] Evidence also suggests that bankfull discharge is responsible for all the other aspects of channel shape because at this stage the channel is operating most efficiently.[7] Hence bankfull discharge can be regarded as the single dominant flow. Unfortunately this does not explain why the channel adjusts its shape and dimensions to this particular flow.

Studies of the magnitude and frequency of transport processes offer some insight into this problem.[8, 9] Wolman and Miller's[9] observations and calculations have shown that the frequency of occurrence of the flow

73

which collectively does most work equates with the frequency of bankfull flow. It logically follows, therefore, that the bankfull discharge can be classed as the dominant one because, in the long term, it is responsible for the transport of the largest volume of sediment through the section.

Although bankfull discharge, or the flow doing most work, could define the design discharge, their values are usually unknown for reconstruction or design purposes. However, if the frequency of bankfull flow could be defined for stable channels, it would be possible to use the discharge associated with this flow frequency for design purposes.

For rivers in England and Wales Nixon[3] calculated that bankfull flow was, on average, equalled or exceeded 0·6 per cent of the days of record, or 2·2 days/year, whilst Wolman and Leopold's [10] data obtained from American rivers indicated an average return period of 1·5 years based on the annual flood series.

Comparisons between these two values have been made but they tend to be meaningless because the two sets of data are statistically imcompatible. The former is obtained from continuous data and the latter from discrete instantaneous events. Even when the data are compatible it will be essential to ensure that only stable channels are analysed and that a common definition of bankfull stage is utilised before comparisons are made.

Two basic issues arise from these studies. First, in view of the amount of scatter associated with each average value, is the frequency of bankfull flow constant for all types of channel? Second, which frequency distribution is the most appropriate one for defining the frequency of bankfull flow? These questions can only be answered after analysing the factors which control the flow doing most work.

7.3   Factors affecting the value and frequency of bankfull discharge

For stable channels the value and frequency of occurrence of the flow doing most work will reflect the nature of the two curves which define the total sediment load for the period in question. These controlling curves are: (a) flow duration curve and (b) sediment load/discharge curve (sediment rating curve), which combine to give (c) collective sediment load/discharge curve. Typical curves are plotted in Fig. 7.1 and point A corresponds to the flow doing most work during the period in question.

The sediment rating curve is usually a power function of the form

$$Q_s = k \, (Q - Q_c)^n$$

where Q_s is the sediment load, Q the discharge, and Q_c the critical discharge for sediment transport. The values of the coefficient k and exponent n are dependent on the type of sediment being transported. If coarse suspended and bed load are predominant the larger discharges will contribute a greater share of the total load and the flow doing most work will be relatively large (Fig. 7.1, point A). This arises because the coefficient of the sediment rating curve is small whilst the exponent has a value of greater than unity. If wash and fine suspended sediment loads are transported by the same flow regime the flow doing most work would be considerably smaller and its frequency of occurrence increased (Fig. 7.2, point B) because the coefficient is large and the exponent is less than unity. For bed load it is apparent that the very large flows are too infrequent to collectively transport large volumes of material, whilst the very frequent flows are associated with too small a load. Hence the intermediate flows are responsible for the greatest amount of work. As the calibre of the load is reduced the more frequent flows become responsible for the transport of the greatest amount of sediment.

The nature of the flow duration curve will also affect the value and frequency of bankfull discharge. Changes in flow variability have the most significant effect; the larger its value the greater the influence of the high flows (Fig. 7.3, point C) and *vice versa* (Fig. 7.3, point D). In contrast variations in meanflow can only affect the value of bankfull discharge and not its frequency of occurrence.

This indicates that the frequency of occurrence of the flow doing most work, and hence bankfull discharge, can vary quite considerably even for stable channels. Within any one region, however, its value is expected to be quite conservative.

For unstable channels the frequency of bankfull flow is complicated by the interdependence of the system variables. Instability occurs due to the excess or deficit of sediment input over output, and the channel will react to any inbalance of this kind by modifying its hydraulic geometry and sediment output by erosion or deposition.

Consider first of all the erosional system. If sediment input declines slightly at a particular section erosion will commence. Immediately sediment output will increase due to degradation increasing bankfull channel slope and flow depth and, thereby, the average shear stress. Although backwater effects will encourage upstream erosion and an increase in sediment input, during this early phase positive feedback will override the upslope negative-feedback component allowing erosion to proceed at a progressively faster rate. This arises because the increase in shear stress more than offsets the increase in input load. As soon as the

75

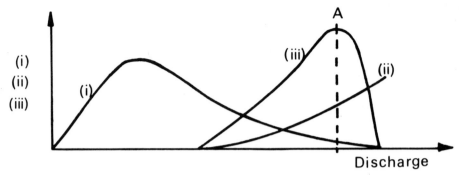

Fig. 7.1   Flow doing most work: bed load predominant

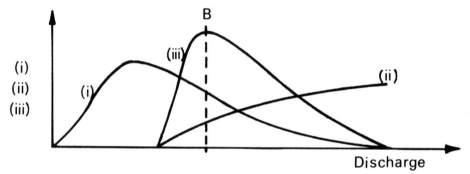

Fig. 7.2   Flow doing most work: wash and suspended load predominant

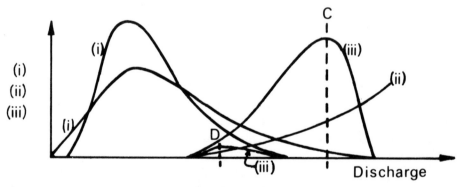

Fig. 7.3   Flow doing most work: effect of variations in flow regime

KEY   (i) Frequency   (ii) Instantaneous Sediment Discharge
         (iii) Collective Sediment Discharge

76

point of maximum erosion migrates upstream the roles are reversed and negative feedback becomes dominant. Channel slope is reduced by this process and this, together with the progressive reduction in the rate of increase in flow depth, results in a progressive decline in the rate of increase in sediment output. Eventually sediment output will achieve a peak value and .thereafter decline until it balances the increasing input. This new equilibrium is characterised by a larger sediment discharge, bed material size and cross-sectional dimensions, and a smaller channel slope.[7]

The effect of these changes on the flow doing most work can be illustrated diagrammatically. As sediment input declines erosion commences and this is illustrated by the divergence of the input and output sediment-load rating curves (Fig. 7.4). The flow doing most work is altered by this process and it is obtained by subtracting the total sediment input from the output curve (Fig. 7.4). Upstream erosion is soon responsible for an increase in sediment input, hence the exponent of the input sediment load/discharge curve is increased. At the same time flow variability increases due to the reduction in the amount of flood attenuation as the channel is incised. The new equilibrium is achieved when the coefficients and exponents of the sediment rating curves are identical (Fig. 7.5).

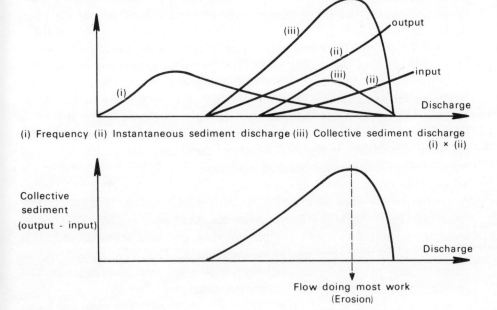

Fig. 7.4   Change in value of flow doing most work during erosion

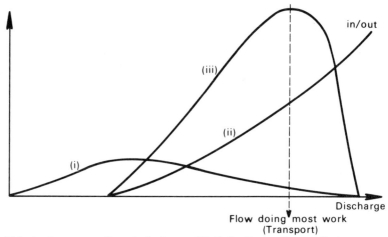

(i) Frequency (ii) Instantaneous sediment discharge (iii) Collective sediment discharge

Fig. 7.5 Flow doing most work after erosion

As the flow doing most work, or more precisely erosion, increases during the erosional phase the dimensions of the channel are modified so that bankfull discharge equates with that doing most work. When erosion ceases the flow doing most work will be that flow which, in the long term, is responsible for the transmission of the greatest volume of material (Fig. 7.5).

Aggradation, on the contrary, occurs as a result of increased sediment input. Initially sediment output declines because aggradation reduces the bankfull channel slope and flow depth and hence the capacity of the river to transport sediment. Positive feedback will predominate at this stage because the shear stress declines at a faster rate than the input load is reduced by headward deposition, and this accelerates aggradation. Negative feedback will only become dominant after the point of maximum deposition has worked upstream. The latter is responsible for an increase in channel slope and this, in conjunction with a progressive reduction in the rate of decrease in flow depth, results in a progressive reduction in the rate of decrease in sediment output. By this process sediment output declines to a minimum value and then increases until it is in equilibrium with the declining input load. This new equilibrium is characterised by a smaller sediment discharge, bed material size and cross-sectional dimensions and a larger channel slope.[7]

As before, the effect of these changes on the flow doing most work can be shown diagrammatically. When aggradation commences, due to the increased sediment input, the exponent of the input rating curve increases whilst that of the output curve declines (Fig. 7.6). The flow responsible for the greatest amount of deposition is reduced in the process (Fig. 7.6). Upstream deposition soon causes a reduction in sediment input and thereafter the input and output sediment-rating curves are convergent. Channel capacity is reduced during this period with the result that flood waves are more attenuated and flow variability is decreased. Ultimately an equilibrium state is achieved when the input and output sediment-rating curves are identical (Fig. 7.7).

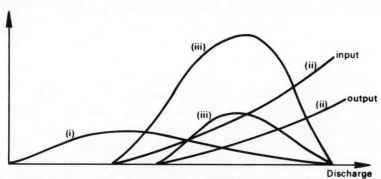

(i) Frequency (ii) Instantaneous sediment discharge (iii) Collective sediment discharge

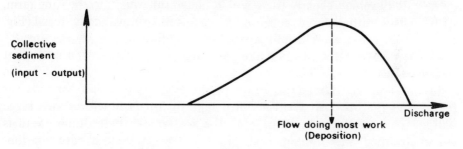

Fig. 7.6   Change in value of flow doing most work during deposition

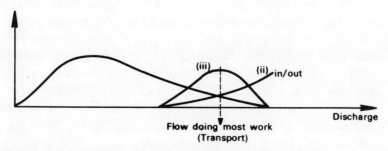

(i) Frequency (ii) Instantaneous sediment discharge (iii) Collective sediment discharge

Fig. 7.7   Flow doing most work after deposition

79

During the aggradational phase the flow responsible for the greatest volume of deposition declines and the channel is modified to accommodate this change. Consequently the flow doing most work, deposition in this case, will equate with the bankfull discharge. When equilibrium is established the flow doing most work will be responsible for the transmission of the largest volume of material (Fig. 7.7).

Thus the frequency of bankfull discharge will also depend on the degree of instability of the channel. Actively eroding sections will have a less frequent bankfull discharge, whilst depositing sites will overtop their banks more frequently than stable channels.

7.4   Frequency of bankfull discharge

Although this explains why the frequency of bankfull flow can vary between sites it does not identify which distribution is best suited for defining its frequency of occurrence. Two possibilities exist, either a daily flow duration curve or a flood frequency distribution.

If the daily flow duration curve is used to calculate the flow doing most work it follows that the sediment rating curve should also be based on average daily values. Clearly there would be considerable scatter associated with such a rating curve because, for a given average daily flow, the passage of a flood wave would give a higher sediment load than a steady discharge. This scatter would make any calculation of the total sediment load very inaccurate.

In order to overcome this problem the time base would have to be reduced so that discharges do not fluctuate significantly within each time period. This would reduce some of the scatter on the sediment rating curve although the fundamental problem of differences between the sediment loads associated with the rising and falling stages would still exist. Wolman and Miller[9] advocated the use of this shorter time period when they used sediment volumes associated with individual flood peaks in some of their calculations. They argued that it offers a more realistic way of calculating the flow doing most work because the relatively low and steady flows are ignored so that flood flows can be given their rightful weighting. If this is the case then it is likely that the return period of bankfull flow will correlate best with a flood frequency distribution based on discrete flood data rather than a percentage flow duration value obtained from the average daily discharge distribution.

To test this hypothesis and define the frequency of bankfull flow, field data were obtained for the bankfull discharge at 78 sites on the rivers

Wye, Severn and Tweed.[7] As the majority of these sites were not at gauging stations direct comparisons between bankfull discharge and the various flow duration and flood frequency discharges could not be made. Instead it was necessary to try to predict regional runoff patterns so that comparisons could be made.

For the three rivers the flow records of all the gauging stations on the trunk stream were analysed in order to obtain their flow duration and annual flood frequency curves. The records were standardised to the longest record within each basin using Searcy's method[11] for the flow duration series and Dalrymple's method[12] for the annual flood frequency series.

To construct the regional runoff patterns a simple model was established linking runoff and the contributing basin area of the form

$$Q = CA^n$$

where Q is the discharge (cumecs) and A the basin area (square kilometres).

For the flow duration data it was possible to fit straight lines through the data points using regression techniques (Figs. 7.8, 7.9, 7.10). Because of the confidence shown in these equations, slopes and correlation coefficients being significantly greater than zero at the 95 per cent level, the prediction of flow duration curves for any point along the trunk stream is simple and accurate.[13]

The data for the flood frequency flows can also be plotted against the contributing basin areas. Although the same basic trend is evident in these graphs it was not possible to fit a straight line through the scatter of points (Figs. 7.11, 7.12, 7.13). In particular the graphs for the Wye and Severn show some rather anomalous patterns in the areas downstream from Erwood and Abermule. This is due to flood attenuation and results from increased channel and overbank storage within flood plain areas. Wherever there is considerable local storage capacity flood peaks may be reduced in a downstream direction and this is the case on the Wye between Erwood and Belmont and between Abermule and Montford on the Severn. Local variability of this nature precludes the possibility of fitting straight-line relationships to the data. Instead each data point was linked by a straight line even though this is not an ideal solution.

These graphs can be directly compared with those of bankfull discharge plotted against the contributing basin area (Figs. 7.14, 7.15, 7.16). This proves that the intermediate flood flows are responsible for the three-dimensional geometry of natural channels because bankfull discharge is closely associated with the 1·5 year flood on the annual series.

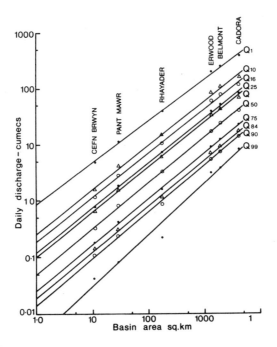

Fig. 7.8   River Wye – downstream daily flow duration curves (1937–62)

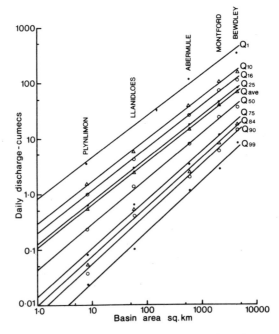

Fig. 7.9   River Severn – downstream daily flow duration curves (1937–66)

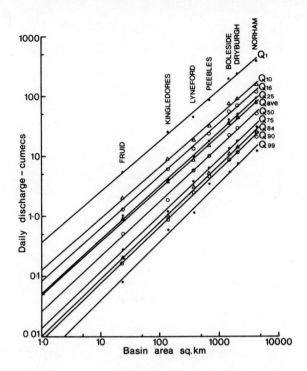

Fig. 7.10   River Tweed — downstream daily flow duration curves (1952–65)

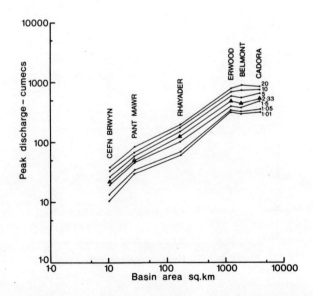

Fig. 7.11   River Wye — downstream flood frequency curves (1937–64)

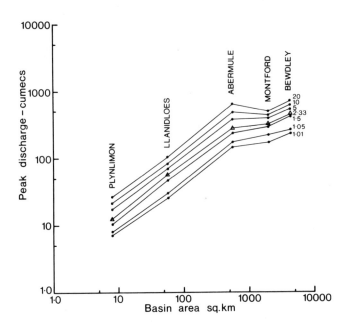

Fig. 7.12 River Severn — downstream flood frequency curves (1937—65)

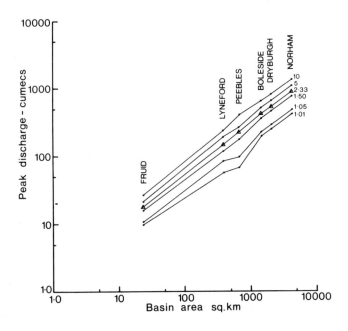

Fig. 7.13 River Tweed — downstream flood frequency curves (1951—66)

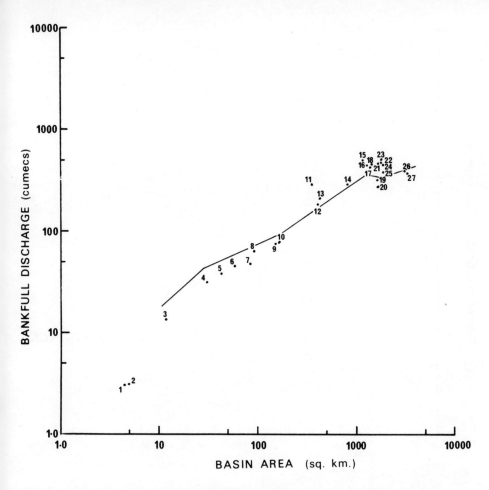

Fig. 7.14   River Wye — downstream variations in bankfull discharge

The scatter of data points about this line reflects the rather inaccurate definition of the regional flood pattern and also the influence of channel instability on the recurrence interval of bankfull flow. Eroding sites plot above the line and depositing ones below it.

7.5   Design discharge

This analysis indicates that the design discharge for stable natural channels with cobble beds in the 1·5 year flood based on the annual series. In addition the design sediment discharge will be the input load associated with this flow. However, application of these values for design purposes

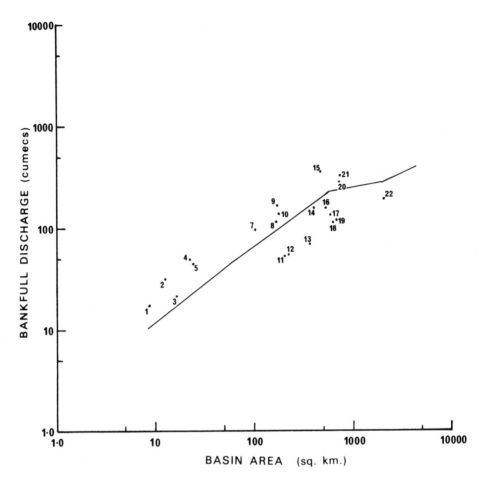

Fig. 7.15   River Severn – downstream variations in bankfull discharge

requires some clarification.

It is not usually necessary to redesign a reach of stable channel unless it is being straightened or protected for flood relief or navigational purposes. In this situation the original bankfull flow and sediment load could be utilised in the design equations.

Redesign is usually carried out for eroding or depositing sections in order to stabilise them. In eroding channels the bankfull flow will be large with a low return period. To stabilise this type of channel it is necessary to reduce its capacity and also its ability to transport sediment. Regional flood runoff patterns will provide a value of 1·5 year flood and this, together with the input load associated with the flow, will enable a new channel to be constructed. Conversely, depositing sections will have a

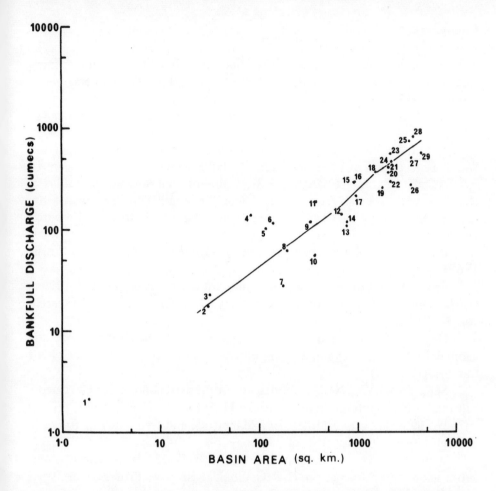

Fig. 7.16   River Tweed — downstream variations in bankfull discharge

more frequent return period which means that the channel capacity and its transporting ability has to be increased in order to establish an equilibrium condition. As before, the 1·5 year flood and its input sediment load will enable a new channel to be constructed.

These techniques will only succeed if the whole length of the unstable reach is redesigned. If only a part of the unstable section is reconstructed the solution will only be a temporary one because the input load is not controlled. For sites which were originally eroding the new channel will aggrade because the sediment input will increase due to continued upstream erosion. Similarly for sites which had been depositing the new channel will degrade because sediment input will decline as a result of upstream deposition.

87

References

[1] Inglis, Sir Claude C., Meanders and their bearing on river training (Maritime and Waterways Paper No. 7, Institution of Civil Engineers, January 1947).

[2] Inglis, Sir Claude C., The behaviour and control of rivers and canals (Research Publication No. 13 of the Central Board of Irrigation, India 1949).

[3] Nixon, M., A study of the bankfull discharge of rivers in England and Wales (Proceedings of the Institution of Civil Engineers 12, 1959).

[4] Ackers, P. and Charlton, F.G., Dimensional analysis of alluvial channels with special reference to meander length (Proceedings of the American Society of Civil Engineers, Journal of Hydraulics Research Division 8 [3] 1970).

[5] Blench, T., Mobile bed fluviology (University of Alberta Press, 1969).

[6] Pruis, A. and de Vries, M., On dominant discharge concepts for rivers (14th Congress of the International Association for Hydraulic Research, vol. 3, 1971).

[7] Hey, R.D., An analysis of the factors influencing the hydraulic geometry of river channels, unpublished PhD thesis, University of Cambridge, 1972).

[8] Schaffernak, F., Neue Grundlagen für die Berechnung der Geschiedeführung in Flussläufen (Frank Denticke [Leipzig and Wien], 1922).

[9] Wolman, M.G. and Miller, J.P., Magnitude and frequency of forces in geologic processes (Journal of Geology 68, 1960).

[10] Wolman, M.G. and Leopold, L.B., River flood plains: some observations on their formation (US Geological Survey, Professional Paper 282−C, 1959).

[11] Searcy, J.K., Flow duration curves (US Geological Survey, Water Supply Paper 1542−A, 1959).

[12] Dalrymple, T., Flood frequency analysis (US Geological Survey, Water Supply Paper 1543−A, 1960).

[13] Hey, R.D., Flow frequency prediction and the development of regional runoff patterns, paper presented to the British Association for the Advancement of Science, Exeter 1969).

8 The Use of a Hydrologic Simulation Model in the Control of a Water – Resource System

Dr D.G. JAMIESON

8.1 Introduction

Ever since the science of hydrology came into being there has been a particular fascination with the relationship between rainfall and stream-flow. It was quickly appreciated that the same amount of rainfall over an area would not necessarily produce the same amount of runoff and that the initial wetness of the catchment played an important role. It was a matter for common observation that if there had been no rainfall for several days prior to the storm-event in question then less runoff occurred than had it rained the previous day. This fact did not explain all of the differences that occurred between runoff totals from similar rainfall events. In particular, there was a noticeable tendency for comparable rainfall events to produce more runoff during the winter months than the summer months. Moreover, it was observed that a larger percentage of rainfall appeared as runoff with the shorter but higher-intensity storms. Had regression techniques been appreciated in those early years, there would have been no need for the laborious 'coaxial correlation' method which graphically related rainfall amount to total runoff using the initial state of the catchment (antecedent precipitation index), month of the year and rainfall duration as parameters.[1]

Unfortunately this means of predicting the total amount of runoff only partially fulfilled the objective of being able to forecast the temporal distribution of flow rates in general and peak flow rate in particular. Previously, it had been noticed that individual catchments displayed characteristic hydrograph shapes,[2] which were to some extent dependent on the duration of heavy rainfall. This gave rise to the concept of the unit hydrograph[3] based on the principles of superposition and proportionality. It was only relatively recently[4] that an explicit representation of unit hydrograph theory was given from the standpoint of linear, time-invariant systems. This procedure of using coaxial correlation to determine total amount of runoff followed by scaling the appropriate duration unit hydrograph is still in common use for flow forecasting.

Concurrent with this total approach to the problem of flow forecasting, researchers had been trying to explain the observed behaviour of individual subsystems which comprise the land-phase of the hydrologic cycle. Typical examples were Horton[5] with his experiments on infiltration and Zoch[6] with his linear representation of flow routing. However, for obvious computorial reasons, it was not until after the advent of the computer era that attempts were made to produce deterministic models of the complete land-phase. One of the best known models, which typifies the general purpose simulation approach for converting rainfall to runoff, is the Stanford Mark IV.[7]

It has only recently been appreciated that these large, general purpose models are not ideal for real time flow forecasting. Instead, purpose built models have been developed for implementation on small control computers. Such models need not be explanatory since their only purpose is to provide flow forecasts in real time. However, they should be economic on computer store, robust and capable of continual updating. It is perhaps more appropriate to regard this class of model as an element of a feed-forward control system for operating water resources schemes rather than an isolated flow-forecasting procedure. This paper outlines one such attempt to operate a series of multi-purpose reservoirs which regulate the River Dee in North Wales (Fig. 8.1). [8, 9]

8.2   Multi-purpose reservoir operation: River Dee

8.2.1   *On-line data processing*

The success of operating a multi-purpose reservoir system in real time is dependent upon minimal delay between a change of state in the hydrologic system occurring and the appropriate decision being implemented. This is especially true when flooding is imminent. With this in mind the first phase of a comprehensive telemetry scheme has been installed in the Dee catchment (Fig. 8.2) and is operational; phase two is currently being designed and could include radar as the prime rainfall sensor rather than the telemetering rain-gauges indicated. The number of outstations required to define the existing state of the system is large and requires an automated scheme for on-line processing of the telemetered data. Rainfall amounts, reservoir levels, river and tributary levels are relayed to the

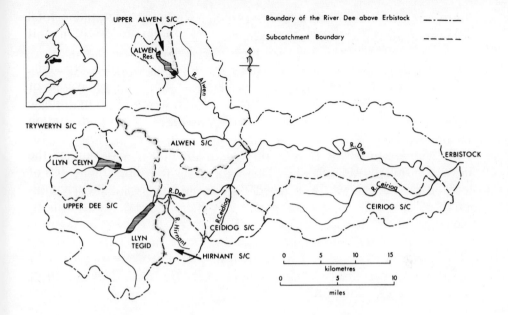

Fig. 8.1   The River Dee multi-purpose reservoir system

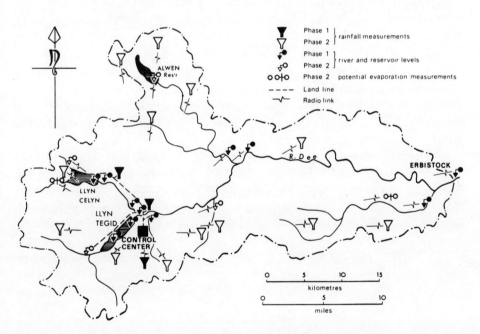

Fig. 8.2   Phase 1 and proposed Phase 2 of the Dee telemetry scheme

91

control centre every half hour by land-line or radio depending on the distance of the outstation from the centre.

The optimal control of the reservoir sluices depends on the ability to forecast future flow sequences. Therefore the framework of the short-term control strategy comprises a hydrologic simulation package mnemonically referred to as DISPRIN (Dee Investigation Simulation Programme for Regulating Integrated Networks). This acts on the telemetered rainfall data and upstream tributary flows to produce forecast hydrographs which are routed through reservoirs, if appropriate, and down the main river channel. These forecasts form the input to the decision mechanism which is based on dynamic programming. Thus the action of the small control computer every half hour is firstly to scan the telemetry scheme to ascertain the existing state of the system, secondly to forecast the future state of the system and finally to decide the optimal releases from the reservoirs. Ultimately it may be possible to dispense with the manual operation of the reservoir outflow sluices and substitute on-line control by computer.

8.2.2 *Flow forecasting*

The simulation package, DISPRIN, is constructed in a modular form. Programmes representing sub-catchments, reservoirs, tributaries and main river channel can be linked in an order corresponding to the physical system. The linkage code describing how these various components are joined together is flexible enough to accommodate most configurations. Should a new reservoir be constructed or an existing direct-supply reservoir be converted to a multi-purpose reservoir, altering the pro-gramme entails little more than modifying the linkage code and a few parameters. A schematic representation of DISPRIN as applied to the River Dee system is given in Fig. 8.3.

The rainfall-runoff process on each sub-catchment is represented by a cascade of linear and non-linear elements which takes into account the processes of the flow regimes, overland flow, quick-return flow and base flow. The model is semi-distributed in that it allows for areal variations in rainfall, soil characteristics and evaporation. All the non-linearity is contained within the accounting procedure. The flow routing is entirely linear and is achieved by cascading through two unequal linear elements for which the impulse reponse is

$$u(0, t) = \frac{e^{-t/K} - e^{-t/K_c}}{K - K_c}$$

The storage coefficient K pertains to the imaginary storage simulating the particular flow regime in question and the storage coefficient K_c pertains to the common channel into which they cascade. The forecast sub-catchment hydrograph is assembled by the superposition of all three flow regimes.

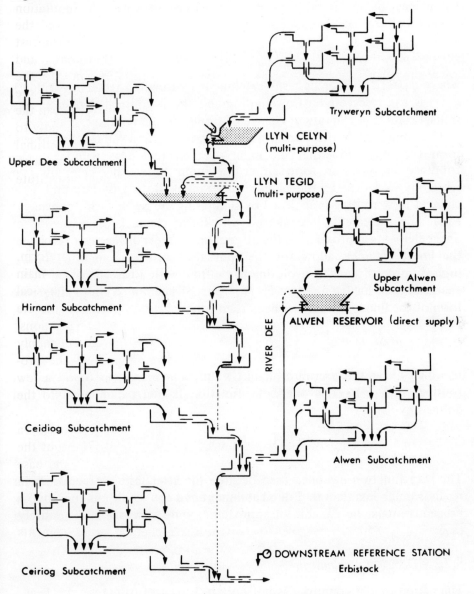

Fig. 8.3   DISPRIN as applied to the River Dee system

Reservoirs, which may be multi-purpose or direct-supply, can be incorporated in parallel or series. Each reservoir is defined by its storage-level relationship and can have either a broad-crested weir or a bellmouth spillway. For reservoir levels in excess or crest level, the routing of forecast sub-catchment hydrographs through the reservoir is achieved by means of an iterative search procedure to solve the continuity equation

$$q_1(t) = q_2(t) + \frac{ds}{dt}$$

where $q_1(t)$ is the forecast sub-catchment hydrograph (reservoir inflow), $q_2(t)$ is the reservoir outflow hydrograph (both controlled releases and spillage) and $\frac{ds}{dt}$ is the rate of change of storage in the reservoir.

The combined outflow from a reservoir or a natural sub-catchment can form the input to either the main river channel or a tributary. The tributary in turn can form either the input to another reservoir (for reservoirs in series) or the main river channel. Both tributary and main channel flow routing is achieved by simulating the reach with a cascade of equal linear elements interspersed with linear channels. The cascade of linear elements approximates the attenuation effects of the river reach and the linear channels allow for the translation effects. The flow routing procedure consists of convoluting the inflow with a cascade of 'n' linear elements each having an identical storage coefficient k. A finite difference form of the linear cascade has been used where

$$u(\Delta t, t) = \frac{1}{K} \cdot \left\{ \frac{\Delta t}{K} \right\}^{n-1} \cdot \frac{1}{tB(n, t)} \cdots \left\{ 1 - \frac{t}{K} \right\}^{t}$$

in which t is an integer (multiple of the unit time increment Δt chosen for routing) and $B(n, t)$ is the beta function having parameters n, t and defined by

$$\int_0^1 x^{n-1} (1-x)^{t-1} dx \qquad n > 0 \qquad t > 0$$

The beta function has been used because the attenuating effect of a river reach is much less than that of a catchment and any viable channel routing procedure must be capable of approaching pure translation as a limiting case.

8.2.3 Decision mechanism

The action of the computer is not only to forecast future reservoir levels, tributary and river flows but also to calculate the optimal reservoir

94

releases on the basis of those forecasts. Since the Dee system is prone to flooding around the edge of Llyn Tegid as well as in the vicinity of Erbistock, it is not immediately obvious what form the optimal reservoir action should take when inundation is probable. Therefore the high-flow decision mechanism has been posed as a dynamic programming formulation which has been simplified to three state variables and one decision variable. At any instant of time the system can be described by Llyn Tegid level s, the Erbistock flow rate q, and the rate of release from Llyn Tegid r. If the minimum cost attainable between now and the time horizon is defined as f_m (s, q, r) and the relevant cost is the maximum cost incurred at either Llyn Tegid $R(s)$ or Erbistock $E(q)$, the decision d (defined as the change in the current rate of release) would be to minimise this maximum. Hence:

$$f_m(s,q,r) = \min_d \left\{ \max \left[R(s), E(q), f_{m-1} \left(T(s,q,r \mid d) \right) \right] \right\}$$

or:

$$f_m (s,q,r) = \max \left\{ R(s), E(q), \min_d f_{m-1} \left[T(s,1,r \mid d) \right] \right\}$$

where $T(s, q, r \mid d)$ denotes the values of s, q, r, adjusted according to the decision d. The f_m (s, q, r) can be evaluated for successive m starting with f_0 $(s, q, r) = \max \left\{ R(s), E(q) \right\}$, all r, given the transformation T.

8.2.4 *Computing requirements*

DISPRIN is currently written in Fortran IV and can be implemented on an ICL 1902A computer (32k 24-bit words). The core storage requirement is independent of the complexity of the water-resource system to which DISPRIN is applied but the processing time and disk storage requirements are directly proportional not only to the number of sub-catchments but also to the number of reservoirs.

Eventually the programme will be re-written in machine language for the small computer that will control the operating scheme. The computing system for the River Dee application has still to be decided. The existing PDP 8s (8k 12-bit words, 32k words disk storage) which was only intended to control the telemetry, has insufficient core store for the on-line data processing. One possible solution is to use the PDP 8s as a front-end processor to control the telemetry as before linked to a PDP 11 (32k 16-bit words) for the data processing. Whatever computing system is installed, it is estimated that the telemetry scheme will require 3 minutes of computing time, leaving a minimum of 27 minutes to update the flow forecasts and compute the optimal releases, prior to the next telemetry scan.

8.3 Conclusion

With the computer relieving the reservoir manager of repetitive forecasts and decision-making, more of his time will be available to monitor the performance of the system for which his experience is best suited. The computer will bring unusual input values or forecasts to the attention of the manager who, ideally, should have the facility to edit them. In this way the computer will be an aid to management rather than a replacement.

References

[1] Linsley, R.K., Kohler, M.A. and Paulus, J.L.H., Applied Hydrology (McGraw-Hill, New York 1949).
[2] Report of the Committee on Floods (Journal of the Boston Society for Civil Engineering 17 [4] 1930).
[3] Sherman, L.K., Streamflow from rainfall by the unit-graph method (Engineering News Record 108, 1932).
[4] Dooge, J.C.I., A general theory of the unit hydrograph (Journal of Geophysical Research 64 [2], 1959).
[5] Horton, R.E., Analysis of run off plot experiments with varying infiltration capacity (Transactions of the American Geophysical Union 20, 1939).
[6] Zoch, R.T., On the relation between rainfall and streamflow (Monthly Weather Review 62 [9], 1934).
[7] Crawford, N.K. and Linsley, R.K., Digital simulation in hydrology (Stanford Watershed Model 4, Technical Report 39, Department of Civil Engineering Stanford University, California 1966).
[8] Jamieson, D.G., Operation of multi-purpose reservoir systems for water-supply and flood alleviation (Water Resources 8 [4], 1972).
[9] Jamieson, D.G. and Wilkinson, J.C., A short term control strategy for multi-purpose reservoir systems (Water Resources Research 8 [4], 1972).

9 Stochastic Modelling and Simulation Techniques in Water Resource Systems Planning

Dr P.E. O'CONNELL

9.1 Introduction

Simulation was born long before the electronic digital computer, and finds its origin in the early days of mathematical statistics. In the early half of the nineteenth century the subject of statistics consisted largely of the collection and display, in graphical form, of data from such fields as economics and actuarial science. The histogram or frequency chart emerged as a useful tool for the graphical display of data and, with the realisation that a histogram could be explained as a practical consequence of the laws of probability, statistics entered a new era. The idea of a probability distribution had been contrived by mathematicians, and could be interpreted as a description of an infinite number of items. As histograms are composed of a finite number of items, a histogram came to be thought of as a representative of a sample from an underlying theoretical probability distribution. Mathematical statisticians then had as their goal the description of a probability distribution, given only a sample from it. Uncertain early attempts to solve this problem required some experimental verification and, in response to this need, the sampling experiment emerged. A close approximation to a probability distribution was created, samples were taken, combined and transformed in suitable ways and the resulting frequency chart of sampled values compared with the predictions of theory.[1]

The advent of the electronic digital computer, and the development of suitable random-number generators for use thereon, widened the potential of the sampling experiment enormously. While formidable advances have been made through applying sophisticated techniques of mathematical analysis in statistics, many problems still emerge which cannot be solved by analysis, and for which the sampling experiment represents the only feasible means of solution. The field of hydrology is a ready source of such problems.

9.2   Synthetic streamflow generation

The efficient design and operation of a water resource system inevitably demands the quantification of the temporal and spatial behaviour of streamflow within the system. Probability theory is frequently employed as a means of quantifying the inherent variability and complexity of streamflow. Such a quantification affords a means of formulating an objective methodology for assessing the inherent risks and uncertainties associated with hydrological design, which must frequently be undertaken in the face of inadequate data.

A description of streamflow in terms of probabilistic laws necessitates that streamflow be hypothesised as a stochastic process; in this context, the stochastic process represents a mathematical or stochastic model of streamflow. For purposes of application, a stochastic model must be specified in terms of a set of parameters, which specify in turn the probability law of the stochastic process; in this form the model is sometimes referred to as a generating process. The values of the parameters will be unknown, and statistical estimates of these parameters must be abstracted from the observed historic record. The stochastic model can then be combined with the sampling of random numbers on a digital computer to yield sequences of synthetic flows. These sequences of synthetic flows can then be viewed as likely projections of future flows within a water resource system, and will hopefully contain critical periods of low or high flow which might not be expected to occur within short historic records. The response of a water resource system to such critical periods of flow can thus be more readily assessed.

Stochastic techniques of flow synthesis are frequently referred to collectively as synthetic hydrology; it is important to note, however, that while very many synthetic flows may be generated, new information is not created. Synthetic hydrology is merely a sophisticated technique for fully utilising the information contained in historic records.

The time unit for which synthetic flows are to be generated will generally be dictated by the problem to be solved. In the design and operation of water resource systems, daily, monthly or annual flows are invariably used, depending on what time unit sensitivity tests demand. However, daily flows frequently exhibit characteristics, such as recession effects, which have been averaged out on a monthly or annual time scale, and consequently different approaches may have to be used for different time units. Seasonal effects have to be modelled in monthly or daily flows. Persistence, which is the tendency for high flows to follow high flows and low flows to follow low flows, is present to a greater or lesser extent in most streamflow sequences, and must be quantified and modelled properly to ensure that realistic synthetic flows are generated. Persistence tends to decrease as the time interval over which streamflow is averaged is increased.

Thomas and Fiering[2] were apparently the first to combine the use of an electronic digital computer, the sampling of random numbers on the computer and a model which took some account of seasonality and persistence in streamflow, in order to generate synthetic flows for use in the design of water resource systems. They suggested that their model, the lag-one Markov or autoregressive process, could be used for generating monthly, seasonal or annual flows. Since then, some deficiencies in the lag-one Markov model as a generating process for streamflow have been identified, and more sophisticated models have been advanced which overcome these deficiences.

9.3 Generation of annual flows

9.3.1 *The lag-one Markov process*

For the generation of annual synthetic flows, the univariate lag-one Markov process is formulated as

$$(X_t - \mu) = (X_{t-1} - \mu) + \sigma \sqrt{1 - \rho^2} \, \epsilon_t \qquad (9.1)$$

where X_t and X_{t-1} are the flows for times t and $(t-1)$ respectively, ϵ_t is an independently distributed random variable independent of X_{t-1}, and μ, σ and ρ are the mean, standard deviation and lag-one autocorrelation of the process. Estimates of the latter parameters, denoted as $\hat{\mu}$, $\hat{\sigma}$ and $\hat{\rho}$, respectively, are derived from a historic sequence of annual flows. To generate synthetic flows using equation (9.1), the term ϵ_t is sampled from the appropriate distribution using a random number generator. Annual flows are quite often approximately normally distributed; if ϵ_t is sampled from a normal distribution, then X_t will be normal, and synthetic flows will resemble historic flows in terms of $\hat{\mu}$, $\hat{\sigma}$ and $\hat{\rho}$.

Techniques for generating synthetic flows when the historic flows are skewed have been presented by Matalas[3] who has also developed a multi-site extension of equation (9.1) for generating synthetic flows at several sites within a river basin. The multi-site model ensures that cross-correlations between the flows at the various sites are modelled.

99

9.3.2 *Fractional Gaussian noise*

The autocorrelation function of the lag-one Markov process, which is given as

$$\rho_k = \rho^k \tag{9.2}$$

where ρ is the lag-one autocorrelation coefficient, and k is the lag, dictates the type of persistence modelled within synthetic sequences generated by equation (9.1). A typical value of p for annual streamflow is 0·3; thus, from equation (9.2) it can be seen that the persistence modelled by the lag-one Markov process is essentially short-term, as ρ_k approaches zero extremely quickly. However, the studies of Hurst,[4, 5] based on some 800 geophysical time series ranging in length from 40 to 2,000 years, provide strong evidence of long-term persistence.[6] A parameter h was used by Hurst to quantify the low-frequency movements observed in long geophysical time series, with $0 < h < 1$. Long-term persistence is synonymous with the presence of low frequencies, and is typified by values of h in the range 0·5 $< h < 1$ while values of h in the range $0 < h \leqslant 0·5$ are synonymous with short-term persistence. Hurst's extensive studies yielded an average value of 0·73 for h; however, for the lag-one Markov process, h equals 0·5, which implies that the process cannot adequately model long-term persistence. Mandelbrot and Wallis[6] proposed discrete-time fractional Gaussian noise (*dfGn*) as a model of Hurst's time series, with the parameter h explicitly incorporated and with an autocorrelation function which decays very slowly. In theory, *dfGn* possesses an infinite memory, and approximations to *dfGn* with finite memories must be used for generating synthetic flows. Some of these approximations are cumbersome and expensive to compute; an example is the filtered *dfGn* approximation proposed by Matalas and Wallis[7] as

$$X_t = (h - 0·5) \sum_{u=pt-M}^{pt-1} (pt - u)^{h-1·5} \epsilon_u \tag{9.3}$$

where $0·5 < h < 1$, M is a memory parameter, ϵ_u is sampled from a N (0, 1) distribution, and $p > 1$ is an integer. Matalas and Wallis[7] have shown how the process given by equation (9.3) may be formulated so as to preserve estimates of the mean, variance, skewness, lag-one auto-correlation and Hurst coefficient h. However, the estimation of h presents formidable difficulties.[8]

9.3.3 *The ARIMA (1, 0, 1) process*

The complexity of approximations to *dfGn* has tended to inhibit their widespread use as generating processes. A simple first-order autoregressive moving average process or, in Box and Jenkins'[9] terminology, an ARIMA (1, 0, 1) process, has also been found to be a suitable model for Hurst's time series, [10] enabling both short-term and long-term effects to be reproduced in synthetic sequences. The process is defined as

$$X_t = \phi X_{t-1} + \epsilon_t - \Theta \epsilon_{t-1} \qquad (9.4)$$

where ϕ and Θ are parameters which enable estimates of both ρ and h to be modelled within synthetic sequences. The process is attractive because of its elegant simplicity and, for $\Theta = O$, it subsumes the lag-one Markov process, over which it enjoys considerable advantages. The necessary documentation for generating synthetic sequences which preserve estimates of μ, σ, ρ and h has been given by O'Connell[11].

9.4   Generation of monthly flows

9.4.1   *The Thomas-Fiering model*

The basic generating processes used for generating annual flows can generally be suitably adapted for generating monthly flows. Thomas and Fiering[2] assumed that flows for each calendar month are generated by a lag-one Markov process. The process thus preserves the seasonality in monthly means, variances and lag-one autocorrelations, and is formulated as

$$\frac{X_{t+1} - \mu_{p+1}}{\sigma_{p+1}} = \rho_{p+1}(1) \frac{X_t - \mu_p}{\sigma_p} + \sqrt{1 - \rho_{p+1}^2(1)} \; \epsilon_{t+1} \qquad (9.5)$$

where X_{t+1} and X_t are the monthly flows for times $t+1$ and t respectively; μ_{p+1} and μ_p are the means for months $p+1$ and p, respectively, where $p = 0, 1, \ldots, 11$ and is cyclic, σ_{p+1} and σ_p are the standard deviations for months $p+1$ and p, respectively, and $\rho_{p+1}(1)^p$ is the lag-one autocorrelation for month $p+1$. The term ϵ_{t+1} is again an independent random variable with zero mean and unit variance. As monthly flows exhibit higher skewnesses than annual flows, the preservation of skewness will generally be of interest, and can be achieved through using techniques proposed by Matalas.[3]

A multi-site extension of equation (9.5) has been developed by Bernier.[12]

9.5   Generation of daily flows

9.5.1   *The shot-noise model*

The successful simulation of daily flows is more difficult than that of monthly or annual flows, primarily because some complex effects, such as recessions, are more pronounced on a daily time scale. An attractive and promising approach has been developed by Weiss[13] under a contract between the former Water Resources Board and the Departments of Mathematics and Civil Engineering, Imperial College, University of London. The basic shot-noise process is a continuous time process, and is defined as

$$X(t) = \sum_{r=N(-\infty)}^{N(t)} y_r\, e^{-b(t-\tau_r)} \tag{9.6}$$

The process derives from a series of events occuring at random times τ_r defined by a Poisson process $N(t)$ with rate ν. Associated with each time τ_r is a magnitude y_r which is random and follows an exponential distribution with mean Θ. Finally, y_r produces a response or pulse in the flow defined as $e^{-b(t-\tau_r)}$. A loose physical interpretation in hydrological terms is that the times τ_r represent the beginnings of rainstorms, with the variables y_r loosely corresponding to the amount of water in a rainstorm. The function $e^{-b(t-\tau_r)}$ then represents the system transfer function.

For application purposes, an averaged shot-noise process is defined as

$$X_t = \int_{t-1}^{t} X(\tau)\, d\tau \tag{9.7}$$

The mean, variance and lag-one autocorrelation of X_t, which are estimated from the historic daily flows, can then be used to define the parameters ν, Θ and b. The shot noise process can also model recession effects adequately, in contrast to approaches based on a Gaussian distribution. Seasonality may be accounted for by assuming that daily flows within each of the twelve calendar months are generated by separate shot-noise processes.

Even though estimates of μ, σ and ρ for daily flows within each calendar month were preserved, a single shot-noise process was found to be inadequate for modelling low flow periods successfully as the recessions approached zero flow too rapidly.[13, 14]   A double shot-noise

102

process was thus proposed consisting of a sum of two independent shot-noise processes. One of these processes, the 'fast' process, corresponds loosely to a surface runoff mechanism, while the 'slow' process vaguely corresponds to a groundwater discharge mechanism. The double shot noise model was found to be a reasonable model of daily stream flow; a graphical comparison can be made between some historic data in Fig. 9.1 and some synthetic data in Fig. 9.2. However, a criticism of the model is that the fast and slow processes are independent. The equations for defining the parameters of the double shot-noise process are given by Weiss [13] for the multi-site as well as the single site case. An algorithm for generating the shot noise process has also been documented. [13, 14]

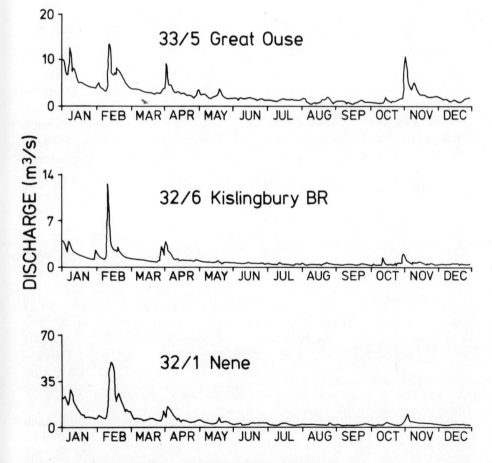

Fig. 9.1   Daily streamflows, East Anglia, 1953

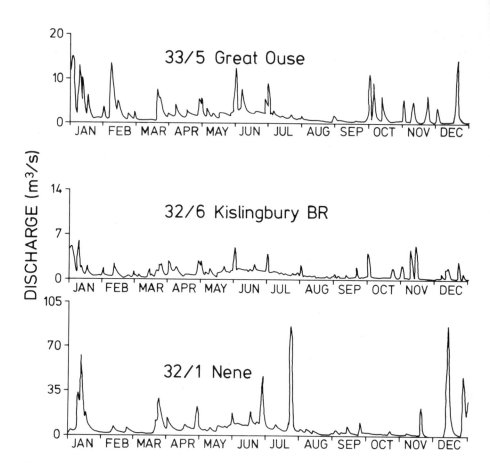

Fig. 9.2   Double shot-noise model, synthetic daily data

9.6   Water resource system design and operation

In the past twenty years there has been a tremendous increase in the world's population attended by a consequent threat of a shortage of a number of natural resources. Water resources are not an exception, and the demand for more accurate evaluation of water resource system design has become more acute in the face of increasing demands for water products and services. The design problem has in the past fallen largely within the domain of engineering hydrology; however, in recent years economic theory has come to play a major role in system planning. The interacting roles of engineering hydrology and economics can best be studied through the methodology of systems analysis or operational research, which has now become widely accepted in the planning and management of water resources. The increasing use of techniques of optimisation and simulation, underlying systems analysis, in the field of water resources, has been closely linked with the development of high-speed large-memory digital computers. Techniques of simulation and optimisation, which afforded a study of the interactions between engineering hydrology and economics, were perhaps first applied on a large scale by the Harvard Water Programme. [15]

An excellent review of the conjoint use of simulation and optimisation techniques in water resource system planning and management has been given by Roefs. [16] He identified a certain sequence of decisions in the planning process:

(a)   the specification of the project to be built;
(b)   the time at which the project should be built;
(c)   the size to which the project should be built;
(d)   the target output which should be set;
(e)   the operation rules for the project; and
(f)   the 'real-time' operational control decisions.

The first three decisions may be characterised as planning decisions. The fourth decision may be regarded as a risk allocation decision, while the fifth decision is the operation plan. The sixth decision may be viewed as a 'real-time' management decision, which is the adjustment of decisions within a fine time scale to fit the operation rules. [16] However, the planning process is complicated by the fact that the planning decisions are interdependent, and are also dependent on the fourth and fifth decisions. In other words the project size cannot be decided without considering the definition of an optimal target for that project and the definition of an optimal set of operating rules for that project and target.

In general, the overall optimal design and operation of a water resource system will be too formidable a problem to permit an optimal solution. However, simulation affords a promising course of action which may be viable in certain cases. If, for example, in the case of a single reservoir system, the reservoir site and timing of construction happened to be known, then the reservoir size and target output could be defined through an iterative process suggested by Roefs (Fig. 9.3). This process is outlined in the following series of steps:

(a)   assume a reservoir size;
(b)   assume a target output;
(c)   for this reservoir size and target yield:

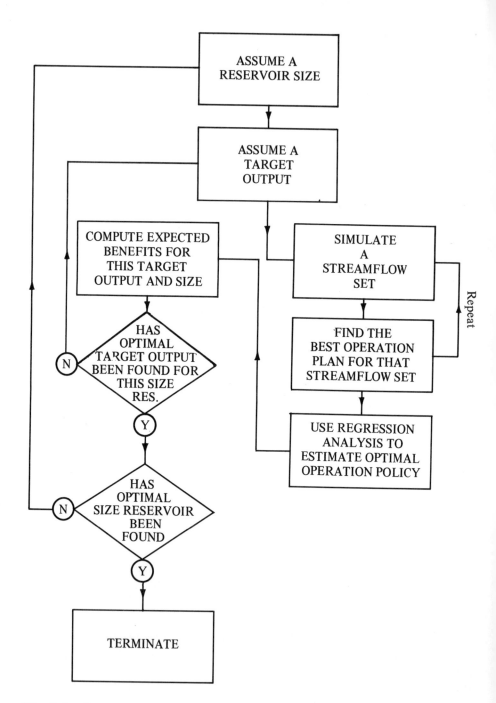

Fig. 9.3   Iterative process to define optimum reservoir size and target output (after Roefs [16])

(i)   simulate a streamflow sequence;

(ii)   find the best operation plan for that streamflow set;

(iii)   repeat steps (i) and (ii) several times; and

(iv)   use a regression analysis to determine the optimum operation plan;

(d)   estimate benefits for the assumed target output and size;

(e)   repeat steps b–d until the optimal target output for a given size has been found;

(f)   estimate benefits for the reservoir at this size;

(g)   repeat steps a–f until the optimal reservoir size is found.

Essentially, an optimisation–simulation technique for defining operating rules is embedded within the overall iterative process.

In a more complex design situation, the number of alternative designs which can be defined will generally be enormous, and the design problem and that of finding operating rules have generally been tackled separately. Nevertheless, in investigating designs, the straight simulation approach has been widely used, mainly because the number of feasible designs can be reduced considerably through the skill and experience of the planner. However, it will generally be impossible to prove formally that the design is optimal.

9.6.1 *Applications*

In sharp contrast to the multiplicity of theoretical papers on generating synthetic flows, relatively little has been published showing actual solutions of engineering problems by the use of such techniques. A stochastic simulation approach was adopted by O'Donnell, Hall and O'Connell[17] for (i) investigation into the effect of a reservoir in the headwaters on the flow of the River Dart in south-west England, and (ii) a flood magnitude frequency study of the River Vardar in Yugoslavia.

In case (i), daily flows were generated using a time series analysis approach similar to that proposed by Quimpo.[18] The properties of the flows which were of primary interest in this investigation, namely long-term average flows and flow duration curves, were successfully modelled.

In case (ii) a simulation approach was adopted because traditional distribution-fitting of annual maximum flows could not successfully establish the magnitude of a design flood at Skopje, Yugoslavia. Daily flows were again simulated using a time series model similar to that used in case (i). For this problem emphasis was placed on the extremal properties of the flows which were successfully reproduced. A total of

1,080 years of daily flows were generated, and a more acceptable solution than that provided by traditional approaches was obtained.

The application of synthetic data generation in the analysis of large-scale water resource systems has been undertaken by the former Water Resources Board of England and Wales. [19] Initially, mixed-integer programming models are used to identify a limited number of near-optimal least-cost solutions of satisfying the forecasted water demands. [20] These potential solutions are then explored through extensive simulation experiments. Up to the present, daily flows have been generated using an approach similar to that proposed by Quimpo; [18] however, the double shot-noise model discussed in section 9.5.1 is now being incorporated into the simulation programmes, enabling appropriate temporal and spatial properties of the flows to be preserved (Sexton, personal communication). Of particular interest is the reproduction of observed low-flow properties at all sites, which has been quite successfully achieved with the double shot-noise model.

9.7 Conclusions

In recent years, formidable advances have been made in the field of synthetic hydrology, and new models such as fractional Gaussian noise, the ARIMA (1, 0, 1) process and the shot-noise process have been developed, which enable important properties of observed flows to be reproduced more accurately in synthetic sequences. However, the model development phase should perhaps now give way to a phase where the performance of models in design situations should be thoroughly evaluated. In the presence of a number of alternative models for generating synthetic flows, the question arises as to which model should be used. In order to gain some insight into this latter problem, a contract has been established between the Water Resources Board and Imperial College with the purpose of providing an algorithm to guide the selection of a suitable model for generating synthetic hydrological data, and to assess the success in fitting the model.

In the case of annual flows, a decision theory approach to the model choice problem has been adopted by O'Connell and Wallis [21] where the choice of model is guided by a loss function. Synthetic hydrology permits the losses accruing from incorrect model choice to be established. However, considerable theoretical difficulties limit the scope of this approach.

References

[1] Tocher, K.D., The Art of Simulation (English Universities Press, London 1963).

[2] Thomas, H.A. and Fiering, M.B., Mathematical synthesis of stream-flow sequences for the analysis of river basins by simulation in A. Maas *et al.* (eds), Design of Water Resource Systems (Harvard University Press, Cambridge 1962).

[3] Matalas, N.C., Mathematical assessment of synthetic hydrology (Water Resources Research 3 [4], 1967).

[4] Hurst, H.E., Long term storage capacity of reservoirs (Transactions of the American Society of Civil Engineers 116, 1951).

[5] Hurst, H.E., Methods of using long term storage in reservoirs (Proceedings of the Institution of Civil Engineers 1, 1956).

[6] Mandelbrot, B.B. and Wallis, J.R., Noah, Joseph and operational hydrology (Water Resources Research 4 [5], 1968).

[7] Matalas, N.C. and Wallis J.R., Statistical properties of multivariate fractional noise processes (Water Resources Research 7 [6], 1971).

[8] Wallis, J.R. and Matalas, N.C., Small sample properties of H and K estimators of the Hurst coefficient h (Water Resources Research 6 [6], 1970).

[9] Box, G.E.P. and Jenkins, G.M., Time series analysis; forecasting and control (Holden-Day Inc., San Francisco, 1970).

[10] O'Connell, P.E., A simple stochastic modelling of Hurst's law (Proceedings of the International Symposium on Mathematical Models in Hydrology, Warsaw, International Association of Scientific Hydrology 1971).

[11] O'Connell, P.E., Stochastic modelling of long-term persistence in streamflow sequences (Internal Report 1974–2, Hydraulics and Hydrology Section, Imperial College, University of London 1974).

[12] Bernier, J., Inventaire des modèles de processes stochastiques applicables à la description des débits journaliers des rivières (Proceedings of the International Symposium on Mathematical Models in Hydrology, Warsaw, International Association of Scientific Hydrology 1971).

[13] Weiss, G., Filtered Poisson processes as models for daily streamflow data, unpublished PhD thesis, Imperial College, University of London 1973).

[14] Weiss, G., Shot-noise models for synthetic generation of multi-site daily streamflow data (Proceedings of the International Symposium on the Design of Water Resources Projects with Inadequate Data, Madrid, UNESCO/WMO 1973).

[15] Maas, A. *et al.*, Design of Water Resource Systems (Harvard University Press, Cambridge 1962).

[16] Roefs, T.G., Reservoir management: the state of the art, (Publication 320–3508, IMB Scientific Centre, Washington D.C. 1968).

[17] O'Donnell, T., Hall, M.J. and O'Connell, P.E., Some applications of stochastic hydrological models (Proceedings of the International Symposium on Mathematical Modelling Techniques, Ottawa, vol. 1, 1972).

[18] Quimpo, R.G., Stochastic model of daily river flow sequences (Hydrology Paper 18, Colorado State University, Fort Collins 1967).

[19] Jamieson, D.G., Radford, P. and Sexton, J.R., The hydrological design of water-resource systems (Water Resources Board Publication, Reading). In press.

[20] O'Neill, P.G., A mathematic programming model for planning a regional water resource system (Journal of the Institution of Water Engineers 26, 1972).

[21] O'Connell, P.E. and Wallis, J.R., Choice of generating mechanisms in synthetic hydrology with inadequate data (Proceedings of the International Symposium on the Design of Water Resources Projects with Inadequate Data, Madrid, UNESCO/WMO 1973).

10 Long Term Changes in the Water Quality of Agricultural Catchments

Dr A.M.C. EDWARDS

10.1 Introduction

It is a widely held belief that modern agricultural practices have led to a deterioration in the chemical and biological quality of rivers draining rural areas. This chapter examines the evidence of insidious background trends which may result from either the increased leaching or greater availability of material to be flushed from the soil. Gradual trends in composition are often difficult to detect from the background variability compared with the effects of more sudden changes, such as the addition of a new effluent outfall. The causes of gradual trends are often difficult to identify and control.

Most of this chapter is concerned with the trends in the concentration of nitrate nitrogen in rivers, for the following reasons.

1   Nitrogen is one of the major plant nutrients and is applied to the land in large quantities as fertiliser and farmyard manure.
2   Nitrogen is one of the nutrients that can cause accelerated eutrophication of rivers and lakes leading to difficulties in water treatment and sometimes to excessive plant growth.
3   Nitrate nitrogen in potable supplies can be toxic, particularly to infants. The recommended upper limits for drinking water range from 10 to 20 mg/l NO_3-N.[1]

Nitrate compounds are mostly highly soluble and move relatively rapidly in drainage waters through the soil. This is in marked contrast to phosphates, which have a low solubility and are readily absorbed on clay minerals. Nitrate is the principal nitrogen species in solution in rivers not seriously contaminated by sewage or industrial effluent.

Evidence for increases in nitrate concentration is first discussed from published data and then the patterns observed over the last twenty to thirty years for the River Stour in Essex and Suffolk (eastern England) are examined in more detail.

10.2 Trends in nitrate concentration in British and American rivers

The major problem in investigating long-term trends of any dissolved constituent in river water is the lack of reliable data. Widespread environmental monitoring is a fairly recent scientific exercise. Many records are either fragmentary or have inconsistencies resulting from a change in the site of a sampling station or of analytical method. There are for most common dissolved constituents in river waters several analytical techniques, some of which are unreliable. This fact, along with instrument and operator errors, means that a scatter of results are often found when replicate determinations are made on the same sample by different laboratories.[2] A range of concentration of 1–2 mg/l NO_3–N about a sample with 10 mg/l NO_3–N is not unusual and discrepancies of 5–10 mg/l NO_3–N are not unknown. Houghton[3] gives some examples of how a laboratory's change of analytical methods can distort a data record. In the case of some records the frequency of sampling is insufficient to pick out significant trends from other variations. The composition of rivers may vary with flow, and strong annual cycles in concentration are sometimes present.

The American Water Works Association enquiry into nitrogen and phosphorus compounds in surface waters in the USA came to the conclusion that there was no evidence, from the rather poor data available, of any universal upward trend in nitrate concentration since the beginning of the century.[4] The enquiry did find specific cases of marked increases though some were due to urbanisation. Much of the scanty early data from the USA is summarised in Clarke[5] but details of frequency of sampling and analytical techniques are lacking. The nitrate concentration of the Mississippi seems to have had a similar range at the beginning of the century to at least that recorded in the 1950s. The Mississippi does gain a proportion of its runoff from areas of limited agricultural value in the West. Increases in the input of the nutrient into rivers may be partly masked by its assimilation by plants. Bower and Wilcox[6] cite results that indicate that nitrate loads and concentrations have declined in some catchments of the Rio Grande over the last thirty years while the application of nitrogenous fertilisers has doubled. The policy of the Illinois State Water Survey since 1945 has been to collect samples from each of its 76 stations at monthly intervals for periods of five years.[7] Some stations have had more than one five-year sampling episode during the post-war period, but the data record is basically composed of a series of fragments from different locations. This is an example of how, for the sake of economy and to maximise the spatial cover, a sampling design has been adopted that rules out the quantitative assessment of one important water-resource parameter, trend in concentration. Harmeson and Larson[7] think, however, that there has been serious deterioration in quality, on the evidence that in recent years more infringements of the Illinois potability limit (10 mg/l NO_3–N) have been recorded than at the beginning of the period.

In Britain Tomlinson[8] has summarised the nitrate data available since the 1950s from 17 rivers, using the records of water undertakings and the Trent River Authority. He found a significant positive trend of mean annual nitrate concentration with time for six rivers, a downward trend for one river, and no significant correlation for the other eleven. Tomlinson went on to correlate annual fertiliser purchases in the counties the rivers drained and the mean annual nitrate concentration. Again no general relationships exist between the two variables. Owens[9] plotted mass flow (concentration times river discharge) of nitrogen per unit area against discharge for the years 1957 and 1967 for the Great Ouse, 1958 and 1968 for some Essex rivers and 1963 and 1967 for some Yorkshire ones. Although in all cases the fertiliser application had increased greatly, there were no significant changes in the mass of nitrogen transported. Owens et al.[10] used a similar approach in comparing nitrogenous fertiliser application rate with mass per unit area of nitrogen transported by 29 rivers draining predominantly agricultural catchments. There was no significant correlation. Again care is needed in interpreting these results, as nitrogen fertiliser application rates are on a county basis, hence giving only a rough guide to the increased mass of nitrogen introduced by modern agricultural techniques into the soil-plant system of each catchment.

Evidence has recently been presented showing significant upward trends in the nitrate levels of a number of public water supply rivers in south-east England. Examples are the rivers of the Great Ouse basin,[11] the Thames and Lee[12] and the Essex Stour. All these rivers contain nitrogen from effluents but probably also have an increasing mass derived from land drainage.

10.3   The River Stour

The Stour at Langham in Essex (near Colchester) drains a catchment of 570 km^2 and has a mean annual runoff of 115 mm. The Essex Water Company (formerly the South Essex Water Company) has collected river samples at this site at weekly intervals since the 1930s. The nature of this data record and the possible inconsistencies that may have occurred prior to 1950 due to changes in analytical methods are described by Houghton. [14] The Stour was one of the rivers where Tomlinson[8] found a significant correlation between mean annual nitrate concentration and both time and fertiliser application rate. Edwards and Thornes [13] used the weekly observations from 1951 to 1970 of pH, conductivity, chloride, nitrate, carbonate and non-carbonate hardness, ammoniacal nitrogen and permanganate value in a study of the application of time series techniques to water quality data. A significant linear correlation of concentration against time existed for both the weekly observations and mean annual values for all the chemical variables except pH and carbonate hardness (mostly from the solution of calcium carbonate minerals). There has been a similar trend in discharge — weighted concentration and no trend in river flow. These upward trends in concentration are in no way accounted for by the increases in sewage effluents going into the river. [14] Houghton has also observed a rise over the years of algal productivity that has led to a decline in performance of the slow sand filters at the waterworks.

The mean annual nitrate values smooth out the variability in the series due to the annual cycle. The sample mean based on 52 samples per year is estimated to give a very good prediction of the actual mean concentration (about ±0·5 mg/l NO_3N). The mean concentrations of nitrate, chloride and non-carbonate hardness are plotted on Figs. 10.1, 10.2 and 10.3. The mean annual concentrations of nitrate and non-carbonate hardness were both markedly higher during the wet years of 1957 and 1959 that followed dry ones. There is, however, no simple relationship between mean annual concentration and runoff, and the increases in nitrate and non-carbonate hardness concentration in recent years cannot be explained by changes in river discharge.

It can be seen from Fig. 10.1 that there seems to have been a take-off in mean annual nitrate concentration from 1965. In fact over the period 1948 to 1964 there was no significant trend in concentration. (Table 10.1). Prior to 1948 it is thought that some of the higher nitrate observations could have been slightly underestimated by the analytical method used.

During the 1960s there was a general phasing out of the use of ammonium sulphate fertilisers, which were superseded by ammonium nitrates. In Suffolk there was a decrease in the application rate of sulphur from 0·4 tonne/km^2 as S in 1963 to 0·05 tonne/km^2 in 1971. The amount applied to the land is small compared with the load of the river, approximately 10 tonnes/km^2 as S in 1970. It is thus unlikely that the trend in non-carbonate hardness is a result of fertiliser use. The magnitude

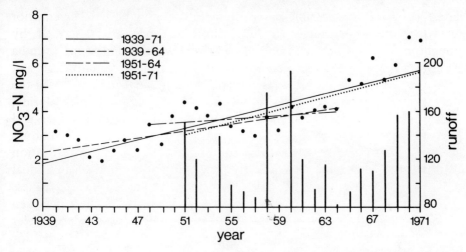

Fig. 10.1   Mean annual nitrate nitrogen concentration and runoff, River Stour.

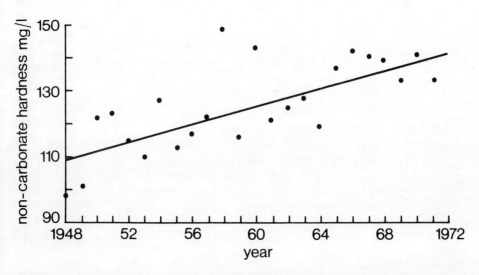

Fig. 10.2   Mean annual non-carbonate hardness concentration, River Stour

115

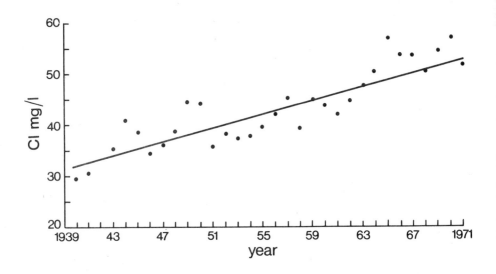

Fig. 10.3   Mean annual chloride concentration, River Stour

Table 10.1

Regression and correlation coefficients of time (years)
and mean annual concentration (mg l^{-1}

Constituent	Time period	Slope coefficient	Intercept	Correlation coefficient	Significance level (%)	Number of pairs of values
NO_3-N	1939–71	0·116	1·881	0·84	0·1	33
NO_3-N	1951–71	0·148	1·111	0·772	0·1	21
NO_3-N	1939–64	0·067	2·381	0·690	0·1	26
NO_3-N	1951–64	−0·002	3·830	−0·020	N.S.	14
Cl	1939–71	0·733	30·185	0·905	0·1	33
Non-carbonate hardness (as $CaCO_3$	1948–71	1·354	96·474	0·717	0·1	24

N.S. = not significant.

Time is the independent variable, year 1 = 1939.

of the increase in non-carbonate hardness is of an order that makes it extremely unlikely to be the result of ion-exchange mechanisms in the soil following the application of ammonium nitrate. The rate of deposition of sulphur from the atmosphere can be a significant amount in the sulphur budget of agricultural land. Garland[15] estimates a dry deposition rate of sulphur dioxide of 5·5 tonnes/km^2/year as S, and Edwards[16] estimated the amount in Norfolk deposited from rainfall to be 1·6 tonnes/km^2 as S in 1970. It is thought unlikely that there has been any increase in atmospheric deposition of sulphur during the 1950s and 1960s.[15]

The amount of nitrogenous fertiliser added to farmland in Suffolk in 1970 was 9·1 tonnes/km^2 as N compared with 5·2 tonnes/km^2 in 1963. The load of nitrate carried by the river was approximately 2·0 tonnes/km^2 as N in 1970. The reason for the increase in chloride concentration over the years is uncertain. Potassium chloride is added as a fertiliser but potassium determinations have not been regularly made on water from the Stour. The mass balance of nitrate, non-carbonate hardness and chloride indicates that the increases in these constituents cannot be accounted for by increases in the effluent input. The concentrations, and hence loads, of nitrate and non-carbonate hardness are highest at times of high flow when the effluents receive maximum dilution. 95 per cent of the nitrate load in 1970 was transported in the months January to April, November and December.

Superimposed upon the upward trend of nitrate and non-carbonate hardness (mostly from the solution of calcium sulphate minerals) is a strong seasonal cycle of relatively low concentration in summer and peaks coinciding with the largest winter flows. Similar patterns have been observed for other rivers in eastern England, for example the Great Ouse.[11] The number of occasions when concentrations greater than 10 mg/l NO_3–N have been reported from the Stour also appears to have risen (Table 10.2). This is an important, gradual change in quality as the water company has a policy of keeping the concentration of finished water to less than 10 mg/l NO_3–N by mixing the river water with borehole supplies of low nitrate concentration.

The close correlation between the concentrations of nitrate and non-carbonate hardness seems to indicate that the annual cycle is a phenomenon of leaching rather than of biological depletion or storage. Sulphur is a minor plant nutrient compared to nitrogen and it seems unlikely that uptake by aquatic organisms could affect the relatively high concentrations in the Stour. Edwards[17] noticed no depletion of nitrate concentration in the River Yare (Norfolk) during algal blooms though both phosphorus and silicon concentration (and hence mass) were

117

markedly reduced. Owens *et al.* [10] however, think that the low nitrate concentration in summer in the Stour and similar rivers could result partly from the uptake of the nutrient by acquatic plants or even from denitrification.

Table 10.2

Observations of 'high' nitrate—nitrogen concentrations in
the River Stour

Year	$>7\text{mgl}^{-1}\text{NO}_3\text{-N}$	$>10\text{mgl}^{-1}\text{NO}_3\text{-N}$
1951	10	0
1952	13	0
1953	6	0
1954	10	3
1955	3	0
1956	2	0
1957	5	1
1958	4	0
1959	4	2
1960	9	4
1961	2	0
1962	8	1
1963	2	1
1964	6	1
1965	14	9
1966	13	5
1967	19	8
1968	10	5
1969	21	3
1970	23	18

Heavy rain immediately after the application of nitrogenous fertilisers (mostly in March or April) can lead to a large mass of nitrate being washed from the soil. During the summer a store of nutrients will accumulate in the soil due to microbiological activity. Large amounts of material may be removed after the soil moisture deficit has been replenished. Edwards [16] observed the highest nitrate concentrations (up to 14 mg/l $\text{NO}_3\text{-N}$) in the Norfolk rivers during the second and third winter flush of the soil but not during the first. Potassium increased in concentration during the first storm hydrographs but was diluted by later ones. Observed nitrate concentrations during the early winter storms are no higher for the Stour than during later ones.

The nitrate and to a lesser extent sulphate minerals are highly soluble and located in the superficial deposits and soil covering the solid geology (chalk). The nitrates are concentrated in the upper horizons of the soil by biological activity and sulphates are particularly abundant in glacial drift. The concentrations of nitrate and non-carbonate hardness are greatest in the rivers when the drainage network is at its maximum extent through the soil. The greatest stores of nitrate will accumulate in the zones of the soil which are furthest from the channels and ditches and which, in the East Anglian catchments of very subdued relief, only intermittently contribute to the drainage. This mechanism may account for the very high concentration (and hence loads) recorded at times of high flow. It is, however, difficult to explain the low concentrations of nitrate in summer baseflow, which must be originally derived from winter infiltration. Part of the baseflow could pass through the soil after most of the nitrate available for solution has been removed. The solubility and availability of minerals in the soil and the frequency of leaching of various parts of a catchment lead to the variations in mass contributed to the main rivers and hence lead to variations in concentration. These mechanisms are still rather poorly understood.

10.4   Discussion and conclusion

The leaching of solutes from the soil to contribute to the load of rivers is part of the cycling of nutrients through agricultural ecosystems. Fig. 10.4 shows both inputs to and outputs from the soil-plant subsystem. Most nitrogen in the soil is in an organic form and the decay of vegetative matter produces soil humus and available nutrients. These transformations are by bacterial activity and hence governed by temperature. Nitrate ions, unlike the positively charged ammonium ions that are absorbed on to the soil humus material, move through the soil in proportion to the net amount of water passing through it. The release of nitrate from the soil-plant system depends on the type of land use, soil constituency and drainage, and the mode of tillage. The supply of nitrate nitrogen to lowland rivers in agricultural catchments is likely to be far more complicated than just a response to an increase in one input (the introduction of artificial fertiliser).

The fact that: (a) negligible amounts of ammonium sulphate fertiliser are applied to the soil in East Anglia; (b) sulphur is a minor nutrient for both terrestrial and acquatic plants compared with nitrogen; (c) both the

119

nitrate and sulphate minerals are relatively soluble (the former more so that the latter) and are thought to occur primarily in the superficial deposits and soil; and (d) there is a close association between nitrate and non-carbonate hardness concentrations both in terms of trend and annual cycle; could indicate that correlation between river nitrate concentration and fertiliser application rate in the Stour catchment since the 1950s may not be a casual relationship.

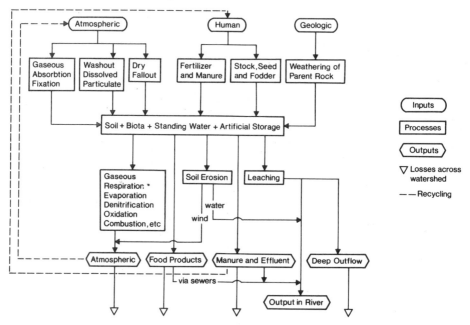

Fig. 10.4   Inputs and outputs of an agricultural catchment ecosystem

It is interesting to speculate on what changes over the years in the soil-plant system could also have led to the upward trends in nitrate and non-carbonate hardness concentrations in the Stour.

1   The capacity of the soil-plant system to absorb nitrogen can be exceeded by over-applying both artificial fertiliser and animal manure and slurry. Haith [18] states that the C/N ratio in soils is important in governing the dual processes of mineralisation and immobilisation that are the transfer mechanisms between the organic and inorganic soil-nitrogen budgets. The ability of nitrogen to be absorbed into organic matter falls as the C/N ratio falls, and hence more nitrogen is available in a highly soluble form for leaching. There is some concern in Britain that there has been a decline in the amount of organic matter present in the soil, and this could lead to a lowering of the ability to assimilate nitrogenous fertilisers. Not

all agriculturalists agree that this has been a general or serious trend. [19]

2   The pattern of tillage affects the liberation of nitrate from organic matter. [20] Increased area and depth of ploughing accelerates the decay of residues and may change the pattern of water movement in the soil. It should be noted that Owens *et al.* [10] were not able to find any significant difference in the data available from English rivers between the load of nitrate per unit area in catchments with either mainly arable land use or pasture.

3   Tile drainage will affect the movement of water through the soil and hence leaching. It is generally thought that drainage increases the loss of nitrogen. The reduction of waterlogging and the increased aeration may increase microbiological activity.

It is suggested that the last two mechanisms could be significant in affecting the nitrate and non-carbonate hardness concentrations recorded in the Stour.

The mechanisms governing the supply of nitrate to rivers draining rural catchments are very complicated, and care is needed in interpreting the relationships between variables even if they have good statistical correlation. Much work has been undertaken on the nature of nitrogen in the soil but there seems to be a lack of work on relating the removal processes from the soil to the chemistry of rivers. Long-term monitoring is required to identify trends and to give a warning to water abstractors of when undesirable nitrate concentrations are likely to occur. Monitoring, however, needs to be supplemented by more detailed work on the cycling of nitrogen and other constituents through ecosystems.

References

[1] Winton, E.F., Tardiff, R.G. and McGabe, L.J., Nitrate in drinking water (Journal of the American Water Works Association 63, 1971).

[2] Finnecy, E.E. and Nicolson, N.J., Evaluation of analytical methods (Proceedings of the Society of Water Treatment Examiners 17, 1968).

[3] Houghton, G.U., The River Stour (Essex and Suffolk) — hardness, chloride and nitrate content (Proceedings of the Society of Water Treatment Examiners 13, 1964).

[4] Task Group Report, Sources of nitrogen and phosphorus in water supplies (Journal of the American Water Works Association 59, 1967).

[5] Clarke, F.W., Composition of river and lake waters of the United States (US Geological Survey Professional Paper 124, 1924).

[6] Bower, C.A. and Wilcox, L.B., Nitrate content of the Upper Rio Grande as influenced by nitrogen fertilisation of adjacent beds (Proceedings of the Soil Science Society of America 33, 1969).

[7] Harmeson, R.H. and Larson, T.E., Existing levels of nitrates in waters — the Illinois situation (Proceedings of the Twelfth Sanitary Engineering Conference, University of Illinois 1970).

[8] Tomlinson, T.E., Trends in nitrate concentrations in English rivers in relation to fertiliser use (Proceedings of the Society of Water Treatment Examiners 19, 1970).

[9] Owens, M., Nutrient balances in rivers (Proceedings of the Society of Water Treatment Examiners 19, 1970).

[10] Owens, M., Garland, J.H.N., Hart, I.C. and Wood, G., Nutrient budgets in rivers (Symposia of the Zoological Society of London 29, 1972).

[11] Billington, R.H., Livesey, J.B. and Taylor, N., Abstractions for Water Supplies in the Great Ouse Basin (Proceedings of the Symposium on Sewage Effluent as a Water Resource, Institute of Public Health Engineering, London 1973).

[12] Scorer, R., Nitrogen: a problem of decreasing dilution (*New Scientist* 62, 1974).

[13] Edwards, A.M.C. and Thornes, J.B., Annual cycle in riverwater quality: a time series approach (Water Resource Research 9, 1973).

[14] Houghton, G.U., Long-term increases in planktonic growth in the Essex River Stour (Proceedings of the Society of Water Treatment Examiners 21, 1972).

[15] Garland, J.A., see Chapter 13.

[16] Edwards, A.M.C., The variation of dissolved constituents with discharge in some Norfolk rivers (Journal of Hydrology 18, 1973).

[17] Edwards, A.M.C., Dissolved load and tentative solute budgets of some Norfolk catchments (Journal of Hydrology 18, 1973).

[18] Haith, D.A., Optimal control of nitrogen losses from land disposal areas (American Society of Civil Engineers, Journal of the Environmental Engineering Division, EET, 1973).

[19] Cooke, G.W., Fertilisers and society (Proceedings of the Fertiliser Society 121, 1972).

[20] Aldrich, S.R., The influence of cropping patterns, soil management and fertiliser on nitrates (Proceedings of the Twelfth Sanitary Engineering Conference, University of Illinois 1970).

11 The Effect of Climatic and Other Environmental Changes on Water Quality in Rural Areas

F.H.W. GREEN

The genesis of the work discussed in this chapter was observation of changes in watercourses in parts of East Anglia, and some changes in flora and fauna suspected to be due to these changes, together with related changes in soil water levels. The following things were, for instance, matters of common observation: shallow watercourses no longer holding water; widespread deepening of roadside and field-side ditches; extensive mole and tile field-drainage operations; and changes in the flora and fauna of streams and rivers. A matter of less common observation, but one of concern to botanists, was floristic changes, including the extinction — widespread or local — of various species of plants which were known to favour a high water level in the soil. For instance, Perring[1] cites very rare species which have declined rapidly and species showing major areal declines from 1900 onwards, and in the case of some species he attributes the declines to drainage activity. Hooper[2] has examined very carefully the dates of extinction of various plants, and concludes that there is no significant correlation with climatic variations, and he too concludes that drainage is the important factor.

In the first week of August 1971 the Advisory Centre for Education in Cambridge in conjunction with the *Sunday Times*, organised a children's survey of water pollution. This resulted in more than 4,000 returns for England and Wales with sufficient numbers of observations in each county to be statistically significant; checks against knowledge from other sources supported the general validity of the results, some of which are shown in Figs. 11.1 and 11.2. This survey provided partial quantification for some of the features of common observation mentioned above.

The next step was to try to discover, and quantify, physical features which could account for the observed spatial and temporal variations. A start was made with land drainage, and the first findings are described in the paper in the *Journal of Environmental Management*.[3] Two of the

123

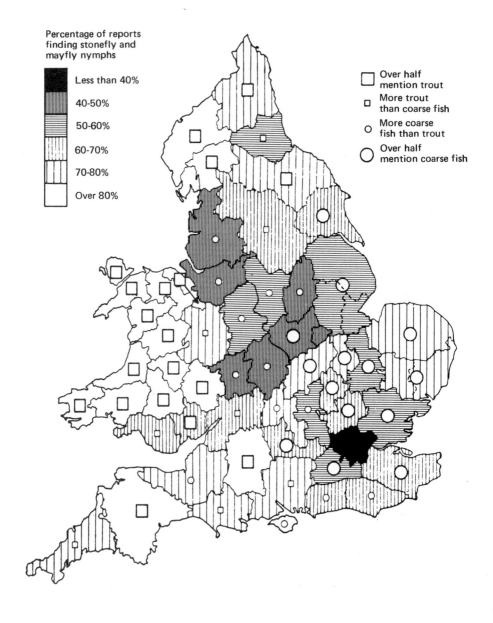

Fig. 11.1 Findings of an amateur survey in 1971, percentage of reports
finding Stonefly and Mayfly nymph

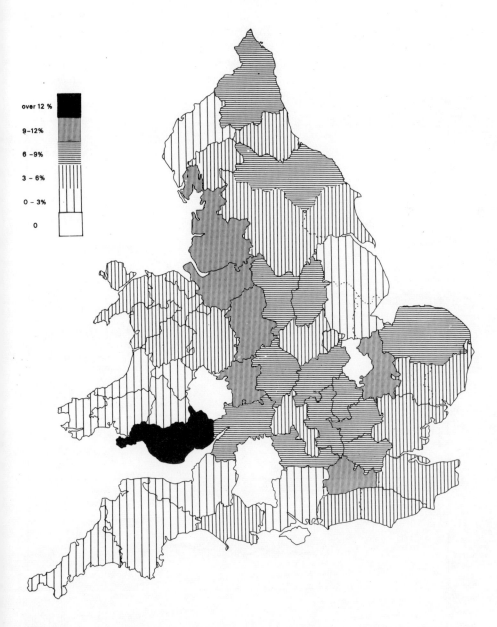

over 12 %

9 – 12%

6 – 9%

3 – 6%

0 – 3%

0

Fig. 11.2 Findings of an amateur survey in 1971, percentage of streams showing no sign of life

125

figures from that paper are reproduced here as Figs. 11.3 and 11.4. Figure 11.3 shows the countrywide increase in field drainage since 1951/52 together with the curves for certain Ministry of Agriculture, Fisheries and Food (MAFF) Divisional areas. It will be noticed how the annual rate of field drainage is steadily increasing, notably in many areas since about 1967. There are also correlations to be observed with various climatic events, such as the increase in drainage in Essex following the floods of 1953, and in some areas the slight falling-off in the dry year 1959, and in the dry years of the mid-sixties.

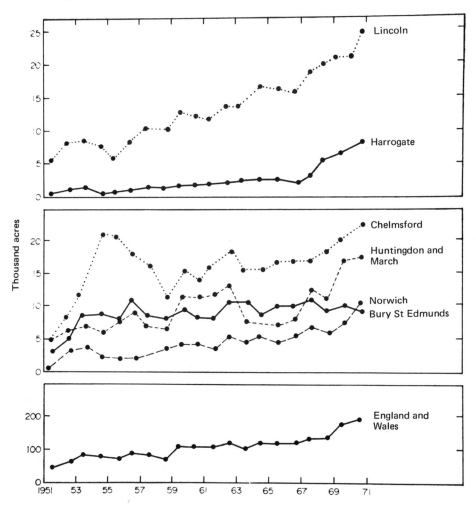

Fig. 11.3 Acres to benefit by underdrainage, England and Wales, and certain MAFF divisional areas

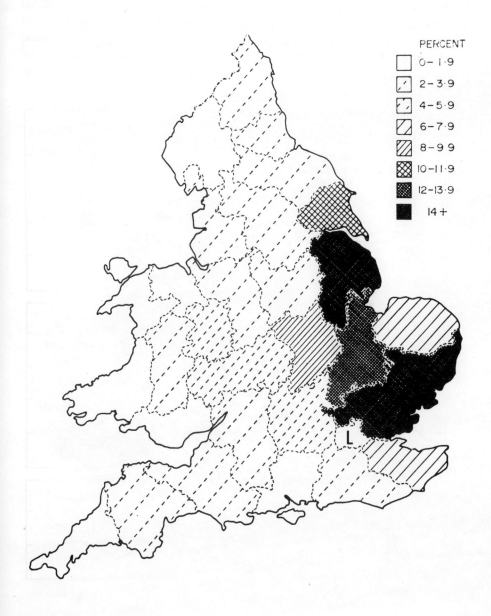

PERCENT
0 – 1·9
2 – 3·9
4 – 5·9
6 – 7·9
8 – 9·9
10 – 11·9
12 – 13·9
14 +

L

Fig. 11.4   Proportion total area underdrained 1951/52–1970/72

Fig. 11.4 shows how an approximate correlation begins to be observed between areas of more intense field drainage and areas of greater 'pollution' on watercourses. Thus moderate 'pollution' is characteristic of those parts of eastern England where there has been much drainage activity. But Fig. 11.2 shows that really bad pollution is not characteristic of these areas, bad pollution being more prevalent in areas where there is much industrial effluent and relatively high amounts of sewage disposal in populous areas.

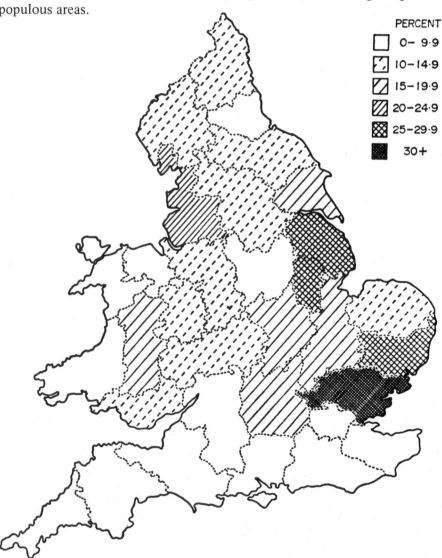

Fig. 11.5   Proportion arable underdrained 1951/52—1970/71

It was a natural next step to see whether there were any *general* climatic trends coinciding with the increase in drainage activity. Firstly, Lamb's[4] classification of weather types was consulted. This shows clearly a marked decrease since about 1950 in days of *westerly* type and a notable increase, particularly since about 1967, of days of *anticyclonic* type (see Figs. 11.5 and 11.6). These facts are not meaningful until one has examined their hydrological consequences. The most relevant consequence is found to be a marked increase since 1967 in the proportion of rain which falls in short periods of heavy rainfall.[5] This is illustrated for Brigstock in the valley of Harper's Brook, Northamptonshire, in Fig. 11.7.

The next thing was to try to find data to support the general observation that flow in watercourses has become subject to greater irregularities in recent years. Use was made of the large number of analyses of flow records which have been made by the Institute of Hydrology. Unfortunately in Britain there is only a limited number of reliable records dating back as much as ten years, but it did soon become clear that many streams exhibited an increased number of days when the flow exceeded any arbitrary high threshold. This is illustrated by the case of Harper's Brook in Fig. 11.8, which has been updated by data kindly supplied by the Welland and Nene River Authority.

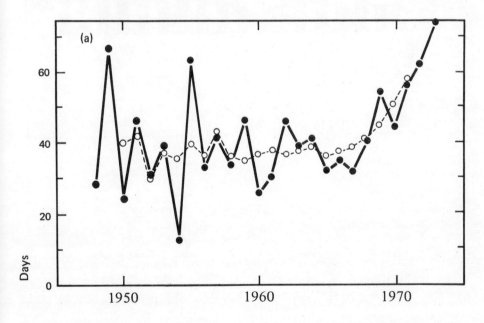

Fig. 11.6 Number of anticyclonic days over central British Isles, June–October (dashed line is 5-year moving average).

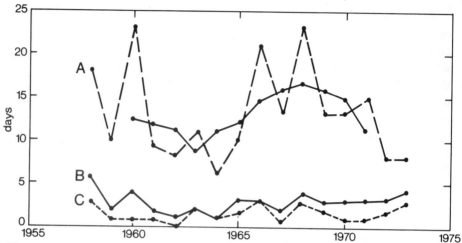

Fig. 11.7 Brigstock, Northants, in the catchment of Harper's Brook. Number of days when rainfall was (A) 10 mm or more, (B) 20 mm or more, (C) 25 mm or more. Five-year moving average is also shown for (A).

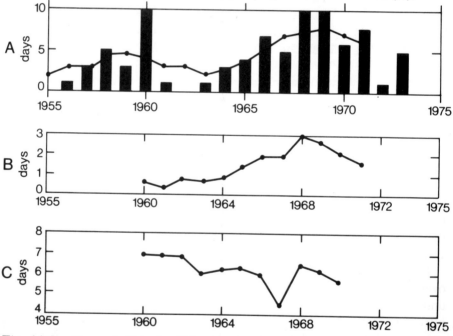

Fig. 11.8 Harper's Brook: (A) number of days flow reached 3·6 cumecs; (B) number of days when flow reached 3·6 cumecs without antecedent rainfall of 10 mm in 24 hours; and (C) number of days when antecedent rainfall of 10 mm produced a flow of 3·6 cumecs subtracted from number of days when it did not

Although unfortunately the Brigstock raingauge records commenced only in 1958, it will be seen immediately from this that there is a correspondence between the increase in days with heavy rain and days when the threshold (in this case 3.6 cumecs) was exceeded. However, there is evidence as shown in Fig. 11.8 that the increased number of days with flow exceeding the threshold is not entirely accounted for by changes in rainfall characteristics. So there must be an additional cause, which is very likely field drainage. This has been found to have been more active since about 1968 than it had been since the middle fifties. Meanwhile, one may say that some streams which show similar flow changes to Harper's Brook, where it is known that there has been only a small amount of field drainage during the period, are found in widely separated parts of England and Wales; this supports the view that climatic factor has been effective. Conversely there are some streams in areas where drainage activity has been relatively intense, which do not show the same kind of flow changes; here presumably neither the climatic nor land drainage factor has had marked effect, at least according to the criteria used. The matter is still being investigated, and will be the subject of a further paper.

Although all the data so far used concern flow in watercourses, it must be presumed that the average level of the water-table in fields has been lowered; indeed the main objective of the field drainage is to remove surplus water as quickly as possible.

To turn to water *quality*, and the nature of stream-beds, the assumptions to be tested were (a) that turbidity conditions in streams were being changed — i.e. more solid matter would enter watercourses during periods of rapid runoff from the land; (b) that the form of the stream-beds was being changed — i.e. by more intense variation between rapid movement of bed-load, and stagnant conditions; and (c) that fertilisers and chemicals applied to fields would be increasingly finding their way into watercourses. Assumptions (a) and (b) have not yet been systematically investigated, but a start has been made with (c).

Data were obtained from MAFF concerning application of fertilisers over the period 1952/53 to the present day. The annual amounts per acre under crops and grass are shown in Fig. 11.9. Concentrating attention on nitrogenous fertilisers, it will at once be seen that there is a general coincidence between increase in the application of nitrogen, the increase in field drainage, and the climatic changes described above.

Although the application of nitrogen continues to be greatest in arable areas, there has been a marked increase in its application to grassland. The total application to all land under crops and grass is shown for 1970—73

131

in Fig. 11.10, and the increase over 14 years in grassland counties is shown in Fig. 11.11.

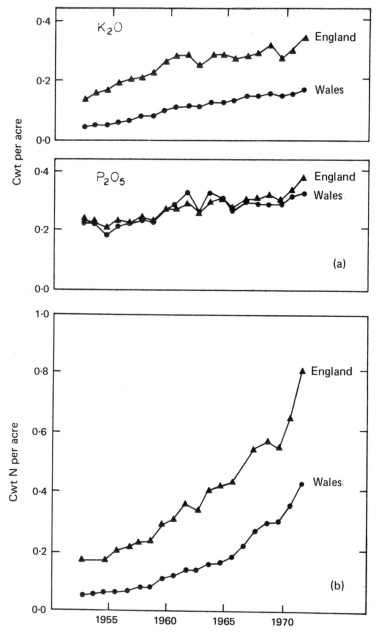

Fig. 11.9   Cwt K_2O and P_2O_5 (soluble plus insoluble) per acre under crops and grass. Cwt N applied per acre under crops and grass

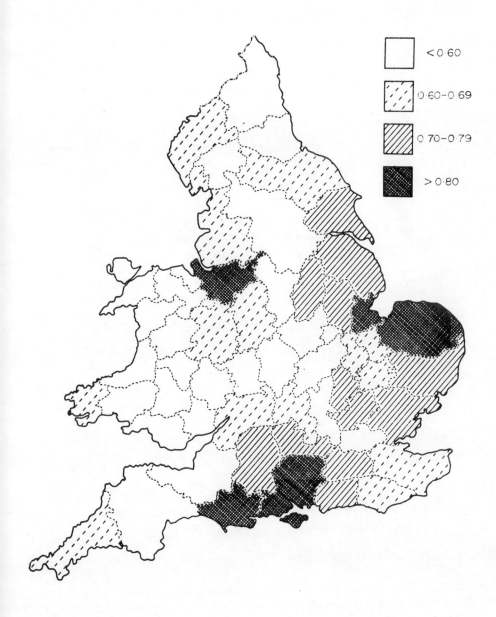

Fig. 11.10   N applied, in cwt per acre of crops and grass 1970–71

Legend:
- < 0·60
- 0·60–0·69
- 0·70–0·79
- > 0·80

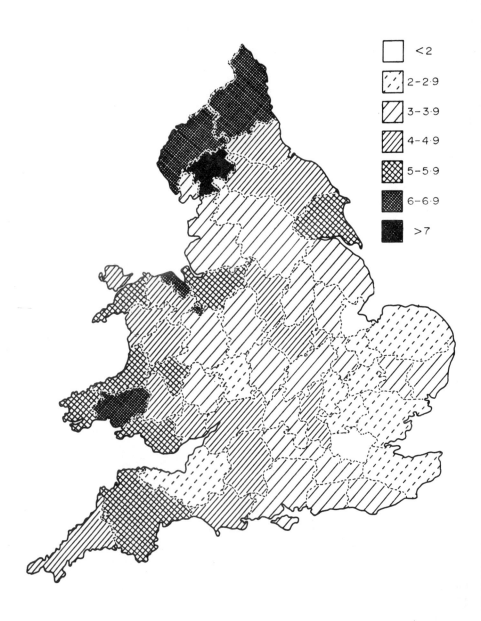

Fig. 11.11 Cwt N per acre under crops and grass. Figures for year 1971/72
divided by figures for year 1957/58

134

Although comparison of Figs. 11.4 and 11.10 shows that there has been in eastern England a generally high amount of nitrogen application in areas with considerable under-drainage, there has also been high application in counties such as Norfolk, Hampshire and Cheshire where field-drainage activity has been small or modest. The Wessex area for instance has not needed much field-drainage because most of its area has soil which is naturally freely drained. Reference back to Figs. 11.1 and 11.2 shows that it is an area where the pollution index is low. The hypothesis suggested is that chemical fertilisers applied to the land are not in this area getting into watercourses in increasing or undesirable amounts. Many of the watercourses are spring-fed. Similar remarks apply to Norfolk; in the case of Cheshire, the pollution factor for the country as a whole is high, but this is because of industrial activity in parts of the country.

It was to be considered whether increased amounts of pesticides were finding there way into watercourses, but so far it has not been possible to obtain data to test this.

The general conclusion from what has been discussed in this chapter is that various changes, natural and man-made, are taking place with increasing tempo, and they demand more careful evaluation than they have yet been accorded.

References

[1] Perring, F.H., The last seventy years in F.H. Perring (ed.), The Flora of a Changing Britain, (published for the Botanical Society of the British Isles, 1970).

[2] Hooper, M.D., Underdraining claylands: some botanical evidence (submitted for publication 1972).

[3] Green, F.H.W., Aspects of the changing environment: some factors affecting the acquatic environment in recent years (Journal of Environmental Management 1, 1973).

[4] Lamb, H.H., British Isles weather types and a register of the daily sequence of circulation patterns, 1961–1971 (Meteorological Office Geophysical Memoir 116, HMSO 1972; updated by Climatic Research Unit, University of East Anglia in their Monthly Bulletin).

[5] Grindley, J., The rainfall of 1972 (*The Times*, 25 January 1973).

12 River Vegetation and Pollution

Dr Sylvia M. HASLAM

12.1 Introduction

The factors determining the distribution and performance of watercourse macrophytes (larger plants) can be grouped into three categories: (a) catchment geology and flow regime, the latter depending on topography, geology and climate; (b) management practices such as canalisation, dredging, cutting, flow regulation and spraying; and (c) man-made alterations to the chemical or physical quality of the river (not included in (b) as they are not intended for the benefit of the watercourse or its users). This diverse group of factors will be considered in this chapter.

Vegetation can, therefore, be predicted from flow pattern and geology (and management). When the general type of plant community does not conform to prediction, the vegetation is damaged, e.g. by trampling or accidental toxic spillages; or is polluted, frequently eutrophically; or is eliminated by severe damage or pollution.

Macrophytes are common in lowland and some highland rivers. They are easier to record than fish or invertebrates, as they are large and stationary, and there are only about fifty common species. The species present at a site can usually be seen from a bridge, though more detailed sampling may be required.

Macrophyte species are closely correlated with their habitat. Stream habitats are complex, and different species tend to be best correlated with different variables. *Callitriche* spp., for example, are related to shallow water; mosses to stable substrates; *Myriophyllum alterniflorum* to soft waters; *M. spicatum* to harder ones; *Potamogeton pectinatus* to high concentrations of various solutes; and *Ranunculus fluitans* (in highland regions) to large volumes of water. Conseqeuntly, much information on a stream habitat can be deduced from a list of the species present in it. Macrophytes can, therefore, be used for monitoring.

Since macrophytes differ from man, fish and invertebrates, their response to pollution and damage may be expected to differ also. Macrophytes are, for example, more sensitive to boats, and probably less so to high ammonia or biological oxygen demand. They are usually rooted in the soil, and so are affected by the chemical status of both soil and water, unlike many animals used for monitoring.

All lowland, and many highland watercourses are managed by man, and so their vegetation is not 'natural' in the strict sense. It is, however, convenient to term vegetation affected by both the truly natural and the management factors (excluding aquatic herbicides), as natural. The term will be used in this sense in this chapter.

All native British aquatics must, because they are native, have a natural distribution in Britain. No species therefore, not even *Potamogeton pectinatus*, indicates pollution merely by its presence. Pollution is only suspected when a species occurs outside its natural distribution.

When the 'wrong' species are present, the habitat may resemble a different natural one. A chalk stream with eutrophic pollution may bear the same species as a chalk—clay stream, for instance. Or pollution may be greater, and the stream bear only species tolerating the artificial habitat. In the former, the pollution-indicators are in their optimum habitat, but in the latter they are towards the extremes of their ranges.

12.2   Factors determining river vegetation

Topography and rainfall are usually associated in Britain, and the latter can be disregarded for the present purposes. At a simple level, the flow patterns derived from topography can be divided into those of lowland, upland and highland streams. In unpolluted conditions the soil usually has more effect than the water, the nutrients being more concentrated there. Soils derive from the catchment, so their nutrient status varies with the rock types of the catchment. Rock type affects the amount of sediment available for deposition in the stream, and topography then affects the amount actually deposited. In the lowlands, chalk provides little silt, clay much, and sandstone an intermediate amount. In the highlands, most rock types have little sediment, though sandstone has more than most.

Plant nutrients are mainly in the silt and mud fractions of the substrate. Consequently the higher the proportion of silt in the soil, the higher the nutrient status. High trophic status results from a rock producing much sediment, from a silt of high nutrient status, and from flat reaches with much deposition. So the maximum nutrient status is when all three factors are favourable. At lower trophic levels one of these can compensate for the lack of another, as when a flat reach compensates for a rock type producing little silt.

It is usually the surface rocks which affect vegetation. Boulder clay has the same effect as solid clay, and the solid rock below it need not normally be considered. Alluvium likewise conceals the effect of the rock below, though many streams on it are derived from, and hence affected by, other rock types.

In catchments of mixed rock types, the vegetation usually reflects these rocks, in the proportions in which they occur. However, a rock at the headwaters of a stream has more effect than the same area downstream and away from the channel. For instance, the Avon and the Wylye (Avon and Dorset River Authority area) rise on greensand, but have long lengths on chalk. They retain non-chalk species throughout, because of the fertile greensand.

An acid sandstone in an otherwise chalk catchment has less effect than that expected from its area, and sometimes has no effect even when comprising perhaps a quarter of the catchment (excluding the headwater area). The pollution-indicating species of mixed catchments can usually be deduced from those for each of the rocks being those common to both. *Potamogeton pectinatus*, however, occurs naturally in clay—chalk streams, and in large sandstone rivers, etc. Its presence here does not indicate pollution.

Passing downstream, more sediment moves through the habitat and nutrient status increases. Except in the smallest rivers, vegetation noticeably changes. Consequently, natural eutrophication must be considered before pollution can be diagnosed in a downstream region. Natural eutrophication is particularly marked in chalk streams and large upland or semi-highland rivers. Here the more eutrophic species are present downstream only.

Management practices (excluding aquatic herbicides) usually affect the amount, more than the type, of vegetation. After dredging, a plant population (though not necessarily the biomass) is typically restored in two to three years. Cutting seldom affects the presence or absence of a species. Consequently these practices can usually be disregarded for the study of pollution. There is, however, an exception; where alterations to the flow regime remove or create a thick layer of silt on the channel floor, this alters the nutrient status of the habitat, and hence the plant community.

12.3 Types of pollution and the way these affect macrophytes

The main sources of pollution can be classified as follows.

139

1   Solutes: sewage and other eutrophic effluents; industrial non-eutrophic effluents (including road-washings and other minor sources); fertilisers, as eutrophic runnoff; and pesticides and herbicides.
2   Sediments (with or without solutes): increased silt from arable land; heavy sediments with much deposition, e.g. coal dust; and light sediments with little deposition, e.g. paper-mill effluent.
3   Disturbance, with associated sediment and/or solute: boats, cattle, paddling, etc.
4   Heat.

Severely polluted rivers, e.g. the Rhymney (Glamorgan River Authority area), rarely, if ever, bear macrophytes. Macrophytes, therefore, cannot be used to assess or monitor pollution here. The levels of different pollutants which are intolerable for macrophyte species are not yet known.

Rivers which have little normal pollution may occasionally suffer accidental toxic spillages. As the toxic water moves downstream, it is usually present in lethal quantities for only a few hours at any one site. This suffices to kill some or all plant parts in the water, but probably does not affect buried rhizomes. Consequently, the effect resembles that of dredging: removal of parts above ground, followed by regrowth from viable parts left *in situ*, and colonisation from outside. Such pollutions may be disastrous to fish or invertebrates, but the long-term effects on macrophytes are usually negligible, and so they are not considered further here.

Low-level continuous pollution is much worse for plants. Here the pollution never ceases, so the vegetation, over the years, comes to be in equilibrium with the polluted water and soil. The natural vegetation is lost, the polluted community differing in species composition (species performance has not yet been fully investigated). This type of pollution is frequent, but often unrecognised, as macrophytes still occur.

Watercourse pollution is difficult to define. Under natural conditions, many substances enter watercourses. Solutes (nutrients, etc.) are leached from soils, others enter from local high concentrations, e.g. of salt or gypsum. Sediments are washed from the adjoining land, they fall in from banks, and are created by erosion of the channel floor, and by the decomposition of organic matter. Both the quantity and the chemical composition of solutes and sediments vary greatly from place to place.

When human interference alters the incoming solutes and sediments, the effects vary. Adding low concentrations of solutes already present in quantity will not affect the plants. Nor will they be affected by low

140

concentrations of solutes inert to macrophytes. As natural rivers vary in their chemical composition, the same concentrations of a pollutant may affect vegetation in one river (with a low natural concentration of that substance), but have no effect in another (because of its high natural concentration of the substance). Thus pollution can change one natural vegetation type to another, by changing the chemical status of one habitat to that which occurs naturally in a different habitat. This is a characteristic effect of eutrophication in mesotrophic (or oligotrophic) habitats. The same phenomenon occurs with sediment. Increased silting from ploughed land causes an increase in the fertile sediment in streams which, on a rock type or land form with little natural silting, can lead to vegetation more appropriate to those with much natural silting.

Plant communities which do not occur naturally result from low-level pollution by substances affecting macrophytes, but hardly occurring in natural rivers, or from more severe pollution by substances which do occur naturally. The vegetation of course grades into natural types, but in the more extreme instances it consists of only a very few, unusually tolerant species. The most tolerant British species is *Potamogeton pectinatus*. For macrophytes, therefore, watercourse pollution can be defined as the addition of solutes or sediments which alter the chemical status of the habitat or for the animals associated with them. The effects of pollutants entering a watercourse depend on four factors. The quality of the pollutant, its quantity, the dilution occurring in the stream, and the type of river. Stream type is very important for eutrophication effects. Clay streams are the most eutrophic natural ones, followed by those on heavy lowland sandstone, chalk, hard sandstone, and finally on very hard rocks (granites, shales, etc.) which are the most oligotrophic.

12.3.1 *Pollution by solutes alone*

The various sources can be grouped into eutrophic effluents, other effluents, eutrophic runoff and other runoff. Eutrophic effluents may be large-scale, e.g. from city sewage works, or small-scale, e.g. from fertilised watercress beds. As explained above, macrophytes are affected when the additions substantially alter the natural concentrations. It is fairly easy to affect the vegetation in a low-nutrient stream (e.g. on chalk or very hard rock), but massive additions are needed before clay vegetation is altered.

Non-eutrophic effluents are, of course, diverse. Species diversity usually decreases with pollution, *Potamogeton pectinatus* tolerating higher pollution than other species.

Eutrophic runoff arises from crop fertilisers. These have, of course, greatly increased in the past few decades. The evidence is still incomplete, but it appears that the effects develop slowly, possibly altering species distribution after about twenty years in dykes on alluvial plains. Species distribution in streams is probably little affected at present, but as rivers remove runoff more efficiently than do dykes, an effect may develop in the next decade or two. Since eutrophic runoff, unlike eutrophic effluents, comes from many places, the effects on vegetation would be both more widespread, and more difficult to reverse, than those from the effluents. Widespread eutrophication of mesotrophic (and oligotrophic) streams would be most unfortunate for the conservation of natural stream vegetation.

There is no current evidence for the effect on macrophytes of pesticides washed out from the land. Neither are the effects of aquatic herbicides considered here.

12.3.2   *Pollution by sediments, etc.*

Turbidity lessens light penetration, and so decreases or eliminates submerged species requiring high light. Particles may cause abrasion of plant parts, and if the sediment settled, may lead to substrates unstable in flow.

This substrate instability is the most damaging effect of sediment pollution, and is characteristic of coal streams. In coal streams with slow flow and no liability to spate, luxuriant vegetation can occur even with considerable sediment pollution. Where storm flows are frequent or normal flow is fast, however, coal dust repeatedly accumulates and is washed away, and vegetation is absent or sparse. *Potamogeton pectinatus* is the most tolerant species, probably because it can anchor in fine sediment and grow afresh each summer. *Ranunculus penicillatus* is excluded by severe pollution, but can, in appropriate habitats, recolonise rapidly when this ceases.[1] Silt from ploughed fields has a similar, though lesser effect.

12.3.3   *Pollution from sources associated with mechanical disturbance*

Boats are the most harmful of these minor causes. They decrease the total vegetation more than they alter the species composition.

12.3.4   *Pollution from hot effluents*

Where the habitat is not otherwise unsuitable, *Vallisneria spiralis* may occur.

142

12.4 Discussion

Mild pollution has three main effects. Eutrophication introduces species from eutrophic habitats, and removes species characteristic of nutrient-poor ones. Poisons keep species diversity very low, and permit the growth of only the most tolerant species. Unstable substrates come from pollution from heavy sediments and disturbance by boats, etc. *Potamogeton pectinatus* is the commonest species in polluted watercourses, but is not confined to these.

Town sewage and coal mine effluents are the most generally harmful to macrophytes, apart from local instances such as the boats on Norfolk Broads rivers. The worst industrial pollution occurs in the coal-mining areas of the Pennines and South Wales, although there are other bad areas, e.g. near Birmingham. Apart from this, lowland rivers tend to be more polluted than highland ones, as they tend to have denser population and industry, and more intensive agriculture.

Reference

[1] Holmes, N.T.H., Lloyd, E.J.R., Potts, M. and Whitton, B.A., Plants of the River Tyne and future water transfer scheme (*Vasculum* 57, 1972).

13 Dry Deposition and the Atmospheric Cycle of Sulphur Dioxide

Dr J.A. GARLAND

13.1 Introduction

The long-term transport of an air pollutant is controlled by the effectiveness of the mechanisms for its removal from the atmosphere. It has long been known that sulphur is removed from the atmosphere as sulphate in rain, and the rate of removal has been measured for several decades. Some of the earlier results were examined by Meetham,[1] who pointed out the large difference between the quantities emitted to the atmosphere over Great Britain and the measured deposition. Meetham concluded that only a quarter of the sulphur dioxide emitted over a large part of Great Britain is carried away by the wind and 14 per cent deposited in rain. The remaining 60 per cent was deposited on the ground by direct interaction of the molecules with the surface. This removal by direct interaction has become known as dry deposition to distinguish it from deposition in rain.

Few attempts have been made to measure the dry deposition rate directly. Katz and Ledingham[2] have fumigated alfalfa with sulphur dioxide and shown that the plants absorbed the gas, and other studies have measured uptake rates under laboratory conditions (e.g. Spedding[3]). Johansson[4] presented data on the sulphur balance of soil in pots exposed in the field for 5 or 6 years, and deduced deposition velocities from the results. An experimental programme was begun at AERE about 18 months ago, with the aim of measuring the rate of dry deposition of sulphur dioxide directly.

13.2 Experimental methods

Several methods for measuring the dry deposition of sulphur dioxide or of other materials have been suggested. Some of these are summarised in Table 13.1. All the methods have some limitation: the isotope ratio method cannot be applied to vegetation growing in the field, and results from the soil balance and conservative tracer methods are difficult to interpret. The methods employed at AERE have been the gradient method and the radioactive tracer method. The chief limitation of the gradient method is the need for very uniform terrain. Thus, deposition on hedges, small woods and copses cannot be measured by this technique but it is ideal for use over extensive fields, forests or lakes. The radioactive tracer method does not have these limitations, but the safety requirements inhibit its use in large-scale experiments and contamination problems prevent frequent measurements over the same area.

Table 13.1

Some possible methods for the measurement
of dry deposition velocities

Method	Range of application	Details
Radioactive Tracer e.g. $^{35}SO_2$	Medium- or small-scale field or wind tunnel experiments	Labelled Tracer ($^{35}SO_2$) released upwind. Deposition and concentration measurements facilitated by radioactivity
Isotope ratio method	Pot culture	Plants grown in medium containing tracer (e.g. ^{35}S). Reduction in $^{35}S/^{32}S$ ratio is due to $^{32}SO_2$ absorbed from the air
Mass balance	Pots, lysimeter, field or whole river catchment area	Dry deposition = $S_{out} + S_{stored} - S_{rain} - S_{added}$. Uncertainties in measurements of S_{out} and S_{stored} makes large-scale experiments difficult
Conservative tracer	Medium range	E.g. CO_2 emitted with SO_2 in power station plume. Ratio SO_2/CO_2 decreases with distance due to SO_2 loss from plume. Methods of SO_2 removal not distinguished
Eddy correlation	Field experiments	Instantaneous concentration measured together with vertical instantaneous wind component. Mean value of product = SO_2 flux. No suitable sensor available
Gradient method	Extensive uniform area	Flux = Concentration gradient X eddy diffusivity

13.2.1 *The gradient method*

(i) *Principle* The existence of a concentration gradient of sulphur dioxide near the ground was demonstrated by Gilbert[5] when he took measurements at several heights above the grass surface in parkland. Fig. 13.1 shows that the flux of an atmospheric constituent to the ground can be calculated if the eddy diffusivity and concentration gradient are measured simultaneously. The diffusivity is determined by the rate of mixing of the air by turbulent eddies of a range of sizes. It is a function of height and a consequence of wind shear. It can be calculated from the wind profile, using the results of micrometeorology developed to enable the evaporation of water from crops to be measured. When there is no change of temperature with height the profile of wind speed is found to be logarithmic with height and is conventionally written

$$u = \frac{u_*}{k} \ln \frac{Z-d}{Z_0} \qquad (13.1)$$

where u_* is defined in terms of τ, the surface drag.

$$\tau = \rho u_*^2 \qquad (13.2)$$

Here u is the wind speed at height Z; Z_0 is a 'roughness length' as determined by the roughness of the surface; d reflects the effect of tall crops in raising the height of the momentum sink above the surface; ρ is the density of the air; and k is vón Karman's constant, an empirical constant of value 0·4.

Since τ is a downward flux of momentum and since the gradient of momentum per unit volume $\rho \frac{du}{dZ}$ can be derived from equation 13.1, the diffusivity for momentum

$$K_m = \tau / \frac{du}{dZ}\rho = ku_* (Z - d) \qquad (13.3)$$

is derived. If the simplifying assumption that SO_2 diffuses at the same rate as momentum is made, this diffusivity is enough for our purposes, and the necessary parameters u_* and d can be obtained by fitting observations of wind speed profile to equation 13.1.

In situations where a significant difference between the ground surface and the air temperature exists a correction for the change in turbulent mixing arising from buoyancy effects must be included. The simple logarithmic wind profile no longer applies and experiment shows that diffusivities for momentum and heat differ. The dimensionless shears of momentum and heat

147

$$\phi_M = \frac{kZ}{u_*}\frac{du}{dZ}$$

$$\phi_H = -\frac{kZu_*\rho C_p}{H}\frac{dT}{dZ}$$

(13.4)

where H = heat flux and C_p = specific heat of air at constant pressure, have been studied by several workers including Businger *et al.*[6] and Dyer and Hicks.[7] These quantities can be expressed as functions of the Richardson number

$$R_i = \frac{g\frac{dT}{dZ}}{T(\frac{du}{dZ})^2}$$

(13.5)

where T is the absolute temperature, or of the ratio Z/L where L is the Monin–Obukhov length. The empirical relations can be found in the literature. The diffusivities are then given by

$$K_M = \frac{ku_*(Z-d)}{\phi_M} \quad \text{and} \quad K_H = \frac{ku_*(Z-d)}{\phi_H}$$

(13.6)

and can be calculated provided both temperature gradient and wind profile are known.

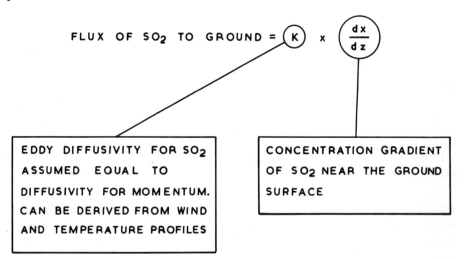

Fig. 13.1   The gradient method

In calculating the diffusivity it is necessary to assume that the fluxes of momentum, heat and sulphur dioxide concentration are constant with height over the range of measurement. This requires an extensive area where the surface properties of roughness and absorptivity for sulphur dioxide are constant for at least 100 times the measurement height upwind. Thus measurements can be made up to 2 or 3 metres in the middle of a large field, but an area of many square kilometres of forest would be required to enable measurements to be made to the necessary heights of some tens of metres above the treetops.

(ii) *Field measurements* The gradients of wind speed, temperature and SO_2 concentration over practicable working ranges of height are quite small so that small differences must be measured. The platinum resistance thermometers used are enclosed in polished metal radiation shields and air is drawn past them with small fans. Measurements are made at five points, namely 20, 50, 100, 200 and 400 cm above the ground surface. The wet-bulb depression is also measured at each height so that evaporation rates can be calculated. The anemometers and the sulphur dioxide sampling points are located 20, 50, 70, 100 and 200 cm from the ground. Data from the anemometers and temperature instruments is recorded automatically every half minute and later averaged over the period of the sulphur dioxide sampling run.

The gas is absorbed and retained in the bubbler after oxidation in 1-volume hydrogen peroxide solution as sulphuric acid. The glass bubbler has a capacity of 125 ml and its inlet tube has been pulled down to a jet approximately 3 mm internal diameter and terminating 2 mm from the bottom of the bubbler. Usually 40 ml of hydrogen peroxide is used in the bubbler, but this volume may be increased if the relative humidity is very low or if sampling runs of appreciably longer than the 1 hour normally used are to be made.

Sulphur dioxide sampled is subsequently determined as sulphate, and particulate sulphates which if allowed to reach the bubbler would interfere in the determination are removed with a 'Microsorban' absolute pre-filter. In order to prevent sulphur dioxide uptake on the pre-filters a heater is fixed to the inlet tube which raises the temperature of the air sampled by approximately 10 °C. During sampling the bubbler is supported in a brass box and polystyrene covers are placed over the filter holder and bubbler head to prevent condensation. The inlet tubes of the sulphur dioxide samplers are directed into the wind to avoid distortion in the profile downwind of the mast.

All five sampling positions are connected to a single pump through critical orifices, and flow rates measured by gas meters in each sample line. The quantity of solution remaining in each bubbler after each experiment is measured by weighing before analysis. Thus the need to transfer to a calibrated flask and make up the solution to a standard volume is avoided.

(iii)   *Analysis* Sulphur dioxide trapped in solution as involatile sulphuric acid is determined by the thoronol method of Persson[8] using a Technicon Autoanalyser. Limits of detection for sulphur dioxide with a 1-hour sampling period at $30\,1\,min^{-1}$ and 40 ml hydrogen peroxide absorbing solution are $1-2\,\mu g\ SO_2\ m^{-3}$ and profiles have in fact been established with sulphur dioxide at levels of $3-4\,\mu g\ m^{-3}$. Evaporative losses of the hydrogen peroxide absorbing solution limit the sampling period with the present apparatus. These, however, could be overcome if longer sampling times were shown to be necessary.

(iv)   *Accuracy* A series of tests using radioactive tracers were made to assess the performance of the sulphur dioxide sampling method. Carryover of spray from the bubbler which would result in the loss of sulphuric acid was shown to be insignificant in experiments with a radioactive tracer (^{137}Cs). With flow rates of $25-30\,1\,min^{-1}$ used in the experiments the uptake of sulphur dioxide was shown to be 95 per cent complete in one bubbler with excellent reproducibility using $^{35}SO_2$. Loss of sulphur dioxide on the pre-filter and internal surfaces of the apparatus was also checked with labelled sulphur dioxide. With the heater in operation a series of tests using $^{35}SO_2$ at the sub-microgram level, relative humidities of up to 90 per cent and with flow rates considerably less than $40\ cm.\ sec^{-1}$ used in sampling, losses of sulphur dioxide in the apparatus were shown to be negligible.

The accuracy and precision of the sulphate determination have been investigated and shown to be good with coefficients of variation at the 1 ppm level of better than 2 per cent and at the 3 ppm level of 0·4 per cent. Precision for the whole process of sampling and analysis were investigated in a series of experiments in the field in which the sampling boom was held horizontally when the same level of sulphur dioxide was sampled at each point. The results obtained are shown in Fig. 13.2. Each point on the graph represents the standard deviation in the atmospheric sulphur dioxide levels measured in one run at the five sampling positions. Clearly the precision is dependent on the sulphur dioxide concentration and decreases from approximately 8 per cent at the $10\,\mu g\ m^{-3}$ level to 4 per cent when sulphur dioxide is present at $100\,\mu g\ m^{-3}$. An atmospheric concentration of $10\mu g\ SO_2\ m^{-3}$ corresponds to a concentration of sulphate in solution of approximately 1 ppm.

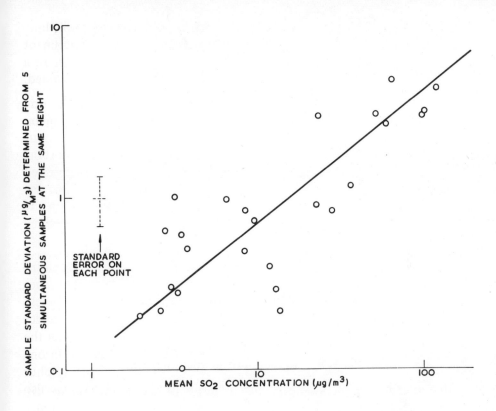

Fig. 13.2   Precision of sulphur dioxide measurements in the field

Regression analysis shows that the standard error in the concentration gradient (expressed as $d\chi/d\ln Z$ since χ is linear in $\ln Z$) is of the form $C\sigma$. Here, σ is the standard error of a single concentration measurement. The value of C depends on the arrangement of samplers. Using five samplers with a factor of ten between the heights of the highest and lowest the value of C is about 0·55. Typically $\sigma/\chi = 0·06$ and $\dfrac{1}{\chi}\dfrac{d\chi}{d\ln Z} = 0·09$, so that $\dfrac{d\chi}{d\ln Z}$ is measured to above 30 per cent (rather better at high concentrations and worse at low). Since the estimation of eddy diffusivity is probably rather more accurate, the probable error in each determination of the flux, or of v_g is about 30 per cent.

(v)   *Results* The profile method described has been used to make four series of measurements. Fig. 13.3 shows a typical set of data plotted on a log-linear plot comprising SO_2 concentration, wind speed and temperature gradient. The information in these curves is used in the manner already described to obtain the flux of sulphur dioxide to the ground.

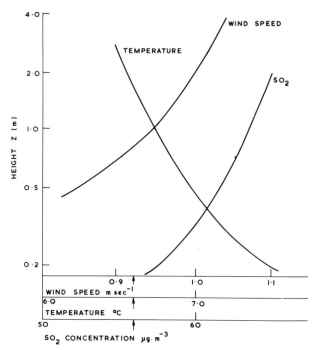

Fig. 13.3   Typical set of data from profile measurements

It is useful to express the results in terms of the deposition velocity $g = \dfrac{\text{flux}}{\text{concentration}}$, since this quantity is independent of concentration provided that the properties of the surface and the wind profile remain constant. It is also convenient to define a resistance of sulphur dioxide transport

$$r = \frac{1}{v_g} \tag{13.7}$$

where r can be considered as a sum of resistances

$$r = r_a + r_b + r_s \tag{13.8}$$

separating the aerodynamic effects r_a and r_b defined below from the purely surface effects, r_s. While r_a and r_b are determined by the wind speed and surface roughness (r_a and r_b decrease with increasing wind speed) r_s depends only on the rate of uptake of the surface for sulphur dioxide. Thus, if the surface were a perfect sink, r_s would be zero. The aerodynamic resistance

$$r_a = \frac{u}{u_*}2 \tag{13.9}$$

152

can be calculated from the wind profile and the boundary-layer resistance. r_b can be found by the approach of Owen and Thomson[9] using empirical values of Chamberlain. [10, 11] Thus r_s can be found by difference. Table 13.2 shows a summary of four sets of measurements with values of v_g and r_s obtained in this way. The very small value of r_s on calcareous soils show that the surface is almost a perfect sink for sulphur dioxide. The large range of values for r_s found for the grass surface is partly due to experimental error but also reflects the changes in the physiological activity of the vegetation.

The mean v_g for all the experiments presented is 0.85 cm s^{-1}. This is similar to 0.61 cm s^{-1}, the mean of fourteen measurements presented by Shepherd. It falls within the range of values suggested by Chamberlain[13] and measured by Katz and Ledingham[2] and Johansson.[4]

Table 13.2

Summary of Deposition Measurements

Type of surface	Time of year	v_g measured m sec^{-1}	Surface resistance* r_s sec m^{-1}
Short grass (Cardington)	March–June	0.0014–0.02	0 –500
Grass (Harwell)	Nov.–Jan.	0.002 –0.013	15–30
Bare calcareous soil	Feb.–March	0.005 –0.022	<50
Pine forest	June	<0.007	>80

*
$$r_s = \frac{1}{V_g} - \frac{u/u_* + B^{-1}}{u_*}$$

13.2.2 The radioactive tracer method

(i) *The method* ^{35}S is a useful tracer because it does not occur naturally in measurable amounts. Thus labelled sulphur dioxide deposited during a brief period can readily be distinguished from the sulphur previously present in vegetation or soil. In addition, nuclear techniques make the isotope easy to measure at very low concentrations.

In field experiments to measure the deposition velocity to grass a small quantity ($\approx$ 1 m mole) of SO_2 containing 50 mC of ^{35}S was released during a period of about 30 minutes at a height of 1 m at a position of 50 m upwind of a prepared sampling area near the centre of the field. The concentration of $^{35}SO_2$ in air was measured above the crop using bubblers containing hydrogen peroxide, from which aliquots were later taken for liquid scintillation counting. The flux of $^{35}SO_2$ to the crop was measured by collecting several measured areas of the crop. The ^{35}S content was determined by extraction of total sulphate and liquid scintillation counting.

(ii) *Results* The ^{35}S method was employed over one of the grass fields used for the gradient experiments. The results, as shown in Table 13.3, suggest consistency between the two methods. Although the measurements were made at different times of the year, and there are large variations between one measurement and the next, the range of results obtained by the two methods is very similar.

The result of the one measurement over a small group of young pine trees shows a low deposition velocity (0·002 m sec^{-1}). That is consistent with the result obtained with the gradient method over Thetford Forest where the difference between sulphur dioxide concentration over a range of heights of 15 m just above the canopy was less than 1 per cent. This result suggests a deposition velocity less than 0·01 m sec^{-1} over the forest.

13.2.3 *Wind tunnel experiments*

(i) *Method* The gradient method was employed to measure the deposition velocity of sulphur dioxide to bare soil in the wind tunnel described by Chamberlain.[10] This system has a 4 m long working section of rectangular cross-section, 30 cm wide and 35 cm high. The base of the working section was occupied by an aluminium trough filled with sieved soil. A pitot tube was used to measure the wind speed profile above the soil near the downstream end of the working section and $^{35}SO_2$ was released slowly into the tunnel during a period of 10 minutes. The $^{35}SO_2$ dosage was measured at several heights from 1 to 10 cm above the surface using bubblers containing hydrogen peroxide solution and the deposition velocity obtained by the gradient method.

Several measurements were made at different wind speeds, and soil moisture contents for three different soils. The soil types were 'S', the Southampton series described by R.A. Jarvis,[14] sampled at a depth of 30 cm in woodland, 'H', the Harwell series and 'U', the Upton series obtained from grassland, described by M.G. Jarvis.[15] They were chosen to cover a wide range of pH.

(ii) *Results* The Results, summarised in Table 13.4, show that only the

Table 13.3

Measurements of the deposition velocity of sulphur dioxide to grass by the radioactive tracer method and the gradient method

Date	Concentration (1) (μg m^{-3})	u_* (m s^{-1})	$u(1)$ (m s^{-1})	z_O (m)	v_g (m s^{-1}) Mean	v_g (m s^{-1}) Error	r (s m^{-1})	r_s (s m^{-1})
Radioactive tracer method								
8 June 1972	—	0·63	4·8	0.040	0·022	±0·0005	45	20
17 July 1972	—	0·40	4·5	0.010	0·0036	±0·0003	280	230
29 August 1972	—	0·40	4·1	0.014	0·0094	±0·0018	106	66
14 September 1972	—	0·37	3·8	0.024	0·017	±0·002	59	11
18 October 1972	—	0·38	3·8	0.026	0·0076	±0·0007	130	76
2 November 1972	—	0·27	2·7	0.014	0·012	±0·0014	83	20
Gradient method								
22 November 1971	12	0·29	3·3	0.0105	0·0079		130	65
22 November 1972	21	0·21	2·3	0.0115	0·0069		150	64
13 December 1972	36	0·29	3·3	0.0105	0·0086		110	53
21 December 1972	34	0·053	0·60	0.012	0·0016		610	330
21 December 1972	71	0·084	0·85	0.012	0·0025		400	220
11 January 1973	20	0·25	2·7	0.012	0·0093		110	37
11 January 1973	14	0·30	3·4	0.009	0·013		77	15
12 January 1973	20	0·24	2·6	0.012	0·012		86	14
12 January 1973	26	0·24	3·0	0.006	0·0073		140	58

155

exceptionally acid soil presented any surface resistance. The results for the calcareous soil are consistent with those obtained in the field over a very similar soil (Table 13.2). Addition of mositure did not appear to enhance SO_2 deposition, and the variation of v_g with wind speed followed equations (13.7) to (13.9).

13.3   Discussion

13.3.1   *Applicability of the profile method*

The profile method is the more convenient of the two methods we have discussed, since it does not involve the use of radioactive material, and it can be used to monitor the deposition velocity frequently over the same surface. It is, therefore, valuable to examine how widely it may be used. The accuracy of a single measurement of v_g, considered in section 13.2.1, subsection (iv), is not great, and several measurements are clearly necessary to obtain a reliable mean value. However, in the Thetford Forest experiment, the mean of thirteen runs was not sufficiently precise to establish the value of the deposition velocity. This failure in the method was due to the small value of r_a/r_s. To use the electrical analogy, the method depends on measuring the potential difference across a part of r_a, but if r_s is too large the current is small and so the proportional difference in potential to be measured is too small. Satisfactory measurements can be made only if the part of r_a accessible to measurement $(r_{a1} - r_{a2} = \frac{1}{ku_*} \ln Z1/Z2$ in neutral conditions) is, say, 10 per cent or more of the total resistance. Over a forest, with $Z_0 = 1$ m, $r_s = 100$ s m^{-1}, $u_* = 1$ m s^{-1} and $Z_2 - d = 4$ m, the upper sampling point would need to be 400 m above ground to accomplish this. Clearly this is not practicable, and in any case the sampler would not be in the constant flux layer, so that the approach used above could not be applied to the data.

   The profile method is also subject to the basic requirement that measurements be made in the constant flux layer, a shallow layer adjacent to the ground in which the pressure gradient has a negligible effect on the wind field compared with the downward diffusion of momentum. The measurements must be made close to a surface of uniform roughness and absorption characteristics since it takes a considerable distance for the wind speed and concentration profiles to reach their equilibrium form after a change of surface characteristics.

Table 13.4

Measurements of the deposition velocity of sulphur dioxide
to bare soil in the wind tunnel

Soil pH	u_{10} (cm sec^{-1})	u_* (cm sec^{-1})	z_0 (cm)	H_2O (% in soil)	v_g (cm sec^{-1})	r (sec cm^{-1})	r_s (sec cm^{-1})	$\frac{r_s}{r}$ (%)
3·62 (S)	384.0	24.7	0.020	2.1	1.08	0.92	0.2	21.0
	598.0	39.4	0.023	2.1	2.6	0.38	0	–
	598.0	39.4	0.023	24.6	1.64	0.61	0.14	23.0
	449.0	30.2	0.026	24.3	1.16	0.87	0.27	31.0
5·68 (H)	458.0	26.3	0.0095	15.02	1.36	0.74	0.006	0.8
	605.0	35.0	0.010	18.4	1.90	0.53	0	–
	365.0	20.1	0.0070	15.3	1.2	0.83	0	–
	365.0	20.1	0.0070	15.9	1.15	0.87	0	–
	460.0	26.6	0.0098	28.4	1.51	0.67	0	–
	610.0	36.6	0.013	30.6	2.05	0.49	0	–
8.0 (U)	611.0	35.6	0.010	14.58	2.10	0.48	0	–
	390.0	23.8	0.014	14.76	1.33	0.75	0	–

13.3.2 *The rate of deposition on to agricultural land*

Sulphur is an essential element for crop growth and substantial amounts are probably not added artificially to the soil now that high-analysis fertilisers predominate. Cowling and Jones[16] have suggested that some British soils do not contain enough sulphur to support intensive crops year after year without any supplement. They also suggest that on sulphur-deficient soils ryegrass grows more quickly if SO_2 is present in low concentration. On the other hand Bell and Clough[17] found that low concentrations can reduce growth under slow growing conditions. It is thus not clear whether sulphur dioxide in the atmosphere aids growth of crops, or whether its effects on vegetation are harmful.

However, it is worth considering what the rate of deposition to the land is. Fortunately, the deposition velocity does not vary very much between the different surfaces considered and the mean value of 0·0085 m s^{-1} for all measurements reported in Tables 13.2 and 13.3 is assumed to apply to agricultural land. A mean concentration of 40 μg m^{-3} then yields a deposition rate of 55 kg of sulphur per hectare per year. Prince and Ross[18] compiled a list of the sulphur requirements of several crops, and it appears that this rate of deposition will be much greater than the sulphur requirements of most crops considered.

13.3.3 *The sulphur balance in the atmosphere above Great Britain*

In the paper referred to in the introduction, Meetham[1] developed a model for the behaviour of sulphur dioxide in the air above a large area of Great Britain. The more remote parts of the country were excluded because of insufficient data. The results are summarised in Fig. 13.4.

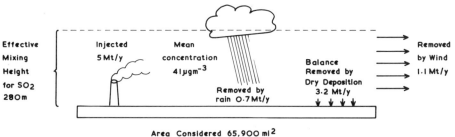

Area Considered 65,900 mi^2

Fig. 13.4 The atmospheric balance for sulphur dioxide over Britain according to Meetham (1950)

The dry deposition rate required to balance input and output of sulphur dioxide in the air above Great Britain implies a deposition velocity of 0·013 m s^{-1}, 50 per cent larger than the mean of the values reported here. In arriving at this figure Meetham was forced to assume, *inter alia*, that carbonaceous smoke particles and sulphur dioxide have similar concentration profiles. Since the sulphur dioxide concentration near the ground is probably reduced as much as 20 to 30 per cent due to deposition, the effective mixing height (the ratio of the mass of material in the column of the atmosphere standing on unit area to the concentration at ground level) for sulphur dioxide is probably larger in this proportion than for smoke. Hence the amount of sulphur dioxide blown away was probably underestimated by 20 to 30 per cent. This would have led to an overestimate in the dry deposition rate and the deposition velocity, but by only 10 per cent. It is also likely that sulphate in particulate form contributes to the sulphur carried away by the wind but was not collected by the sulphur dioxide samplers used. If the mean airborne sulphate concentration is one-quarter the sulphur dioxide level a further 8 per cent correction of Meetham's dry deposition rate results. These reductions may be partly offset by the fact that Meetham makes no allowance for sulphate or sulphur dioxide advected into the volume considered.

While Meetham's approach may overestimate the deposition velocity, it is also likely that a significant error results from the application of the value found in a few experiments over grass and soil to the countryside as a whole, and only by extending the measurements to a much wider variety of surfaces can this inadequacy be made good. However, for the present, one can argue that the experiments over forest suggest that where a very rough surface has a small aerodynamic resistance, the surface resistance increases in compensation, and it may be that the deposition velocities of different vegetated surfaces do not differ too widely.

Before leaving the topic of the sulphur cycle above the United Kingdom it is important to point out that since Meetham's survey there has been a moderate increase in sulphur emissions over the country. Ground level concentrations may not have increased in proportion since the use of tall chimneys and a reduction in the use of coal for domestic heating have raised the mean height of emission. Indeed, Craxford, Gooriah and Weatherley [19] show that the mean concentration in urban areas has decreased. A recent survey by the National Society for Clean Air [20] includes a map of rural concentrations which suggests a mean concentration of about $40 \, \mu\text{g m}^{-3}$. Thus the total amount of sulphur dioxide removed from the air above Great Britain by dry deposition has probably remained unchanged since Meetham's survey though the rate of emission may have increased to approximately 6 M tonne/year. With a deposition velocity of $0.85 \, \text{cm s}^{-1}$ dry deposition would remove 1.9 M tonne/year, equivalent to 40 per cent of the emission in the conditions considered by Meetham but nearer 30 per cent in present-day conditions.

13.3.4 *The global cycle of atmospheric sulphur*

Several authors have examined the balance between known emission and deposition rates of sulphur compounds from the atmosphere. This exercise is important because it indicates how large an effect man's activities are having on the sulphur circulation, and it also tests the completeness of our knowledge of the behaviour of sulphur in the atmosphere. Fig. 13.5, taken from Robinson and Robbins,[21] has been included as an example of a global balance, and the results of these sulphur balance studies are summarised in Table 13.5. All the quantities shown in Fig. 13.5 are based on measurements or calculations of the rates of known mechanisms, with the exception of the hydrogen sulphide emission rates. In each of the studies the emission of this or some other volatile sulphur compound has been assumed to explain the substantial discrepancy between the measured emission and deposition rates, and in each case this emission rate has been found to be greater than the fairly well-known anthropogenic rate. The difficulty of measuring the concentration of hydrogen sulphide has prevented any demonstration that this material is released to the atmosphere, but Eriksson[22] presents some arguments to show that hydrogen sulphide may well be released as a result

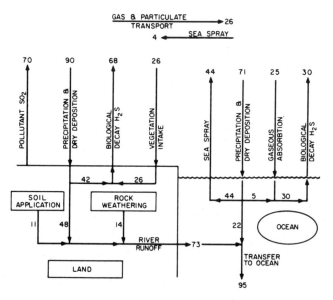

Fig. 13.5   Environmental sulphur circulation

Table 13.5

The atmospheric cycle of sulphur compounds
as derived by several authors

	Robinson and Robbins (1968)		Kellog et al. (1972)		Eriksson (1960)		Robinson and Robbins (modified)	
Sources								
Anthropogenic emission	70		50		39		70	
Sea spray	44		44		44		44	
Natural emission of gaseous sulphur	98		90		267		77	
Removal processes								
Precipitation	130		159		203		130	
Dry deposition of SO$_2$	51		15		147		46	
Dry deposition of sulphate particles	34		10		—		18	

Details of dry deposition estimates

	Land	Sea	Land	Sea	Land	Sea	Land	Sea
Sulphur dioxide sulphur concentration (μg m^{-3})	0.5	0.25	2.9	—	0.7	0.7	0.5	0.25
Deposition velocity (cms^{-1})	1.0	0.9	0.17	0	2.2	0.9	0.85	0.9
Sulphate concentration (μg m^{-3})	—	—	—	—	—	—	1.4	—
Deposition velocity	—	—	—	—	—	—	0.03	—

Unit: 1 tonne sulphur per year

of bacterial decay in soil, mud on the continental shelf, intertidal flats or even the sea surface. Lovelock[23] has recently suggested that the excess emission may be dimethyl sulphide, at least in part.

It is interesting to see what changes in the sulphur balance result from the application of the direct measurement of deposition velocity reported above. The table shows that the mean value for the deposition velocity obtained in the experiments is rather similar to the value used by Robinson and Robbins, and if we accept the concentration used by these authors, the dry deposition rate we calculate does not differ greatly (see the final column of Table 13.5). We have accepted the value of 0.9 cm s^{-1} for sea, based on evaporation rates from the ocean, since Liss[24] has predicted that sulphur dioxide, like water vapour, will find a negligible surface resistance at the pH of sea water. The deposition rate for sulphate particular over land has also been modified, since the size distribution for sulphate particles of Heard and Wiffen[25] combined with the deposition velocity measurements of Chamberlain shows that the small sulphate particles in the contaminated aerosol have a deposition velocity of only 0.03 cm s^{-1}. This finding is supported by the absence of an appreciable concentration gradient for sulphate determined on the pre-filters used in several of the gradient experiments. These changes (Table 13.5) have reduced the natural sulphur emission required to balance the cycle, but it is still larger than the other sources. The greatest remaining uncertainty in its magnitude probably results from the paucity of data on sulphur dioxide and sulphate concentrations in remote locations, although extrapolating the few measurements of deposition velocity to the land surface of the entire globe may also lead to serious error.

13.4   Conclusions

Present measurements indicate a mean deposition velocity for sulphur dioxide to grass and bare soil surfaces of about 0.85 cm s^{-1}. The results of measurements by the gradient method and the radioactive tracer method appear to be consistent.

In the conditions existing at the time of Meetham's study this deposition velocity would lead to dry deposition of about 40 per cent of the sulphur dioxide emitted to the atmosphere above Great Britain. On a world scale it appears that some of the previous estimates of dry deposition may have been rather high, and so the natural emission of gaseous sulphur required to balance known sources and sinks of atmospheric sulphur may have been overestimated.

162

References

[1] Meetham, A.R., Natural removal of pollution from the atmosphere (Quarterly Journal of the Royal Meteorological Society 76, 1950).

[2] Katz, M. and Ledingham, G.A., Effect of sulphur dioxide on vegetation (NCR No. 815, National Research Council of Canada, Ottawa 1939).

[3] Spedding, D.J., Uptake of sulphur dioxide by barley leaves at low sulphur dioxide concentrations (Nature 224, 1969).

[4] Johansson, O., in Annals of the Royal Agricultural College of Sweden 25 (1959).

[5] Gilbert, O.L., Bryophytes as indicators of air pollution in the Tyne Valley (New Phytologist 67, 1968).

[6] Businger, J.A. *et al.*, Flux-profile relationships in the atmospheric surface layer (Journal of Atmospheric Science 28, 1971).

[7] Dyer, A.J. and Hicks, B.B., Flux-gradient relationships in the constant flux layer (Quarterly Journal of the Royal Meteorological Society 96, 1970).

[8] Persson, G.A., Automatic Determination of Low Concentrations of Sulphate for Measuring Sulphur Dioxide in Ambient Air (International Journal of Air and Water Pollution 10, 1966).

[9] Owen, P.R. and Thomson, W.R., in the Journal of Fluid Mechanics Nos. 15, 163, 321.

[10] Chamberlain, A.C., Transport of gases to and from grass and grass-like surfaces (Proceedings of the Royal Society A 290, 1966).

[11] Chamberlain, A.C., Transport of gases to and from surfaces with bluff and wave-like roughness elements (Quarterly Journal of the Royal Meteorological Society 94, 1968).

[12] Shepherd, J.G., Measurement of the deposition of sulphur dioxide onto grass (NW/SSD/RN/257/72, CEGB, North West Region, Manchester 1972).

[13] Chamberlain, A.C., Transport of lycopodium spores and other small particles to rough surfaces (Proceedings of the Royal Society A 296, 1966).

[14] Jarvis, R.A., Soils of the Reading district (New Soil Survey of Great Britain, ARC, Harpenden 1968).

[15] Jarvis, M.G., Soils of the Wantage district (New Soil Survey of Great Britain, ARC, Harpenden). In press.

[16] Cowling, D. and Jones, J., in Soil Science 110, 1970).

[17] Bell, J.N.B. and Clough, W.S., Depression of yield in ryegrass exposed to sulphur dioxide (Nature 241, 1973).

[18] Prince, R. and Ross, F.F., Sulphur in Air and Soil (Water, Air and Soil Pollution 1, 1972).

[19] Craxford, S.R., Gooriah, M.D. and Weatherley M—L., Air pollution in urban areas in the UK (The National Survey of Air Pollution, Report No. 1, Warren Spring Laboratory 1970).

[20] National Society for Clean Air, Sulphur Dioxide (Brighton 1971).

[21] Robinson, E. and Robbins, R.C., Sources, abundance and fate of gaseous atmospheric pollutants (SRI project PR—6755, Stanford Research Institute 1968).

[22] Eriksson, E., The yearly circulation of chloride and sulphur in nature: meteorological, geochemical and pedological implications, Part I, (Tellus 11, 1959); Part II (Tellus 12, 1960).

[23] Lovelock, J.E., Maggs, R.J. and Rasmussen, R.A., in Nature 237, 1972.

[24] Liss, P.S., Exchange of SO_2 between the atmosphere and natural waters (Nature 233, 1971).

[25] Heard, M.J. and Wiffen, R.D., Electron microscopy of natural aerosols and the identification of particulate ammonium sulphate (Atmospheric Environment 3, 1969).

14   Transport of Smoke and Sulphur Dioxide into Rural Areas of England and Wales

R.A. BARNES

14.1   Introduction

Our atmosphere possesses several very efficient mechanisms by which it can purge itself of alien solids and gases. These mechanisms will cope with natural emissions, maintaining an equilibrium concentration in the atmosphere which is called 'background level', and still have latent capacity to deal with a certain degree of anthropogenic emissions. However, man releases his air pollutants in very confined areas. Twenty per cent of the sulphur released by human activities is emitted over central and north-west Europe, which accounts for only 1 per cent of the Earth's total area[1]. With these emissions the atmosphere is unable to readily restore the background concentration, and ambient levels throughout the region rise.

Within the last decade the Scandinavians have become aware of air pollutants arriving in considerable quantities from distant industrial regions of Europe. Great Britain has been named as being particularly responsible in this respect. If the assertions of the Scandinavians are correct, the air in country districts of Great Britain should exhibit concentrations of air pollutants (sulphate, the oxidation product of sulphur dioxide, and soot seem to be particularly important) very much above a background level. Until the middle of the last decade observations of smoke and sulphur dioxide concentrations in country areas of England and Wales were very localised. The establishment after 1965 of an open network of country sites within the National Survey of Smoke and Sulphur Dioxide has provided a comprehensive set of daily data with which to assess the drift of pollutants from their source areas.

14.2 Accuracy of National Survey Data

The National Survey Sampler (The Daily Volumetric Instruments, BS 1747, parts 2 and 3) was developed to monitor the smoke and sulphur dioxide concentrations usually found in urban areas. There is little question that it is suited to this function. However, the accuracy of individual observations, particularly of sulphur dioxide, obtained in country areas where concentrations are usually well below those of towns, is in doubt.

The weakest point in the technique is that net gaseous acidity is measured, not sulphur dioxide concentration. In urban areas where the latter is by far the more important acid gas and concentrations are high, net gaseous acidity will be a very good index of sulphur dioxide concentrations. In country areas minute traces of acid (besides sulphur dioxide) and alkali substances, even from parts of the sampler itself, give rise to spurious indications of sulphur dioxide concentration. The PVC sample line can be a source of acidity,[2, 3] while fractures in the glassware can give rise to alkaline contamination.[4] Fry[5] explains how evaporation of the hydrogen peroxide sampling solution at a country site can give rise to results which indicate a sulphur dioxide concentration in the air where none exists. Should any alkali be present in the air being sampled at a country monitor – ammonia is commonly cited – it will neutralise the acidity due to any sulphur dioxide sampled. Martin and Barber[3] have found that the entire sulphur dioxide acidity at a country site may be lost in this way. Sample line deterioration may also lead to low smoke as well as sulphur dioxide concentrations.[3]

The filter paper used to collect the smoke particles also gives rise to errors in the indicated sulphur dioxide concentration. According to Craxford et al.[6] and Martin and Barber[7] the observed concentration can be low due to the absorption of sulphur dioxide and acid mists by the filter. NAPCA[8] and Martin and Barber believe reaction between the solids deposited on the filter and the gas stream is also important. The density of the stain will affect the volume of air sampled in a 24-hour period, except where a constant flow pump is used. All but four of the twenty-four sites considered in the subsequent analyses have (or had) 'eight-port' samplers with a standard pump and gas meter. By averaging the difference in meter reading over the seven days of unattended operation of these samplers, errors in estimated smoke and sulphur dioxide may reach ± 10 per cent for 24-hour periods when the filter stain was thinner or denser than the average during the seven days.

Individual 24-hour observations of smoke and sulphur dioxide concentrations obtained with National Survey Samplers in country areas could be seriously in error, particularly in the case of sulphur dioxide. But the work of Craxford et al.,[6] Killick,[9] Weatherley [10] and Barnes[4] show that mean concentrations calculated from eighteen observations or more are likely to be representative.

14.3   Analytical methods

14.3.1   *Selection of air pollution sites*

All National Survey country sites classified '02' (completely open country; no sources within one-quarter of a mile) [11] and with a sufficiently long data record to give representative mean concentrations in all eight wind directions were considered for inclusion in the study. Each site was visited to ensure that there were no local environmental factors likely to unduly bias the observations. Martin and Barber, [12] for example, show that samplers with inlets close to foliage indicate anomalously low sulphur dioxide concentrations. Persson [13] finds exposure of large areas of alkali soil by ploughing, etc. has the same effect. In the case of the Castell Mai monitor a strong source of ammonia was identified close to the sampler inlet. The Dean Moor site was found to have a non-standard inlet likely to draw the sample from close to a road surface. The sulphur dioxide observations at Lewknor were recognised as spurious by Warren Spring Laboratory. [14]

The locations of all twenty-four sites used in the study are shown in Fig. 14.1. In addition to the '02' sites, Little Wenlock, a '01' site (open country but not entirely without sources), was used to fill a gap in the site network. Two urban sites, Hereford 2 (A2), and Walsall 14 (C2), later to become Walsall 17, were included for comparison purposes. Neither of the urban sites was in a smoke-controlled area. Daily observations of smoke and sulphur dioxide monitored at each site were then extracted for the period October 1965–March 1969. A2 is a residential area with high-density housing (probably terraced) or with medium-density housing in multiple occupation interspersed with some industrial undertakings and surrounded by other built-up areas. C2 is an industrial area interspersed with domestic premises of high density or in multiple occupation.

14.3.2   *Meteorological data*

Seven meteorological stations (shown in Fig. 14.1) were chosen so that all the air pollution sites lay within 90 km of them and most were closer. A

167

NORTH
SEA

ESKDALEMUIR ▲

IRISH
SEA

□ Dean Moor

Market
Weighton 2 □

Thornton Curtis □

FINNINGLEY ▲

Hayfield 2 □   Caenby □

VALLEY ▲   □ Castell
                    Mai

□ Delamere

SHAWBURY ▲

Kirkby □

Lt. Wenlock □   ■ WALSALL 14/17

MILDENHALL
▲   Sibton □

Ravensden
□

ABERPORTH ▲

HEREFORD 2 ■

Cuddington
□

Lt. Horkesley □

Kelvedon
Hatch □

□ Rhydargeau

Lewknor □

Kilpaison □
Burrows

Sparsholt □   □ Cholsey

BOSCOMBE
DOWN ▲   □ Rogate

□ Askerwell

KEY
□ POLLUTION SITE (RURAL)
■ POLLUTION SITE (URBAN)
▲ METEOROLOGICAL STATION

SCALE
0   km   100

Fig. 14.1   Meteorological and air pollution stations

168

test analysis showed that 24-hour mean wind directions, grouped into eight sectors (excluding those periods where the extreme directions observed differed by more than 67½°), calculated from the 06.00 and 12.00 hours observations only, did not differ to any great extent from those calculated from the 00.00, 06.00, 12.00 and 18.00 hours observations. Using the 06.00 and 12.00 hours observations from the closest of the seven meteorological stations, the mean wind speed and direction for the air pollution sampling period were calculated.

14.3.3 *Analysis of air pollution data*

Using the appropriate mean wind direction and speed, the daily smoke and sulphur dioxide concentrations were classified into one of twenty-five groups. The eight 45° wind directions had three sub-divisions according to wind speed: 2·0—5·5 knots: 5·6—15·0 knots and over 15·0 knots, while the final group was for calm periods (wind speed < 2·0 knots). The classification was carried out separately for the summer (1 April—30 September) and winter (1 October—31 March). Mean smoke and mean sulphur dioxide concentrations were calculated for each wind-speed group of each wind direction and for winds of all three speed groups in each wind direction. Pollution roses were drawn for each site from the latter means and appear as Fig. 14.2. The mean smoke and sulphur dioxide concentrations in periods of calm are shown diagrammatically in Fig. 14.3.

No attempt was made to standardise the number of observations used to calculate the mean concentrations. Obviously the variation in wind frequency between different directions and the difference in continuity of data record between sites resulted in the mean concentrations being derived from a widely ranging number of observations. If standardisation had been employed the means would have not represented the *average* conditions in a given wind direction at a specific site. In order to ascertain the likely difference in accuracy between means calculated from widely differing numbers of observations, ten randomly selected concentrations were used to calculate means at two sites and these were compared with the means derived from the much larger entire data record. The maximum difference was found to be 12 per cent.

The mean concentrations of smoke and sulphur dioxide used to construct the pollution roses were used to calculate a sulphur dioxide/smoke ratio for each wind direction at every site. These ratios aided the identification of sources affecting the site and unreliable data, but are not presented here due to lack of space.

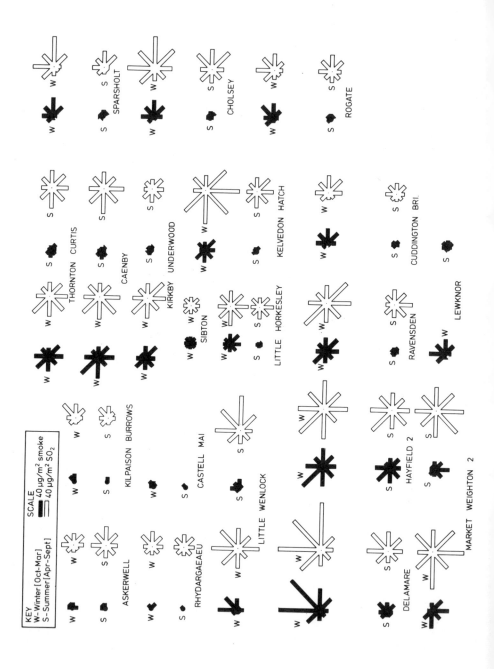

Fig. 14.2 Mean daily pollution concentrations for different wind directions 1965—69

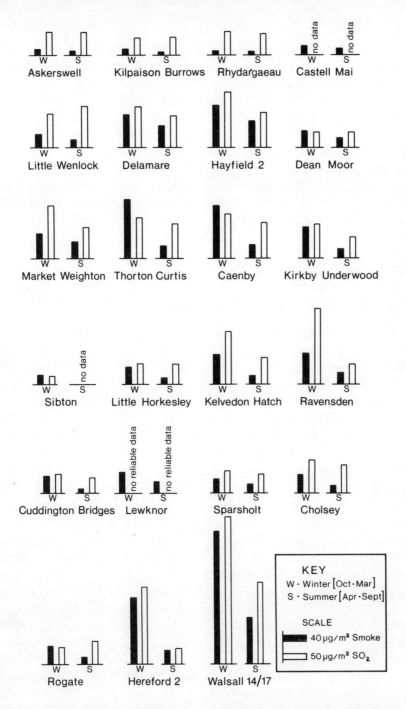

Fig. 14.3   Mean daily pollution concentrations in calms 1965—69

14.3.4 *Source inventory*

As an aid to the interpretation of the analysed data the distribution of emitters likely to affect concentrations at each monitor was sought. The 1: 63,360 scale Ordnance Survey maps, Warren Spring Laboratory site forms (WSL Form 214 AP) and notes made during the site visit were used to establish the location of any sources close to the monitor. Regional maps were inspected to identify the position of towns and cities relative to the site, even if these were tens of kilometres distant. Additionally, maps giving the location of major industrial plants (e.g. power stations, steel works, oil refineries) known to make important contributions to smoke and sulphur dioxide concentrations were obtained from the respective operating organisation.

14.4 Results

14.4.1 *Analysis according to wind direction*

(i) *General pattern* Only a small number of sites studied were found to have mean smoke concentrations, in a majority of wind directions, close to that recognised by other authors as background concentration. The corresponding directional mean sulphur dioxide concentrations were, in every case, found to be greater than the background levels.

Mean concentrations of smoke for both winter and summer, and most wind directions as Askerswell, Kilpaison Burrows, Rhydargaeau and Castell Mai fall close to the figure of 10 μg m^{-3} quoted by Porch *et al.* [15] as being the typical minimum value monitored in the US National Air Sampling Network. However, none of these sites shows itself to be completely free from the effect of anthropogenic smoke emissions. In certain wind directions there is a distinct increase in mean concentrations from summer to winter. Since the mean smoke concentrations in calms are below 15 μg m^{-3} in both seasons, local sources are not indicated. Rhydargaeau is a good example. In summer the mean smoke concentration for south-east and north-west winds is typical of a natural background level. The significant increase in winter indicates that smoke is travelling to Rhydargaeau some 40 km from industrial south-east Wales, and over 180 km from the West Midlands and beyond.

As explained in the second section, little reliance can be placed on the sulphur dioxide concentrations measured by the National Survey instrument. Certain of the features shown by the sulphur dioxide roses drawn for Askerswell, Kilpaison Burrows and Rhydargaeau serve to illustrate this point. While, for the most part, the sulphur dioxide roses have a similar form to· those for mean smoke concentration, they do show two unexpected characteristics. All eight of the summer directional mean concentrations for Askerswell exceed the corresponding winter ones. A similar anomaly occurs in the north and south-west directions at Rhydargaeau. At Askerswell the differences range from 5 to 18 μg m^{-3}. The only apparent explanation is one of observational error, possibly due to the concentration of sulphuric acid, used to bring the hydrogen peroxide to pH 4·5 before exposure, by evaporation of the solute during the 24-hour sampling period. The mechanism by which such an error can develop was described by Fry.[5]

The other unexpected characteristic is the relatively high mean sulphur dioxide concentrations in directions having background smoke levels and no apparent sulphur dioxide source. High sulphur dioxide concentrations in country areas, compared to country smoke and urban sulphur dioxide levels, were noted by Warren Spring Laboratory [16] and are discussed later. There is, of course, a wide variation in the values of background sulphur dioxide concentration found by various investigators. Attempting to draw the different values together, Junge [17] arrives at a value of 6 μg m^{-3} and says that only areas with values less than 10 μg m^{-3} can be considered free from an artificial sulphur dioxide component.

(ii) *Country sites* In general, country areas of England have mean smoke concentrations well above the accepted upper limit of the background level in winter in almost all wind directions. In the summer, background or near-background smoke concentrations are experienced in about half the wind directions, the others showing evidence of smoke transport from upwind industrial sources.

Sulphur dioxide levels in country areas of England and Wales are everywhere greater than the background although in a small number of cases in west Wales and south-west England they do approach it. To a certain extent anomalous data can be used as an explanation but it seems clear that sulphur dioxide is reaching country areas from distant sources and that these sources are, in some cases, contributing little or no smoke to the country air in question.

Excluding country sites close to industrial conurbations (within 25–30 km), mean winter smoke concentrations range up to 50 μg m^{-3} calculated for north winds at Little Wenlock and 57 μg m^{-3} for the north-west winds at Caenby. This level of smoke concentration is typical of the winter mean concentrations for the centre of Hereford (41–77 μg m^{-3}). For many of these sites, the mean winter smoke

173

concentrations in calm conditions are much less than the concentrations for certain wind directions, e.g. 22 μg m^{-3} (calm), 50 μg m^{-3} (north wind) at Little Wenlock; 24 μg m^{-3} (calm), 45 μg m^{-3} (east wind) at Sparsholt. This implies that the high mean concentrations do not originate in any great measure from local sources. When account is taken of the distribution of emitters around the monitor, it is apparent that these concentrations are produced by smoke drifting tens or even hundreds of kilometres.

Country areas close to large industrial conurbations (i.e. within 25–30 km) can expect to receive very high smoke concentration when they come to be downwind of the source in summer or winter. The results from Delamere, Hayfield 2 and Market Weighton 2 illustrate the levels to be expected. The maximum summer mean concentration for Delamere is 32 μg m^{-3} and occurs in north-east winds (Manchester 30 km), and that of 45 μg m^{-3} for Hayfield 2 occurs in north-west winds (Manchester 10 km). As a comparison, the maximum summer mean smoke concentration at Hereford 2 is 25 μg m^{-3}.

The winter mean smoke concentrations at Delamere, Hayfield 2 and Market Weighton 2 show a considerable increase over the summer ones for winds in the direction of nearby industrial conurbations. This points to a greater domestic space heating emission. Mean winter smoke concentrations for north and north-east winds at Delamere (106 μg m^{-3}, 107 μg m^{-3} respectively) exceed four of those calculated for Walsall 14/17. It is interesting to note, however, that while the Walsall 14/17 figure for calm conditions is 230 μg m^{-3}, the mean for Delamere is only 54 μg m^{-3}. This emphasises the exotic nature of the pollution in the latter case.

In certain country areas of England very high mean sulphur dioxide concentrations are likely in winter. Sites in south-east England show typical maxima of over 70 μg m^{-3} in winds blowing from conurbations such as London, Lower Thames-side and the West Midlands. Such values fall within the upper part of the range (59–102 μg m^{-3}) experienced in central Hereford. Although, because of the profusion of sources, it is difficult to say exactly how far upwind the main sulphur dioxide emissions lie, it would seem that they can be over 40 km distant.

With fewer non-urban monitors in northern England, generalisations may be less valid, but it would certainly seem that some country areas experience mean winter sulphur dioxide concentrations even greater than those seen in the South-East. Delamere illustrates the situation. With Runcorn and Widnes lying 15 km away to the north, the mean winter sulphur dioxide concentration in that direction is 110 μg m^{-3}. With east winds, with possible sources 10–30 km distant, the mean concentration is 120 μg m^{-3}. Liverpool, Birkenhead and Port Sunlight, being over 25 km away, give rise to a winter mean sulphur dioxide concentration in north-west winds of 71 μg m^{-3}.

Unlike mean smoke concentrations, those of sulphur dioxide do not show a particularly large fall from winter to summer in country areas. This is probably explained by the more rapid fall-off in smoke concentrations, compared to sulphur dioxide, with increasing distance from an urban area.[16] It can be argued that this, in turn, is the result of industrial emission of sulphur dioxide (industry is the largest emitter of sulphur dioxide yet one of the smallest of smoke) from tall stacks which reduce the contribution of industry to surface sulphur dioxide concentrations in urban areas. However, this may bring about a significant contribution to the surface concentration in country areas.[16] Domestic sources, being the most important source of smoke, emit at low level and therefore affect their immediate environs to a much greater extent. However, while this explanation may hold close (within about 30–40 km) to the source, once the mixing layer is filled, it seems more likely that the relative preponderance of sulphur dioxide at a distance should be attributed to the more rapid removal of smoke from the atmosphere.

In certain situations other factors may also be important: a conurbation burning mainly smokeless fuel would produce much higher downwind sulphur dioxide than smoke concentrations.

(iii) *Sites in eastern England* Five sites in eastern England (Thornton Curtis, Caenby, Kirkby Underwood, Little Horkesley and Ravensden) show a much greater increase among their lowest directional mean smoke concentrations from summer to winter than sites in other parts of the country. This seems to indicate the presence of upwind sources in the direction of summer minimum concentrations which make a major contribution only in winter. The distribution of emitters around Little Horkesley, Ravensden and Thornton Curtis seems to confirm this explanation, but it is difficult to identify sources in the case of the Lincolnshire sites of Caenby and Kirkby Underwood.

South-east winds see an increase in mean smoke concentration from 13–36 μg m^{-3} and from 13–39 μg m^{-3} at Caenby and Kirkby Underwood respectively from summer to winter. A similar pattern is observed in the easterly direction, but with a less marked increase. In north-east winds Caenby and Kirkby Underwood both have mean summer smoke concentrations of 8 μg m^{-3} rising to 23 and 15 μg m^{-3} respectively in winter. An explanation is not immediately forthcoming since the apparent source strength around both sites is greater to the north-east than to the south-east. In attempting to account for this anomaly the figures for the east Suffolk site of Sibton must also be considered. No value is available for the summer period, but in winter a mean concentration for both east and south-east winds of 19 μg m^{-3} is anomalously large compared with those for other directions (e.g. south-west and south 17 μg m^{-3}) when the source distribution is taken into account.

It is possibly not without significance that all three sites lie not far from the coast of eastern England and that it is the east and south-east directions which are anomalous. One explanation would be that smoke drifting from sources in mainland Europe is contributing significantly to the mean concentrations at these sites.

Chamberlain and Penkett [18] observed that ground level concentrations of sulphate and sulphur dioxide were approximately 5 μg m^{-3} and 20 μg m^{-3}, respectively, on the north-east coast of Britain during times of persistent easterly winds. This suggests that these pollutants too may be reaching our shores from continental sources. The results of a survey into air pollution concentrations monitored at seven coastal sites on both sides of the North Sea have shown this to be the case. [19]

14.4.2 Analysis by wind speed

Since the air pollutants sampled at country sites have a distant origin, mean concentrations in calm conditions are generally low. However, as can be seen from Fig. 14.3, this is not so in every case. The mean winter smoke concentration for calm conditions at Caenby, for example, exceeds the highest of the directional means (north-west, 59 μg m^{-3}). As for other examples, this seems to be the result of the upper threshold of wind speed for the calm classification (2 knots) being too high.

Gooriah [20] presents a smoke pollution rose for the 1963/4 winter at Caenby taking all winds between 0 and 11 knots. In the north-west direction (steelworks and town of Scunthorpe 21 km) a mean concentration of 300 μg m^{-3} is given. Since this value is much greater than that calculated for all wind speeds over 2 knots in this paper (59 μg m^{-3}) the suggestion is that smoke drifts to Caenby in very light winds.

Maximum mean concentrations of smoke and sulphur dioxide usually occur at country sites in light winds and decline progressively as the wind speed increases. In some cases, however, mean concentrations increase with wind speed and after reaching a maximum can occur at wind speeds over 15 knots. A similar phenomenon was noted by Zeedijk and Velds. [21] The most important variable determining the wind velocity of maximum mean concentration in a given wind direction appears to be the average mixing height in relation to the distance and strength of the upwind sources.

14.4.3 *Decay rate of smoke and sulphur dioxide concentrations*

Because of the effect of intervening sources it is difficult to obtain a comprehensive picture of the rate at which mean concentrations decay from an area source. However, it some cases it was found to be possible, and these decay rates have been used successfully to predict observed mean concentrations at other country sites. This work will be reported in detail at a later date.

14.5 Conclusion

Very few areas of England and Wales, except the far west, appear free from the effects of urban emissions of smoke and sulphur dioxide. In some country areas the mean concentrations of both these pollutants can be very high and undoubtedly affect the quality of life to a certain extent − tanning of the skin on the beaches of eastern England will certainly be a more protracted process than it is in the transparent air of the west coast. Mean sulphur dioxide concentrations at some country sites in certain wind directions suggest that these areas may, from time to time, experience short-term concentrations within the range of human response. Carnow *et al.* [22] state that there is an increased illness rate of elderly people with severe chronic bronchitis when 24-hour mean sulphur dioxide concentrations reach $140-260 \, \mu g \, m^{-3}$.

References

[1] Rodhe, H., A study of the sulphur budget for the atmosphere over Northern Europe (Tellus 24, 1972).

[2] Marsh, K.J. *et al.*, An experimental study of the emissions from chimneys in Reading, Part II: description of the instrument used (Atmospheric Environment 1, 1967).

[3] Martin, A. and Barber, F., Control of daily sulphur dioxide instruments to minimise possible errors (Atmospheric Environment 5, 1971).

[4] Barnes, R.A., Duplicate measurements of low concentrations of

smoke and sulphur dioxide using two 'National Survey' Samplers with a common inlet (Atmospheric Environment 7, 1973).

[5] Fry, J.D., Determination of SO_2 in the atmosphere by absorption in H_2O_2 solution – the effect of evaporation of the solution during sampling. (CEGB [South-West Region], Scientific Services Department Report P 13702, 1970).

[6] Craxford, S.R. *et al.*, The measurement of atmospheric pollution – the accuracy of the instruments and the significance of the results (Proceedings of the National Society for Clean Air, Harrogate Conference 1960).

[7] Martin, A. and Barber, F., Investigation of SO_2 pollution around a modern power station (Journal of the Institute of Fuel 39, 1966).

[8] NAPCA, Air quality criteria for sulphur oxides (US Department of Health, Education and Welfare 1969).

[9] Killick, C.M., Atmospheric sulphur dioxide by the hydrogen peroxide method: data from two sites six feet apart (Warren Spring Laboratory Report RR/AP/61, 1962).

[10] Weatherley, M-L., Measurement of atmospheric smoke and sulphur dioxide: reproducibility of results (Warren Spring Laboratory Report RR/AP/70, 1962).

[11] Warren Spring Laboratory, Directory of sites used in the investigation of air pollution (Department of Trade and Industry 1971).

[12] Martin, A. and Barber, F., Some measurements of loss of atmospheric SO_2 near foliage (Atmospheric Environment 5, 1971).

[13] Persson, G., The acidity and the concentration of sulphate in precipitation over Europe (Swedish Nature Conservancy 1968).

[14] Warren Spring Laboratory, National Survey of Air Pollution, 1961–1971, vol. 1 (HMSO 1972).

[15] Porch, W.M. *et al.*, Does a background level exist? (Science 170, 1970).

[16] Warren Spring Laboratory, National Survey of Air Pollution, 1961–1971, vol. 2 (HMSO 1972).

[17] Junge, C.E., Air Chemistry and Radio-activity (Academic Press, New York 1963).

[18] Chamberlain, A. and Penkett, S., Atmospheric pollution – present trends and future problems (Contemporary Physics 13, 1972).

[19] Barnes, R.A., Sulphur emissions (Ecologist 4, 1974).

[20] Gooriah, B., Distribution of pollution at some country sites (Warren Spring Laboratory Report LR 58 [AP], 1968).

[21] Zeedijk, H, and Velds, C., The transport of sulphur dioxide over a long distance (Atmospheric Environment 7, 1973).

178

[22] Carnow, B.W. *et al.*, The Chicago Air Pollution Study: SO_2 levels and acute illness in patients with chronic bronchopulmonary disease (Archives of Environmental Health 18, 1969).

15 Measurements of Atmospheric Ozone in Rural Locations

Dr R.A. COX

15.1 Introduction

Measurement of oxidant in the atmosphere has been used for some years in the United States as an indicator of the occurrence of photochemical air pollution in urban environments. Levels of oxidant (chiefly ozone) in excess of 100 ppb (1 ppb = 1 part per 10^9 air) are considered evidence of photochemical pollution arising from reactions in the atmosphere of nitrogen oxides and hydrocarbons from combustion sources. By comparison clean-air ozone concentrations at ground level rarely exceed 50 ppb during daytime and may fall to near zero at night, due to decreased vertical mixing and destruction of ozone at the ground.

Until the late 1960s it had generally been held that photochemical air pollution was unlikely to be encountered in Western Europe because of the lower sunlight intensities, air temperatures and pollutant emissions, compared with, for example, the western United States. However, measurements made in the Netherlands in 1968[1] showed elevated levels of oxidant under anticyclonic conditions which seemed to indicate local photochemical ozone formation in the atmosphere. This prompted us to embark on a programme of atmospheric ozone measurements in southern Britain, and the results of this survey[2] for 1971–73 are briefly presented here.

15.2 Methods

Ozone was measured using detectors based on the chemiluminescent reaction between ozone and ethylene. The instruments give a continuous analogue signal directly proportional to the ozone concentration with a response time of a few seconds and a sensitivity of ≈ 1 ppb. A data-logging system was designed to record the ozone concentration every ten minutes and store the data on punched tape which could be processed at a later date to obtain hourly average concentrations. Ozone was sampled approximately 2 m above the ground at locations away from combustion sources of nitric oxide, which would interfere by depleting the local ozone concentration.

15.3   Results

15.3.1   *1971*

The first series of measurements were made during June–July 1971 at Harwell, Oxfordshire ($51° 35'$ N, $1° 19'$ W). During the period of operation the hourly average ozone concentration varied from zero to maxima of over 10 pphm. Minima were normally recorded during the early hours of the morning and maxima during the afternoon. These times correspond roughly to the daily minimum and maximum extent of vertical mixing in the lower troposphere. On days when atmospheric mixing was good throughout, little diurnal variation in the ozone concentration was observed. When mixing was poor, particularly in anticyclonic conditions, a large diurnal variation in ozone was found. These features are demonstrated in Fig. 15.1, which shows the variation of ozone and also of the air concentration of radon (which is roughly inversely proportional to the extent of vertical mixing) on two days, 26 June on which a depression passed over northern Britain, and 3 July when an anticyclone was stationary over the North sea.

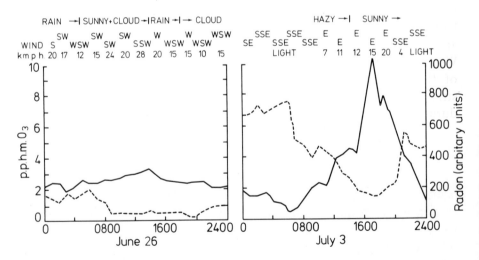

Fig. 15.1   Variation of ozone and radon at Harwell, Oxfordshire, 1971

Table 15.1

Frequency distribution of maximum hourly ozone concentrations – Harwell, 1971

Max. O_3 (ppb)	0 – 1·9	2 – 3·9	4 – 5·9	6 – 7·9	8 – 9·9	10 – 11·9
No. of days	1	14	13	1	4	2

Table 15.1 shows the frequency distribution of the maximum hourly average ozone concentrations on 35 days during the summer of 1971. On 80 per cent of the days ozone concentrations were below 60 ppb and can be considered normal. Although 100 ppb was only exceeded on 2 days, on 6 days the maximum hourly average ozone concentrations was in excess of 80 ppb which is the recommended United States air quality standard, not to be exceeded more than once per year.[3] These data comprised the first observations indicating photochemical oxidant formation over southern Britain.

15.3.2   *1972*

In 1972, the survey was extended inasmuch as data was acquired throughout the summer (May to October) at Harwell and a second monitoring station was set up at Ascot, Berks, which is closer to the Greater London urban region. A similar pattern of ozone concentrations to that found in 1971 was observed, both at Harwell and at Ascot. Of particular interest was the fact that when elevated ozone levels occurred, they were observed at both sites, showing that the phenomenon was influenced primarily by large scale meteorological factors. The maximum levels of ozone observed during these 'episodes' were essentially the same at the two sites; furthermore ozone measurements carried out by the Warren Spring laboratory in Central London also showed ozone maxima of the same magnitude during photochemical episodes. This is demonstrated in Table 15.2 which shows data for the three sites for 4 days during July 1972.

Table 15.2

Comparison of maximum ozone concentrations – Harwell, Ascot, Central London, July 1973

Date	Maximum hourly average O_3 (ppb)		
	London	Ascot	Harwell
12 July	8·5	7·5	6·1
13 July	11·1	12·8	7·0
14 July	8·3	10·5	12·2

15.3.3 *1973*

In 1973 ozone measurements were made at three widely spaced locations on an E–W trajectory across the southern British Isles, in an attempt to determine the extent and magnitude of photochemical ozone production in the region. The locations were Harwell, Oxfordshire, Sibton, Suffolk (52° 03′ N, 1° 05′ E) and Adrigole, Co. Cork, Eire (51° 40′ N, 9° 45′ W). In addition measurements of atmospheric Freon 11 (CCl_3F) were made at Adrigole and at Bowerchalke, near Salisbury, Wiltshire (in collaboration with Professor J.E. Lovelock), which gave valuable information[4] concerning the origin of the air masses present over Southern Ireland and Southern England during the period of the survey.

A summary of the concentrations of ozone observed at the three stations over the period of operation is plotted in Figs. 15.2–15.4, in the form of maximum hourly mean ozone concentration for each day. The occurrence of incidents of elevated ozone concentrations superimposed on a background level (shown by broken lines in Figs. 15.1–15.3), is clearly indicated at each site. This background level is believed to represent the natural ozone content of the lower troposphere over N.W. Europe and, based on the data from the most remote site (Adrigole) the background value was about 40 ppb.

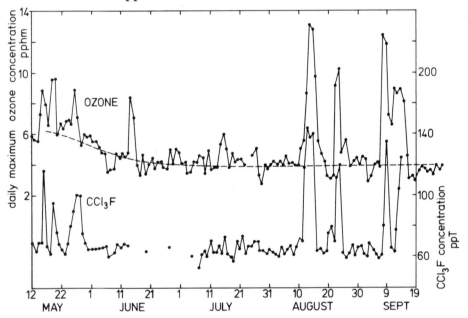

Fig. 15.2 Daily maximum hourly average ozone concentrations and CCl_3F concentrations measured at Adrigole, Co. Cork

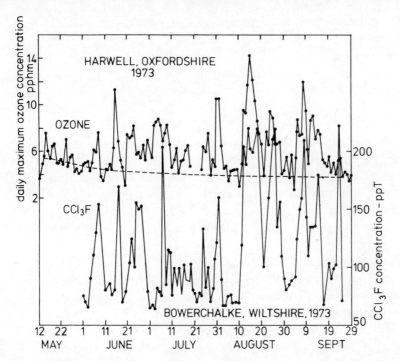

Fig. 15.3   Daily maximum hourly average ozone concentrations and CCl$_3$F concentrations measured at Harwell, Oxfordshire and Bowerchalke, Wiltshire, respectively

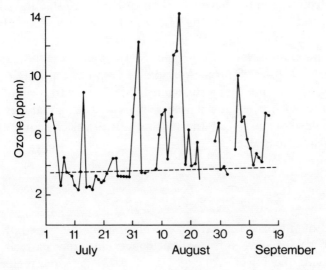

Fig 15.4   Daily maximum hourly average ozone concentrations measured at Sibton, Suffolk

The pattern of the incidents, particularly during August and September, was similar for each of the three sites, confirming that large scale meteorological conditions are an important factor in the occurrence of elevated ozone levels. Also shown in Figs. 15.1 and 15.2 are the Freon 11 concentrations of Adrigole and Bowerchalke. The general pattern of the Freon 11 was similar to the ozone; that is, rather variable levels in Southern England but with longer periods near background at Adrigole. Freon 11 is entirely anthropogenic in origin and behaves essentially as an inert gas in the troposphere. Its concentration therefore gives an unambiguous measure of the extent to which a given air mass is affected by man-made pollutants. The correspondence of the elevated ozone and Freon 11 concentrations, therefore, strongly indicates that the ozone measured was in part due to photochemical reactions between pollutant precursors.

A detailed analysis of the data from the three sites during the period 11–18 August was carried out. During this period a persistent anticyclone became established over the North Sea, replacing a south-westerly air flow by a predominantly easterly drift of continental air over the southern British Isles. A synoptic chart for 12.00 h, 15 August, is illustrated in Fig. 15.5. Elevated ozone levels were observed at all three sites following the establishment of the anticyclone, with its associated reduction of vertical dispersion, on 13 August. The elevated ozone levels observed during the episode at Sibton, situated only 10 km from the Suffolk coast in sparsely populated country, must have had their origin in continental sources. The sources of the emissions giving rise to elevated levels at Harwell and Adrigole are less clear cut and probably include a component from the UK. The maximum levels observed at Harwell were not significantly different from those at Sibton, Adrigole or even Central London (136 ppb on 15 August) showing that a sufficiently high concentration of pollutants had accumulated in the continental air mass to give similar elevated ozone concentrations over much of the southern British Isles, and probably over more extensive areas also.

15.4   Conclusions

The results of the ozone measurement programme described briefly above give some useful new information concerning the pattern of ozone distribution in the lower troposphere over the maritime regions of N.W. Europe, which may have relevance in other regions. It appears that photochemical ozone of anthropogenic origin is not a phenomenon

associated only with urban atmospheres, but under suitable meteorological conditions may occur over wide regional areas. Furthermore,
photochemical ozone and/or its pollutant precursors can be transported
over distances of up to 1,000 km in N.W. Europe and on occasions
continental emissions make a major contribution to photochemical
pollution in the UK.

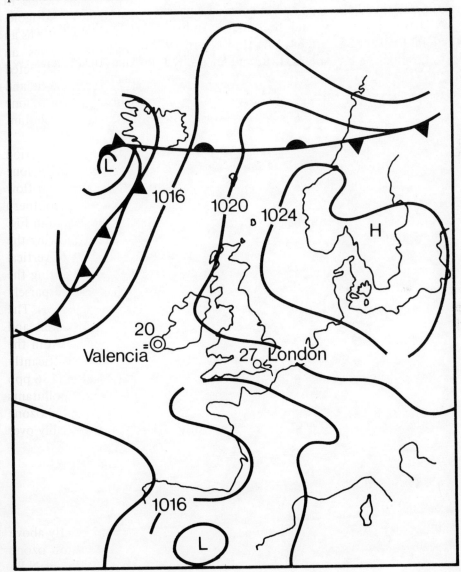

Fig. 15.5   Synoptic chart for 12.00 hours 15 August 1973

References

[1] Wisse, J.A. and Velds, C.A. in an article in Atmospheric Environment 4, 1970.

[2] Part of this survey has already been reported in detail, — Atkins, D.F.H., Cox, R.A. and Eggleton, A.E.J., Nature 235, 1972. The 1973 results will shortly be reported in detail elsewhere.

[3] National Primary and Secondary Ambient Air Quality Standards (Federal Register 36, No. 84, Part II, 30 April 1971).

[4] Lovelock, J.E., Adlard, E.R. and Maggs, R.J. in Analytical Chemistry 43, 1971.

16 Travel and Deposition of Lead Aerosols

Dr A.C. CHAMBERLAIN

16.1 Lead from motor vehicles

Lead is added to petrol as tetra-ethyl lead (TEL) or tetra-methyl lead (TML). During combustion the lead is converted to an aerosol. Some organic lead may also be vaporised from fuel tanks, carburettors and spills of petrol. The chemical form of the particulate lead is a mixture of halides, oxides and sulphates. The physical form depends on the mode of operation of the engine. During cruising at a moderate or high speed, small particles of lead salts may be emitted, but during idling the lead is incorporated in a carbonaceous aerosol, usually in the form of chain-like aggregates.[1] During full-power acceleration and hill climbing, lead and carbon previously trapped in the exhaust system may be released as relatively coarse ($\approx 10\,\mu m$) particles. This is especially likely with high-mileage vehicles.[2]

The lead-carrying aerosol in normal driving conditions is sub-micron in size, and may be expected to disperse in the atmosphere like smoke. In experiments in which the exhaust of a car was passed into a wind tunnel, Habibi[2] found that about 10 per cent of the lead consumed by the engine was deposited in the 40-ft length of the tunnel. The engine was coupled to a dynamometer and operated on a driving cycle typical of city conditions.

About 9,000 tonnes of lead are currently added to petrol in the UK, and about 75 per cent of this amount is emitted to atmosphere.[3]

16.2 Mean concentration of lead to urban areas

Craxford, Weatherley, and Gooriah[4] give the annual emission of smoke in various regions of Britain, and the mean concentration measured at the sampling sites of the National Survey. These sites are mainly in urban areas, but most of them are situated on the roofs of municipal buildings and in open spaces, and not immediately adjacent to main roads.

In Table 16.1 the results of Craxford *et al.*[4] are used to calculate the concentration of lead from motor exhaust on the assumption that the

189

dispersion of the particles is similar to that of smoke in general. In Table 16.2 some recently reported measured values of lead are given. It will be seen that the measured levels are in the range predicted in Table 16.1, suggesting that most of the lead in air in towns comes from exhausts. Colwill[5] found that there was a very close correlation between lead in air and the density of traffic in Reading.

Table 16.1

Emissions and concentrations in air of smoke and lead

		London area	England and Wales	Reference
(a)	Smoke emitted (1968) (tonnes yr^{-1})	2.5×10^4	8.9×10^5	(1)
(b)	Smoke concentration ($\mu g\ m^{-3}$)	40	71 (Urban sites)	(1)
	Petroleum consumption (1970) (tonnes yr^{-1})	1.85×10^6	1.4×10^7	
(c)	Lead emission (tonnes yr^{-1})	900	6,800	(2)
(d)	Lead concentration ($\mu g\ m^{-3}$) (ie. (a) is calculated as bc/a)	1.5	0.55	

(1) Craxford *et al.*[4]
(2) Assuming Pb concentration in petrol $0.46\ g\ l^{-1} = 2.1$ g/gall = 640 ppm by weight, and 75 per cent emission from tail pipe as small particles

16.3   Concentrations near motorways

The concentration of lead in the air near the ground at various distances from a motorway can be calculated from the theory of dispersion of line sources.[6, 7]

The concentration $\chi (x, 0)\ \mu g\ m^{-3}$ at ground level x metres downwind of a line source of strength $Q\ \mu g\ m^{-1}\ s^{-1}$ is given by

$$\chi (x\ 0) = Q/u\overline{h} \qquad (16.1)$$

where u is the wind speed and $\bar{h}$ the equivalent height of the cloud, defined by

$$\bar{h} = \left(\frac{\int_{z=0}^{\infty} \chi(x, z)\, dz}{\chi(x, 0)} \right) \tag{16.2}$$

If the vertical distribution is Gaussian in form,[6] then

$$h = 1.26\, \sigma_z \tag{16.3}$$

where σ_z is the standard deviation of the vertical distribution.

Table 16.2

Lead in air in UK

Location	Pb in air ($\mu g\, m^{-3}$)	Date of measurements	Reference
Main roads			
Fleet Street, London (08.00–19.00 weekdays)	6·3	1971	Lawther et al.[1]
A4, Reading	4·0	1971	Colwill[5]
Jury Street, Warwick	3·5	1963–66	Bullock and Lewis[22]
Other urban sites			
St Bartholomew's Hospital, London	1·0	1971	Lawther et al.[1]
Warwick	0·8	1963–66	Bullock and Lewis[22]
Stockton	0·43	1969	D.H. Atkins[23]
Rural sites	0·05–0·4	1972	Peirson et al.[12] (see Table 16.4)

Sutton[8] gave a semi-empirical formula for σ_z:

$$\sigma_z = \frac{C_z}{\sqrt{2}}\, x^{1-n/2} \tag{16.4}$$

where, in neutral conditions of atmospheric stability, $C_z = 0.12$, $n = 0.25$, and σ_z is in metres.

More recently Pasquill[7] has given a formula

$$\sigma_z/x = ak^2 \, [\ln (c\sigma_z/az_0) - 1]^{-1} \qquad (16.5)$$

where, for flow over grass about 0·1 m high in neutral conditions, $a = 1·3$, k (von Karman's constant) $= 0·4$ $c = 0·6$, $z_0 = 0·01$ m.

Graphs of σ_z derived from equations (16.4) and (16.5) are given in Fig. 16.1. The agreement is close (both formulae are based on the same experimental data, obtained in smoke tests over downland at Porton).

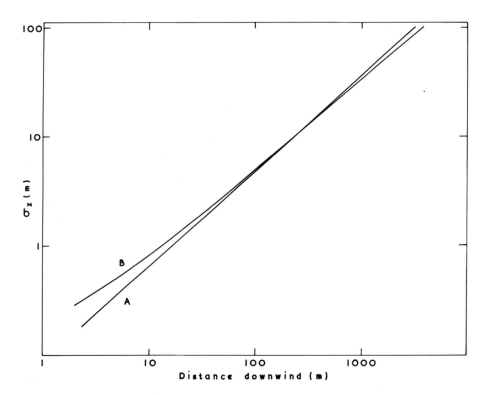

Fig. 16.1 Vertical dispersion of cloud, from line source in neutral stability: (a) Sutton's equation; (b) Pasquill's equation.

Because to a first approximation σ_z is proportional to x, it makes little difference to $\chi(x, 0)$ if the wind does not blow at right angles to the line source. If it blows at an angle Θ, the distance of travel is increased in the ratio $\sin^{-1}\Theta$, but the effective source strength per unit distance cross-wind is also increased in the ratio $\sin^{-1}\Theta$ (Fig. 16.2).

The concentration of lead in air at distance x from the kerb of a highway will now be calculated on the following assumptions:

(a) traffic flow is 1,000 vehicles/hour;
(b) the exhausts of vehicles in the near lane are 2 m from the near kerb and in the far lane 23 m from the near kerb;
(c) vehicles travel at 50 mph, fuel consumption is 20 mpg, lead content of petrol is 0.46 g l^{-1} (2.1 g/gall) and 75 per cent of lead is exhausted; and
(d) the wind speed is 3 m s^{-1} blowing from the road towards the site of measurement and atmospheric stability is neutral.

With these assumptions, the emission of lead is 13.5 μg per m length of road per sec. Bovay[9] takes the emission in Switzerland at $8-10$ μg m^{-1} s^{-1} and Atkins[10] gives data for California which indicate an emission of greater than 20 μg m^{-1} s^{-1} for the same traffic density.

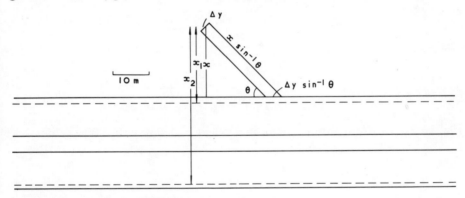

Fig. 16.2   Plan of highway

To calculate χ at distance x m from the nearside kerb of the highway, the sum is taken of the concentration due to two line sources at distances x_1 and x_2, where $x_1 = x + 2$ and $x_2 = x + 23$ (Fig. 16.3). The wind speed is taken as 3 m s^{-1} and equation (16.5) is used for σ_z. It is assumed that the wind is blowing from the road towards the sampling positions. The results are shown in Fig. 16.3.

The results of Fig. 16.3 refer to ideal conditions, a straight road in level country, vehicles cruising at constant speed, and normal dispersion in the atmosphere. Considerably higher concentrations would be found in stable atmospheric conditions with low winds, and lower concentrations in windy weather. The effect of buildings near the road is hard to calculate. In some conditions the effect might be to increase turbulence and dispersion; in others, to hinder dispersion.

193

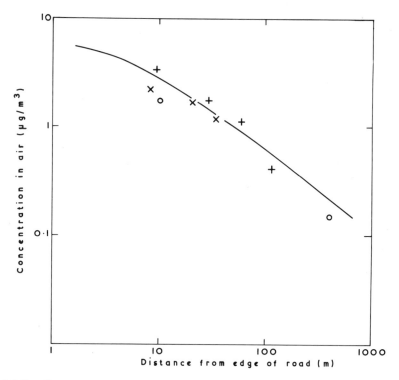

Fig. 16.3 Concentration of lead in air near highway with 1000 vehicles hr^{-1}

16.4 Comparison with measured values of Pb in air near highways

In comparing the results of Fig. 16.3 with measured values, account must be taken of the proportion of the time the wind blows from one side or the other of the road. Also allowance must be made for the background lead in the air.

In Table 16.3 the results are given of three sets of measurements of lead in air near heavily trafficked highways in the USA. The background lead concentration is taken as that measured at the greatest distance from the highway, or with winds blowing towards the highway. With background subtracted, and the results normalised to a standard flow of 1,000 vehicles/hour, the results are in good agreement with Fig. 16.3.

Taken together with the mean levels of Table 16.2, Fig. 16.3 shows that the effect of a single heavily trafficked road on the lead levels in the air will be noticeable out to a distance of about 50 m in towns and perhaps 200 m in the country.

Table 16.3
Measurement of lead in air near highways

Traffic flow (Vehicles/hour)	Distance in metres from edge of highway	Pb in air (μg m^{-3})				Reference
		Sampling station	Background	Excess	Normalised to 1,000 vehicles/hour	
2,000	9.0	5·3	0·9	4·4	2·2	Daines et al.[24]
	22.5	4·2	–	3·3	1·7	
	37.5	3·5	–	2·6	1·3	
4,000	10.6	7·8	1·1	6·7	1·7	Cholak et al.[11]
	400.0	1·7	–	0·6	0·15	
2,400	10.0	10·0	2·2	7·8	3·2	Schuck and Locke[25]
	30.0	6·2	–	4·0	1·7	
	60.0	4·9	–	2·7	1·1	
	1,200.0	3·2	–	1·0	0·4	

16.5   Deposition of lead from exhausts

Aerosol particles may be deposited by sedimentation, by impaction on vegetation and other roughness elements at the ground surface, and by washout in rain. The first two mechanisms, which comprise 'dry deposition', are most effective in the first part of the travel of the aerosol. Washout in rain is relatively more effective at longer distances, especially when the aerosol has diffused up to the height of the rain-forming clouds.

The velocity of deposition of an aerosol is defined thus:

$$v_g = \frac{\text{amount deposited per unit area per second}}{\text{amount per unit volume in air}}$$

Estimates of the deposition of lead near highways are shown in Table 16.4. These are derived from measurements of the air concentration and the fallout of lead near busy roads.[10-12]

Peirson et al. [13] have measured the deposition of lead (and other nuclides) at a number of stations in the UK. The stations were not adjacent to main roads or in heavily built-up areas, though some were in industrialised parts of the country. Horizontal sampling pads, covered with filter paper and protected from rain, were used to measure dry deposition, and the total fallout (wet and dry) was also measured. High-volume air samplers were used to measure air concentration. The results from some of these stations are shown in the lower part of Table 16.4.

The mean velocity of deposition of lead near highways (top part of Table 16.4) was 280 m/day (0.32 cm s^{-1}), and this was mostly dry deposition, since washout by rain is ineffective at short range. There is only slight evidence of variation of v_g with distance from the highways. The high rate of deposition (3,200 μg m^{-2} day) at the site 10 m from the kerb of 175L, reflects the high air concentration and does not imply excessive deposition of large particles.

If this average rate of fallout is assumed to apply to a strip 20 m wide parallel to the road, the rate of deposition in this strip is 3200 $\times$ 20 = 6.4 $\times$ 10$^4 \mu$g m^{-1} day^{-1}, or 0.7 μg m^{-1} s^{-1}. This compares with an emission rate of order 50 μg m^{-1} s^{-1} from vehicles on the highway which carries 4,000 vehicles/hour, on the assumptions about vehicle performance used in 16.1. Apart perhaps for some large particles detached from the exhaust system, only a small proportion of the lead from vehicles is deposited in the immediate vicinity from the highway.

Turning to the stations of Peirson et al. [13] in the lower part of Table 16.4, the mean v_g (dry) is 230 m/day and the mean total v_g (including

Table 16.4

Rate of deposition of lead aerosols

Location	Surface	Air concentration (μg m^{-3})	Rate of fallout (μg m^{-2}/day)		v (m/day)		Reference
			Dry	Total	Dry	Total	
Urban							
Cincinnati							
175L	Deposit gauge	7.8	—	3,200	—	410	Cholak et al.[11]
Mt Storm	Deposit gauge	1.7	—	360	—	210	
Kettering Lab.	Deposit gauge	1.1	—	350	—	320	
San Diego							
Downtown	Deposit gauge	2.2	—	950	—	430	Chow[26]
La Jolla	Deposit gauge	0.40	—	66	—	165	
Palo Alto							
Bayshore (dry weather)	Pan	8.0	1,300	—	160	—	P.R. Atkins[10]
London (NWB)	Tank	—	—	300	—	—	Metropolitan Water Board (1968)
Rural							
Chilton, Berks.	funnel (total) filter pad (dry)	0.13	33	106	250	815	Peirson et al.[13]
Gresham, Norfolk	,,	0.15	25	42	166	280	
Arran	,,	0.10	20	75	200	750	
Plynlimon	,,	0.05	27	49	540	980	
Styrrup, Notts.	,,	0.41	62	162	151	395	
Skewen	,,	0.25	34	70	136	280	
Trebanos	,,	0.23	38	174	165	756	

washout) is 600 m/day. For purposes of calculation a dry deposition rate of 250 m/day will be assumed.

The average rate of fallout of lead for Peirson's stations is 100 μg m^{-2} day^{-1}, or 36 mg m^{-2} y^{-1}. The area of the UK (excluding Northern Ireland) is $2 \cdot 1 \times 10^{11}$ m^2. If the stations are representative, the total annual fallout over the UK is 7,000 tonnes, which is the same as the annual emission of lead from exhausts. In fact, some lead is blown to sea, and this is apparently compensated roughly by non-vehicle emissions.

16.6   Contamination of foliage

Some of the fallout of trace elements, and of pollutants, is retained on the leaves of plants. The proportion intercepted, and the persistence, or period of retention, depends on the density, leaf morphology and rate of growth of the crop, and on the particle size and chemical nature of the fallout. It might be supposed that the combination of these factors would be totally unpredictable, but a review of the available evidence [14] on foliar contamination by fallout (including ^{90}Sr, ^{137}Cs, ^{131}I, ^{210}Pb, F) indicates that for cereal and grass crops in good growth conditions the ratio

$$\text{NSC} = \frac{\text{amount of pollutant per kg dry weight in vegetation}}{\text{amount deposited per m}^2 \text{ of ground area per day}}$$

is often found to have a value in the range 30–80 m^2 days kg.$^{-1}$ More specifically, evidence collected by Jaworowski [15] of the rate of fallout of ^{210}Pb activity and the specific activity in grass indicates a value of about 50 m^2 days kg^{-1}.

Higher NSC values in the range 100–1,000 m^2 days kg^{-1} are found to apply where vegetation is slow growing for climatic reasons. This is partly because the period of exposure to fallout is then greater and partly because the persistence or half-life of retention appears to be greater when growth is slow. This is certainly true of the slow growing mosses and lichens, which have an affinity for metals. [16]

Much lower NSC values apply to crops such as cabbage, in which most of the edible part is protected from foliar uptake, and low values also apply to fruit and root crops.

Combining NSC = 50 m^2 days kg^{-1} with v_g = 250 m/day, the following relation is obtained between the lead level in grass, or leafy crops, and the mean concentration in air:

$$C \text{ (ppm dry wt)} = 12 \cdot 5 \times (\mu\text{g m}^{-3}) \qquad (16.6)$$

In Table 16.5, results are summarised of measurements of C and χ near highways. The ratio C/χ is in fair agreement with equation (16.6), except for the results of Motto [17] obtained near a graded highway. It is possible that the particle size of lead emitted from full-power engines is larger than normal.

Table 16.5

Lead in air and in foliage of leafy crops

Crop	Lead in air (μg m^{-3}) (χ)	Lead in crop (ppm dry weight) (C)	(C/χ)	Reference
Grass	2·32	15·0	6·5	Dedolph èt al.[27]
	1·71	8·4	4·9	
	1·07	7·9	7·4	
			Mean 6·3	
Oat chaff	2·3	31·4	13·7	Ter Harr[28]
	1·7	15·5	9·1	
	1·1	12·8	11·6	
			Mean 11·5	
Corn leaves	7·3	329·0	45·0	Motto[7]
(soil culture)	3·6	188·0	52·0	
	2·6	85·0	33·0	
(sand culture)	7·3	325·0	44·0	(site near up-grade)
	3·6	146·0	41·0	
	2·6	82·0	32·0	
			Mean 41·0	
Corn leaves	1·4	19·0	14·0	Motto[7]
	1·1	17·0	15·0	
	1·0	14·0	14·0	
	4·5	86·0	19·0	
	2·7	47·0	17·0	
	2·4	36·0	15·0	
	5·2	88·0	17·0	
	3·3	51·0	15·0	
	2·5	40·0	16·0	
			Mean 15·8	

16.7 Toxic effects on animals

According to Hammond and Aronson [18], symptoms of intoxication occur in horses and cattle if the lead content of herbage exceeds about 150 ppm. Using the above relation between C and χ, the corresponding mean air concentration is 12 μg m^{-3}, assuming the lead to be in micron-sized particles. If the particles are larger, a lower concentration would be required to give the same contamination.

Persons exposed to 12 μg m^{-3} of lead in air would have a higher than normal lead intake. assuming a breathing rate of 20 m^3/day (person engaged in manual labour), and 30 per cent uptake from the lung, the amount of lead entering the blood stream would be 80 μg/day, compared with about 30 μg/day normal uptake via the gut. [19] Although undesirable, this enhanced uptake would be unlikely to have toxic effects. The industrial MAC of lead (persons exposed 40h/week) is 150 μg m^{-3}. Thus toxic effects on farm animals are likely to be seen at levels of airborne lead which would not produce immediate symptoms in man.

16.8 Summary of rates of fallout of lead

In Table 16.6 the orders of magnitude of the fallout at various types of site are exposed. The fallout within 10 m of a very heavily used motorway may be 50 times higher than in remote districts of the UK. Little data has been published on the fallout near lead smelters in the UK, but Goodman and Roberts [16] and Burkitt et al. [20] have published measurements of the lead in grass in such situations. Applying the NSC factor of 50, very approximate estimates can be made, and these are given at the foot of Table 16.6. Very recently, Roberts [19] has given results of a survey of deposition of lead near a smelter at Toronto, and these are also given in Table 16.6

16.9 Contamination of reservoirs

It is sometimes claimed that fallout of lead from exhausts may contaminate reservoirs adjacent to main roads. Taking the extreme fallout rate of 3,200 μg m^{-2} day from Table 16.4, and assuming that the water in the reservoir is 10 m deep and stays there for a mean time of 100 days, the lead content of the water will be 3 $\times$ 10^4 μg m^{-3}, or 0·03 mg l^{-1}. The WHO standard for lead in drinking water is 0·1 mg l^{-1}, and their level is not infrequently approached in soft-water districts, due to solution of

200

lead from pipes. The contamination of reservoirs by lead, even if they are sited alongside motorways, is a small risk.

Table 16.6

Fallout of lead in various locations

Location	Rate of fallout (μg Pb m^{-2} day)	Reference
10 m from road with 4,000 vehicles/hour	3,200	Cholak et al.[11]
Chicago (Airport)	460	Lazrus et al.[28]
London (MWB)	300	
Sites not in towns, but in industrial regions (Trebanos, Styrrup)	160	Table 16.4
Rural sites, far from industry	50	Table 16.4
0·1 km from smelter (Toronto)	40,000	Roberts[19]
0·3 km from another smelter	8,000	Roberts[19]
0·7 km from smelter	16,000*	Goodman and Roberts[16]
1·1 km from smelter	4,000*	Burkitt et al.[20]

* Estimated indirectly from lead contamination of grass, namely 800 and 200 ppm dry weight respectively.

16.10   Trends of airborne lead with time

Despite correlations between lead and traffic density, there is evidence that lead in air has not increased greatly in recent years.

Cholak et al.[11] found a decline in Cincinnati between 1946 and 1966, and Lee and Tallis[21] have shown by analysis of lead in peat that levels have changed little since about 1850. It is probable that the emission from vehicles has been balanced by a reduction in lead from smelters and from the burning of coal.

References

[1] Lawther, P.J., Commins, B.T., Ellison, J.McK. and Biles, R., Airborne lead and its uptake by inhalation (Institute of Petroleum 1972).

[2] Habibi, K., Characterisation of particulate lead in vehicle exhaust —: experimental techniques (Environmental Science and Technology 4, 1970).

[3] Stubbs, R.L., Sources of lead in the environment (Institute of Petroleum 1972).

[4] Craxford, S.R., Weatherley, M-L, and Gooriah, B.D., The national survey of air pollution (Report No. 1, Warren Spring Laboratory 1970).

[5] Colwill, D.M., Atmospheric pollution from vehicle emissions: measurements in Reading 1971 (Transport and Road Research Laboratory Report LR 541, 1973).

[6] Pasquill, F., The estimation of the dispersion of windborne material (Meteorological Magazine 90, 1961).

[7] Pasquill, F., Atmospheric dispersion of pollution (Quarterly Journal of the Royal Meteorological Society 97, 1971).

[8] Sutton, O.G., The theoretical distribution of airborne pollution from factory chimneys (Quarterly journal of the Royal Meteorological Society 73, 1947).

[9] Bovay, E., Les dépôts de plomb sur la végétation le long des autoroutes (Mitteilungen aus dem Gebiet der Lebensmitteluntersuchung und -hygiene 61, 1970).

[10] Atkins, P.R., Lead in a suburban environment (Journal of the Air Pollution Control Association 19, 1969).

[11] Cholak, J., Schafer, L.J. and Yeager, D., The air transport of lead compounds present in automobile exhaust gases (American Industrial Hygiene Journal 1968).

[12] Chow, T.J., Environmental pollution from industrial lead (International Conference on Geochemistry and Hydrochemistry, Tokyo 1970).

[13] Peirson, D.H. et al., (1973). To be published.

[14] Chamberlain, A.C., Interception and retention of radioactive aerosols by vegetation (Atmospheric Environment 4, 1970).

[15] Jaworowski, Z., Stable and radioactive lead in environment and human body (Atomic Energy Review 7, 1969).

[16] Goodman, G.T. and Roberts, T.M., Plants, soils as indicators of metals in the air (Nature 231, 1971).

[17] Motto, H.L., Daines, R.H., Chilko, D.M. and Motto, C.K., Lead in soils and plants: its relationship to traffic volume and proximity to highways (Environmental Science and Technology 4, 1970).

202

[18] Hammond, P.B. and Aronson, A.L., Lead poisoning in cattle and horses in the vicinity of a smelter (Annals of the New York Academy of Science 3, 1964).

[19] Roberts, T.M., Abnormal lead distributions and effects on the human population (Report 2, University of Toronto 1973).

[20] Burkitt, A., Lester, P. and Nickless, G., Distribution of heavy metals in the vicinity of an industrial complex (Nature 238, 1972).

[21] Lee, J.A. and Tallis, J.H., Regional and historical aspects of lead pollution in Britain (Nature 246, 1973).

[22] Bollock, J. and Lewis, W.M., The influence of traffic on atmospheric pollution (Atmospheric Environment, 2, 1968).

[23] Atkins, D.H., unpublished data, 1973.

[24] Daines, R.H., Motto, H., and Chilko, D.M., Atmospheric lead: its relation to traffic volume and proximity to highways (Environmental Science and Technology, 4, 1970).

[25] Schuck, E.A. and Locke, J.K., Relationship of automotive lead particulates to certain consumer crops (Environmental Science and Technology, 4, 1970).

[26] Chow, T.J., Environmental pollution from industrial lead (International Conference on Geochemistry and Hydrochemistry, Tokyo 1970).

[27] Dedolph, R., Ter Haar, G., Holtzman, R. and Lucas, H., Sources of lead in perennial rye grass and radicles (Environmental Science and Technology, 4, 1970).

[28] Ter Haar, G., Air as a source of lead in edible crops (Environmental Science and Technology, 4, 1970).

17 Analysis of Rainfall Data for Storm Drainage Design — a Survey

B.G. WALES-SMITH

17.1 Introduction

The analyses discussed are mainly appropriate to the design of storm-water drainage for fairly small areas and thus the emphasis is on high-intensity, short-duration rainfall. It should not be forgotten that long duration rainfall events also are important in such contexts as river basin management and fenland drainage.

From the pioneer work of Symons[1] near the end of the nineteenth century and Mill[2] some 20 years later, rainfall event classification developed in step with the availability of suitable data. The well-known Birmingham and Ministry of Health[3] curves were produced and Bilham,[4] in 1936, published an analysis based on systematic rain-recorder data tabulations. He extrapolated from his data and smoothed out regional variations but did not develop point-to-area relationships or intensity-duration profiles. Even so, Bilham's work will always remain a landmark in the development of the subject. More recently, other workers have carried out analyses of rainfall data (references [5-9] are important examples), all aimed at enhancing knowledge and improving techniques. Holland[7] refined the Bilham formula for intensities above about 32 mm h^{-1}.

From the early 1950s there was collaboration between the Road Research Laboratory (RRL), the Hydraulics Research Station and the Meteorological Office. Important results were the production of some provisional storm profiles[10] and the study of point-to-area relationships.[11] A simple method of applying a point-to-area factor was provided in reference [12] published in 1968. RRL (now TRRL) developed computer-based methods of modelling rainfall and run-off.

In 1973 the Construction Industry Research and Information Association held a colloquium covering the whole field of storm-water drainage design.[13] The meteorological problem is to summarise and generalise actual rainfall situations to produce realistic input on design storms for computer models of drainflow. Stall and Huff [14] have demonstrated a very good approach to the problem.

17.2 Important recent and current developments

17.2.1 *Rain recorder data*

At the Nuclear Physics Laboratory, Oxford, a very advanced installation known as the Precision Encoding and Pattern Recognition (PEPR) system is being used to convert past rain recorder data to a computer medium. Within about three years roughly a million daily rainfall charts, assembled from all parts of the country, will have been microfilmed, and converted to digitised form, on magnetic tape, with negligible loss of detail for rainfall durations as short as 5 min. For the first time a very large amount of data, much of it hitherto scarcely analysed at all, will be available for computer analysis. The total body of such data available corresponds to well over 5,000 station-years, compared with the 180 used by Bilham in 1936.

The development of automatic instruments recording in detail on magnetic tape, and producing data which can be readily translated into computer input, has now reached a very promising stage. The potential exists for data from remote areas to become available from instruments unattended for periods as long as 3 months.

17.2.2 *The Dee Weather Radar Project*

This cooperative project, in which the Meteorological Office has taken a leading part, has achieved its primary aim of demonstrating the areal rainfall on a space scale appropriate to requirements for water management and river regulations can be measured quantitatively by radar, as shown by Harrold, English and Nicholass. [15] Much further work is needed in order to develop a real-time computer-based operational system with a network of radars, but there is great promise of a valuable practical outcome in time.

17.2.3 *UK flood studies work*

Following recommendations made by a committee of the Institution of Civil Engineers, [16] two teams — one of hydrologists at the Institute of Hydrology, the other of meteorologists at the Meteorological Office — have completed a three-year programme of work covering the whole field

206

of drainage and flooding problems up to the scale of the major river basins in the UK. [17] Material on short-period intense rainfall relevant to urban storm-water drainage design is included. This is by far the most comprehensive attack on the rainfall-runoff group of problems which has yet been attempted for the UK. The meteorological aspects are discussed in section 17.4.

17.2.4 *Frequency and distribution of intense rainfall, using daily totals*

For the United Kingdom Rodda [18] has mapped estimated daily falls with frequencies of once every 10, 20, 50 and 100 years, and also the largest recorded daily falls in the period 1881–1964.

17.3   Definitions, development and methods

17.3.1 *Rainfall events*

A rainfall 'event' here denotes the occurrence of a given fall of rain in a given period of time. (A fall of 25 mm in 30 min could also be expressed as an average intensity (or rate) of 50 mm h^{-1} maintained for 30 min.) Since rain (especially heavier rain) hardly ever falls at a fixed rate for very long, the fall of 25 mm in 30 min could have contained a heavier fall of, for example, 15 mm in 10 min.

The probability (probability per year) of a given rainfall event occurring implies its 'return period'. Thus we speak of the 100-year, 15-min 'storm'; an amount of rainfall expected to be reached or to be exceeded in 15-min, on average, once every 100 years (here $n = 100$, $t = 15$, probability = $1/100$).

17.3.2 *Probabilities of given rainfall events anywhere in an area, at a specified point and over the whole area*

Rainfall events with given specifications occur less frequently at many gauging points in an area simultaneously than at only one specified point where rainfall events occur less frequently than at any point in the area, as summarised below:

Rainfall event occurs at	Any point in the area	A chosen point in the area	Every point in the area (i.e. over whole area)
Return period	Relatively short	Longer	Much longer
Frequency	Fairly high	Lower	Much lower

An engineer may have to plan the storm drainage of a fairly small area in which the occurrence of more than r mm of rain in t min at any point is important. Techniques for making (a) specified point, (b) areal and (c) any-point estimates have been developed.

17.3.3   *Areal reduction factors*

Holland [11] proposed a formula for estimating areal smoothing. The formula is quoted in the Appendix to Hydrological Memorandum No. 33 which also contains graphs to assist in the calculation of the area factor to be applied to values in the 'point fall' tables. Recent work by the Meteorological Office Flood Studies team indicates that Holland's areal factors need significant modification.

17.3.4   *Rainfall event frequency tables from single records*

During the 1960s the Meteorological Office responded to requests for rainfall intensity–duration–frequency guidance for specified locations by the graphical analysis of single good-quality autographic records. The results were given as amounts of rain to be reached or exceeded, in given durations, on average once every n years and as percentages of values given by the (revised) Bilham formula. Although the best available at the time, the method had certain obvious shortcomings of which the following are important.

1   The results are influenced by the actual period covered by the data and by the length of that period. The period might have been one containing few extreme events, between two other periods having greater variation in rainfall.

2   The results can only be applied, with confidence, to the place where the measurements were made. Quite often the gauging point and the specified location were not the same and some subjective adjustment and/or interpolation between two or more rainfall records was needed to try to take account of the effects of topographical differences between the gauge site(s) and the specified location.

Although objective techniques have since been developed for obtaining intensity–duration–frequency relationships for any chosen point in the UK, single-record analyses are still of value for comparing rainfalls at given points over given periods.

17.3.5   *The design storm profile*

To calculate a realistic hydrograph [10] a representative curve is required relating rate of rainfall and time from start of rainfall; this is called a storm profile. Profiles are related to their storm centres or peaks; values on the time scale before peak being signed negative and those after peak positive.

The Meteorological Office produced 1-year (once a year), 5-year and 10-year profiles from a preliminary analysis of data from a grid of rainfall recorders, making use of the basic Bilham relationships (Section 17.3.7). In response to inquiries the Meteorological Office has, in the past, analysed tabulations of good quality autographic records and, by reference to the amount by which falls at the recording point were above or below Bilham values for 15 min duration, has advised on simple modifications to the profiles.

17.3.6 Storm profiles in RRL Road Note 35

The provisional profiles mentioned in 17.3.5 are shown on page 16 of RRL Road Note 35, for 1–, 5– and 10–year return periods for 2–h Storms. Four sets of 120 storm-curve ordinate values corresponding to 1–, 5–, 10– and 30–year return periods were tabulated. Each value corresponds to a minute, thus the 60th and 61st values (from the top of a column) are rainfall intensities centred ½ min before and ½ min after storm peak.

17.3.7 The profiles and the Bilham formula

The rates of rainfall corresponding to 15 min duration for the various return periods are related on the basis of values given by the original Bilham formula. If we take values centred 7½ min before and after peak from the tabulated values referred to in Section 17.3.6 we obtain:

Return Period	1–yr		5–yr		10–yr		
7½ min from peak	Before	After	Before	After	Before	After	
Intensity	0·48	0·62	0·85	1·10	1·08	1·39	in h^{-1}
Mean intensity	0·550		0·975		1·235		

$$\frac{0.550}{0.975} = 0.564 \qquad\qquad \frac{0.550}{1.235} = 0.445$$

If we now take the rates for 15 min duration from the original Bilham formula we have:

Return period	1–yr	5–yr	10–yr	
Intensity	1·11	1·97	2·48	in h^{-1}

$$\frac{1 \cdot 11}{1 \cdot 97} = 0 \cdot 563 \qquad\qquad \frac{1 \cdot 11}{2 \cdot 48} = 0 \cdot 447$$

The peak rates of rainfall on the RRL profiles are related to one another in the same manner:

Return period	1—yr	5—yr	10—yr
Peak rate	2·18	3·86	4·86 in h^{-1}

$$\frac{2 \cdot 18}{3 \cdot 86} = 0 \cdot 565 \qquad\qquad \frac{2 \cdot 18}{4 \cdot 86} = 0 \cdot 449$$

17.3.8   *RRL Road Note 35 — use of design rate of rainfall and storm profiles*

Appendix 1 of the above Note advises as follows:

Selection of design rate of rainfall
(i)   For use with the 'rational' (Lloyd-Davies) formula — employs the mean rate of rainfall during the storm, the duration of the storm being equal to the time of concentration of the area to the point for which the calculation is being made. The method of calculating the time concentration is described in Appendix 2.

The note goes on to advise the use of the Bilham formula or the results of careful analyses of accurate local records

(ii)   For use with the RRL hydrograph method — it is necessary to employ a curve relating the rate of rainfall with the time from the start of the rainfall (called a 'storm profile').

The method is explained in the note, however, RRL Road Note 5 is under revision.

17.4   UK Flood Studies Project

The Meteorological Office has carried out extensive research in the fields of rainfall intensity—duration—frequency relationships, point—to—areal rainfall relationships, storm (intensity—duration) profiles and on other topics relevant to flooding. The final report [17] is expected to be published in 1975 and it is probable that several related papers and articles will also appear in due course. The following short account of a few aspects and some general results of the work is given. Some of the methods have already been used by the Hydrometeorological Enquiries Section of the

210

Meteorological Office in response to requests for rainfall estimates for storm-drainage design.

17.4.1 *Intensity—duration—frequency relationships*

Compared with earlier techniques used in the UK, the one developed by the Flood Studies Team has the advantage of objectivity. Whilst including the effects of topography and geographical position on rainfall, the new approach by analysis of large amounts of data, supported by reasonable assumptions and statistical treatment, removes the sort of bias which occurs when a single, limited-period record is investigated.

17.4.2 *Outline of analysis*

Because the vast majority of the data are daily totals (rainfall day = 09.00—09.00 GMT), a first step was the determination and mapping (over the UK) of 2-day M5 (the 2-day annual maximum rainfall total reached or exceeded, on average, once in 5 years); 1-hour M5 was also mapped. Linking relationships were obtained between 2-day M5 and falls with other durations and return periods.

17.4.3 *Estimation of the frequencies of extreme events*

From, for example, 60 years of data there is little problem in estimating events with return periods of up to 5 or 10 years. Estimates can be made using extreme-value statistical theory, up to return periods commensurate with the length of the data period. If, however, events which may reasonably be claimed to be independent of one another are considered (say annual maximum 2-day rainfall at a network of widely separated stations) the assumption that station years of data may be regarded as years of data at a station has been considered reasonable. 175 stations were taken to represent one area where the 2-day M5 values are similar. All stations had complete data for the same 60-year period. If these annual maxima of 2-day rainfall were independent it is reasonable to assume that they give a fair approximation to the population of a very long series of annual 2-day one station maxima, even though 10,500 years of record at one, area-representative (or median) station are not obtained by such a method. Good estimates of events as rare as those with return periods 500 and 1000 years are obtained. Estimates of rainfall yields, at chosen locations, from storms of (theoretical) maximum efficiency were made for various durations and compared with the greatest (corresponding) measured falls.

17.4.4 *To derive factors to obtain estimates of areal rainfall events from 'point' events*

Investigations on data from widely differing regions in the United Kingdom showed that the areal reduction factors depend upon the size of the area and the duration of the rainfall, but not significantly upon region or return period.

17.4.5 *Storm profiles*

Analysis of large numbers of storms showed that there is no systematic variation of mean profile with return period and that there are no important changes of mean profile with change of storm duration.

The analysis yielded percentile profiles of 'sharpness'; these are rainfall intensity vs. time profiles which are exceeded in terms of sharpness with given frequencies. A mean symmetrical profile can be prepared for any chosen value of mean rainfall intensity, total storm duration and sharpness of profile. The proportion of storm rainfall falling within any given proportion of the storm duration can also be readily estimated. Profiles for areal falls are always flatter than the corresponding ones for point falls, as would be expected. The Report proposes that standard sets of point rainfall profiles be adopted in the UK for summer (May–October) and winter (November–April).

17.4.6 *Preparation of percentile storm profiles*

The largest 1–24 clock–hour–duration storms and also those extending over 4 rainfall days (0900 to 0900 GMT) were tabulated hour by hour in 4-year periods at 33 stations in the UK between 1951 and 1970. Some of the largest 60-minute storms at Cardington and Winchcombe between 1957 and 1967 and some major flood-producing storms in England and Wales, between 1961 and 1970, were also examined.

In order to compare storm profiles the storms were centred on the shortest part of each storm containing 50 per cent of the storm rainfall. Summer and winter storms were treated separately and a set of profiles obtained for each 'season'. The profiles, of which a summer set is shown for average rainfall intensity (rate) 12·3 mm h^{-1} and duration 2 h in Fig. 17.1 are percentiles. The 95 per cent (sharpest) profile, for example, is one which will be equalled or exceeded in terms of sharpness in only 5 per cent of storms. These mean profiles are symmetrical about the peak intensity although this is not a characteristic of many individual storms. The data required to plot summer and winter profiles will be published in the Flood Studies Report. [17]

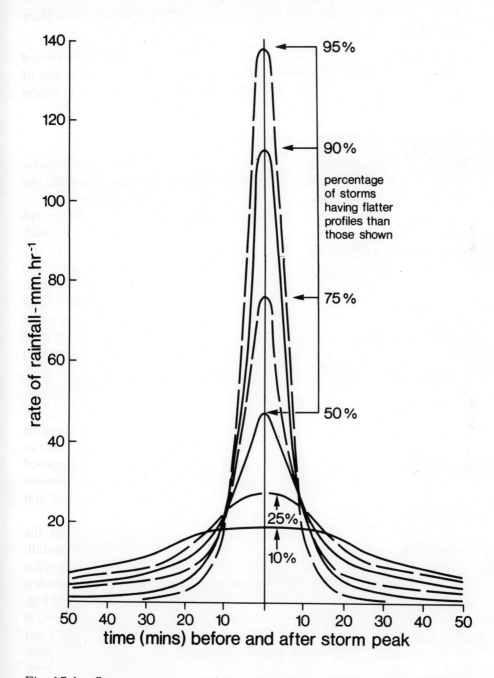

Fig. 17.1   Summer mean rainfall profiles for average intensity 12·3 mm hr^{-1} and duration 2 hours

213

17.4.7 *Proportion of storm rainfall falling within proportion of storm duration*

Fig. 17.2 shows how rainfall is distributed in a storm with 75 percentile degree of sharpness of mean profile, both by proportion of average intensity and percentage of storm duration, and for a 2-hour storm with average intensity 13·5 mm h^{-1}.

17.4.8 *A comparison of the RRL Road Note 35 and the Meteorological Office Profiles*

As many engineers have used the profiles given in RRL Road Note 35 and will wish to know how these old profiles compare with those now proposed, a comparison is made (Fig. 17.3) between the 75 per cent summer profile for a 1-year, 2-h Bilham storm and the corresponding profile from RRL Road Note 35.

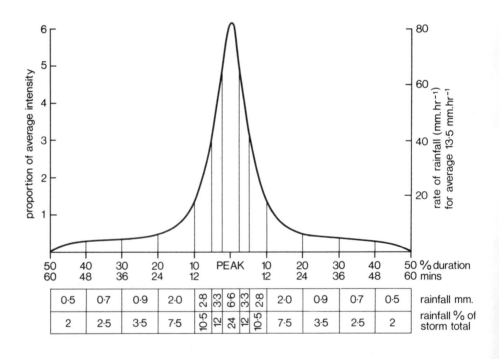

Fig. 17.2 Percentile profile comparing proportion of average storm intensity and percentage of storm duration

214

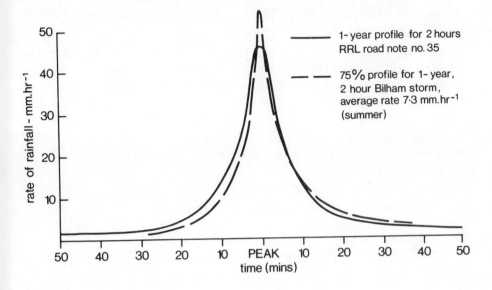

Fig. 17.3   Profile comparison

References

[1]   Symons, G.J., On some intense rains, 1879 to 1888 (British Rainfall 1888, London 1889).

[2]   Mill, H.R., Heavy rains in short periods (British Rainfall 1908, Part II, London 1909).

[3]   Fawcett, E.A., Rainfall and runoff (Report of the Ministry of Health Departmental Committee on Rainfall and Runoff, Journal of the Institute of Municipal and County Engineers 56, 1930; reprinted as Appendix B in Escritt, L.B., Surface Water Sewerage, London 1950).

[4]   Bilham, E.G., Classification of heavy falls of rain in short periods (British Rainfall 1935, London 1936; reprinted as a pamphlet by HMSO, 1962).

[5]   Ashworth, R.G. and O'Flaherty, C.A., Validity of the modified Bilham equation (Journal of the Institute of Municipal and County Engineers, 1973).

[6]   Collinge, V.K., The frequency of heavy rainfalls in the British Isles (Civil Engineering and Public Works Review 56, London 1961).

[7]   Holland, D.J., Rain intensity—frequency relationships in Britain (British Rainfall 1961, Part III, HMSO 1967; (also available in the Meteorological Office Library as Hydrological Memorandum No. 33).

[8] Maclean, D.G., Rainstorm data (Surveyor and Municipal and County Engineers 104, 1945).

[9] Norris, W.H., Sewer design and the frequency of heavy rain (Journal of the Institute of Municipal and County Engineers 75, 1948).

[10] McNaughton, G., Wells, G.S. and Manzoni, H. (Chairman), A guide for engineers to the design of storm sewer systems (Report of the Joint Committee on Rainfall and Runoff of the Road Research Board; Ministry of Housing and Local Government Road Note 35, HMSO 1963).

[11] Holland, D.J., The Cardington rainfall experiment (Meteorological Magazine 96, 1967).

[12] Meteorological Office, Tables of rainfall amounts and intensities for given durations and return periods together with area factor graphs (Appendix to Hydrological Memorandum No. 33, 1968; unpublished, copy available in the Meteorological Office Library).

[13] CIRIA Research Colloquium on rainfall, runoff and surface water drainage of urban catchments, University of Bristol, 2–4 April 1973.

[14] Stall, J.B. and Huff, F.A., The structure of thunderstorm rainfall (Proceedings of the National Water Resources Engineering Meeting, American Society of Civil Engineers, Phoenix, Arizona, 11–15 January 1971).

[15] Harrold, T.W., English, E.J. and Nicholass, C.A., The Dee Weather Radar Project – the measurement of area precipitation using radar (Proceedings of the Symposium on Hydrological problems in Europe, UNESCO/WMO, Geneva 1973; also Weather 28, 1973).

[16] Paton, T.A.L. (Chairman), Floods studies for the United Kingdom (Report of the Committee on Floods in the United Kingdom, Institute of Civil Engineers, London 1967).

[17] Meteorological Office, Flood Studies Report, vol. 2 (Meteorological Studies). To be published in 1975.

[18] Rodda, J.C., A study of magnitude, frequency and distribution of intense rainfall in the United Kingdom (British Rainfall 1966, Part III, HMSO 1973).

18 The Relationship between Rainfall and Runoff on Urban Areas

Dr S.G. NEWTON and Dr R.B. PAINTER

18.1 Introduction

Annual expenditure on storm drainage in the UK currently exceeds £100 million; expenditure in the USA up to the end of this century is estimated to be in excess of $25 billion;[1] annual expenditure in Australia is estimated at $50 million.[2] Compared with such vast sums of money for storm sewerage, very little has been spent on research into design methods. Thus, to design adequate, but not excessive, drainage systems, knowledge of the response of urban areas to rainfall is of great economic importance.

The problem may be divided into two fundamentally different phases. First, given the rainfall distribution, it is necessary to predict the (peak) discharge from a given sewer system at the outfall. A suitable system may then be designed or redesigned by trial and error. Second, it must be decided what storm rain-fall the sewerage is required to transport. This not only poses difficult statistical questions but also raises economic and humanitarian issues concerning the consequences of possible flooding.

18.2 Prediction techniques

A considerable variety of methods are in use throughout the world and the more important of these are briefly described below.

18.2.1 The rational or Lloyd-Davies method

This is one of the earliest methods used in the prediction of storm runoff, put forward by Lloyd-Davies[3] in 1905, and still in use today; for example Aitken[2] states that it is widely used in Australia. Although the rational formula was derived empirically it can be justified both deterministically, under certain conditions, and statistically. If it is assumed that the

217

concentration time for a system represents the time of travel for rainfall input from the remotest point to the outfall, and that the distribution of area with travel time from the outfall is uniform, then

$$Q(t) = \frac{AC}{t_c} \int_{t-t_c}^{t} R(\tau) \, d\tau \tag{18.1}$$

$Q(t)$ is the discharge at outfall, $R(t)$ the rainfall (assumed to be spatially constant), A the impermeable area, t_c the time of concentration, and C a coefficient which represents the percentage runoff and includes a conversion factor for the units. Equation (18.1) is a generalisation of the rational formula for the peak discharge Q_{max}, which is usually stated as follows

$$Q_{max} = CIA \tag{18.2}$$

Where I is the maximum value of the average rainfall over the time of concentration. The formula (18.1) has been derived using the flow conservation equation and a much simplified relationship between flow and cross-sectional area of flow.[4]

A second justification of the rational method was proposed by Schaake, Geyer and Knapp,[5] who suggested that the formula is only meaningful in a statistical context. To compute the discharge Q_N with recurrence interval N years, the storm of duration t_c and the same recurrence interval is employed in formula (18.2). It is in this statistical sense that the rational method is usually applied to design problems and, under this interpretation, it should not be expected that formula (18.2) would accurately predict the discharge for any particular storm.

Following Schaake et al.,[5] frequency distributions of observed rainfall intensities and peak runoff rates were plotted on log-normal probability paper, for data from three of the catchments studied by Watkins.[6] These are shown in Figs. 18.1, 18.2 and 18.3 and they do not display the consistent covergence (indicative of increasing runoff ratio) with increasing recurrence interval that was obtained Aitken[2] and Schaake et al.[5]

18.2.2 The area—time method

If the area of the catchment contributing at time t to the discharge at outfall is $a(t)$, the formula appropriate to this calculation is

$$Q(t) = C \int_{t-t_c}^{t} R(\tau) \, \frac{d}{dt} \{a(t-\tau)\} \, d\tau \tag{18.3}$$

This formula can be derived either by using the intuitive approach employed above for the rational method or by using the more mathematical method given by Newton and Painter.[7]

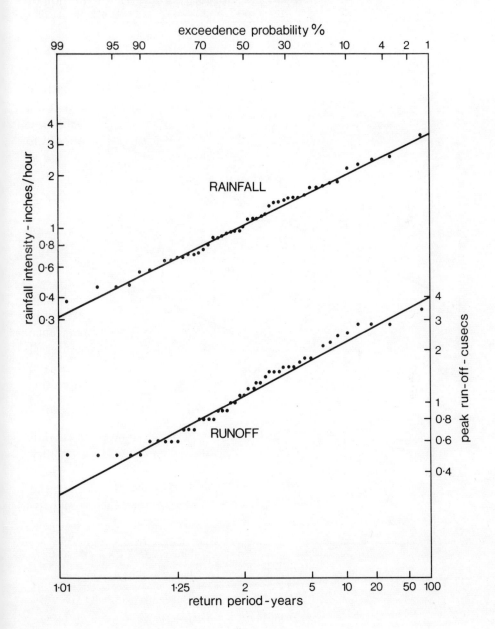

Fig. 18.1   Oxhey Road – rainfall – runoff frequency curves

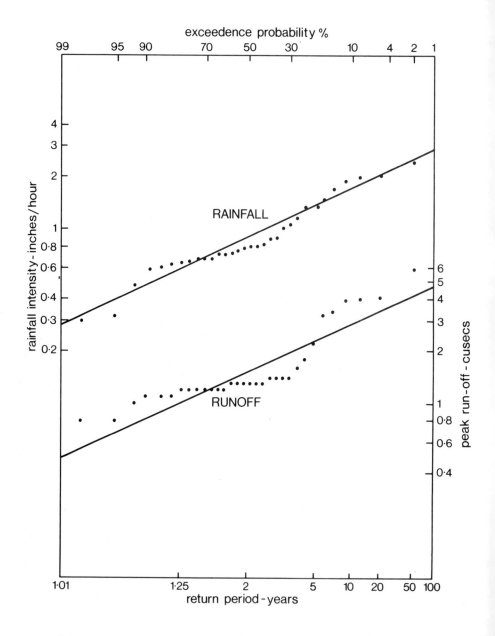

Fig. 18.2   Stevenage – rainfall – runoff frequency curves

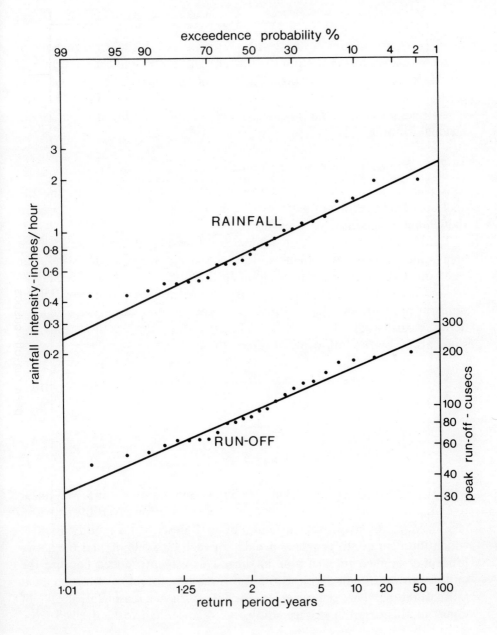

Fig. 18.3   Oxhey Estate – rainfall – runoff frequency curves

It can be shown that equation (18.3) is equivalent to assuming the relationship,

$$Q = c(x) A \qquad (18.4)$$

between flow and area in the trunk sewer, where c is the wave velocity $\dfrac{dQ}{dA}$ and x measures distance from the outfall. This is still a linear relation, but the dependence of c on positions allows for variable slope and pipe diameter and different rates of contribution from various areas. Thus the area—time method is far less restrictive in its assumptions than is the rational formula.

18.2.3 The RRL Hydrograph Method

This technique, developed as the result of considerable research and the analysis of some 286 storms from 12 urban catchments,[6] is widely used in the United Kingdom.

The method consists of calculating the flow due to the rainfall via the area—time formula and then routing the result through the non-linear reservoir formed by the pipe system. In the original work the discharge—storage relation for this reservoir was obtained, under the assumption of uniform proportional depth throughout the system, using the discharge depth relation of the outfall pipe.[7-10] Thus the method may be summarised by the following set of equations.

$$q(t) = C \int_{t-t_c}^{t} R(\tau) \frac{d}{dt} \left\{ a(t-\tau) \right\} d\tau \qquad (18.5)$$

$$\frac{dS}{dt} = q - Q \qquad (18.6)$$

$$S = S(Q) \qquad (18.7)$$

where q, defined by equation (18.5), is the input to the non-linear reservoir of storage S with discharge—storage relation given by equation (18.7). More recently, Watkins and Young[11] described a modification in which uniform depth is assumed only for each pipe length, and the above procedure applied to each pipe in turn. This was introduced because the uniform proportional depth assumption was unsatisfactory for such areas as Kensington, where the sewer system did not have a reasonable degree of taper; in this case the storage—discharge relation had to be derived from recorded recession curves.

In validating the method, Watkins[7-10] multiplied the calculated runoff by the ratio $\dfrac{\text{total runoff}}{\text{total rainfall}}$ (although in later stages it was the rainfall that was modified in this way), and compared the adjusted peak value with that observed. The result of applying the rational formula was also scaled in the same way. This is somewhat unsatisfactory from a design viewpoint since, for the storms analysed by the RRL, the runoff ratio varied from approximately 10 per cent to 130 per cent and the value appropriate to a particular design storm on a proposed sewerage system is difficult to determine. Fig. 18.4 shows the distribution of the number of storms against runoff percentages for the 286 storms analysed by Watkins.[6]

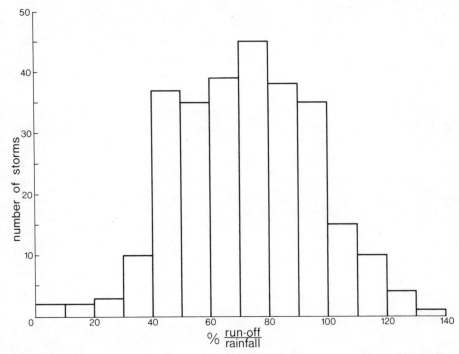

Fig. 18.4   Number of storms and runoff: rainfall — total for twelve RRL catchments

18.2.4   *Simplified RRL calculation*

The most complex part of the above calculation lies in the routing through non-linear storage described by equation (18.6) and relationship (18.7). A simplified procedure is now proposed in which the area—time calculation is applied to the rainfall and the result routed through a *linear* reservoir which approximates to the non-linear reservoir used in the RRL method. Fig. 18.5 shows the relationship between proportional discharge and proportional depth for a circular pipe using the Colebrook—White formula for a typical value of Θ as defined by Ackers,[12] from which reference the values were taken. It can be seen that a linear relation offers a fair approximation to this curve. Thus if Q^* is proportional discharge and D^* proportional depth the suggested approximation is

$$Q^* = D^* \qquad (18.8)$$

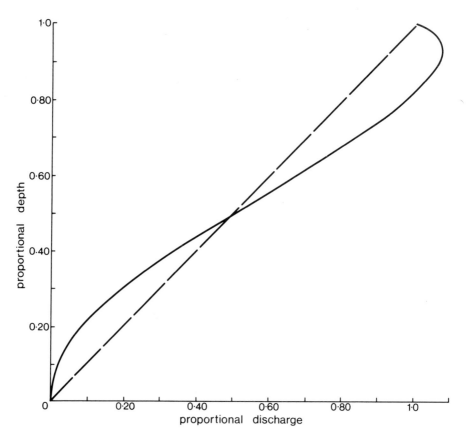

Fig. 18.5   Proportional discharge and proportional depth for a circular pipe

If the total volume of the sewer system is S_m and if the assumption of uniform proportional depth holds then the storage is given by

$$S = D^* S_m \qquad (18.9)$$

Also if Q_m is the full-bore discharge at the outfall, by the definition of Q^*

$$Q = Q^* \cdot Q_m \qquad (18.10)$$

Combining equations (18.8)–(18.10) gives the following linear approx-

224

imation to the storage-discharge relationship:

$$S = \frac{S_m}{Q_m} \cdot Q \qquad (18.11)$$

or

$$S = t_l Q \qquad (18.12)$$

which describes a linear reservoir of lag time $t_l = S\ \dfrac{S_m}{Q_m}$ $\qquad (18.13)$

Figure 18.6 shows the storage–discharge relation for the main area at Oxhey, given by Watkins,[6'] and also the linear relationship as above— demonstrating close agreement.

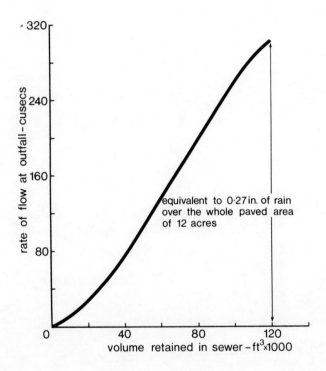

Fig. 18.6   Temporary retention in sewer system — Oxhey estate

Equation (18.6) now has the following solution

$$Q(t) = \frac{1}{t_1} \int_0^t \exp \frac{(\tau - t)}{t_1} \, q(\tau)d\tau \qquad (18.14)$$

which can readily be computed, $q(t)$ having been obtained by the area-time calculation. This technique, which will be termed the ALR method, is considerably simpler than the RRL procedure and could be applied without the need for a computer.

This method was applied to 14 storms at Kidbrooke (using data from Watkins)[8, 9] and the results were found to agree reasonably with those obtained by the RRL, having a correlation coefficient of 0.980.

Fig. 18.7 shows a typical hydrograph for Kidbrooke and Fig. 18.8 is a plot of the peak runoff values obtained by this method against those obtained by the RRL method.

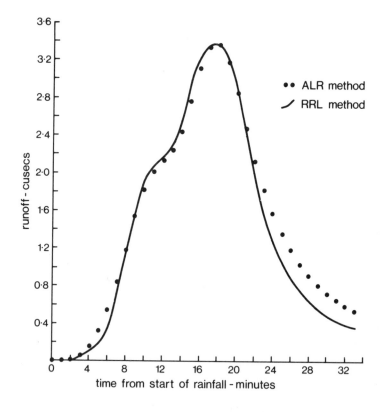

Fig. 18.7   Runoff and time from start of rainfall — Kidbrooke, 27 July 1973

226

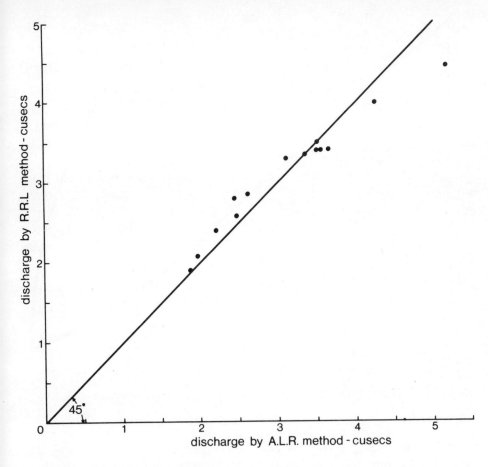

Fig. 18.8 Comparison of discharge by RRL and ALT methods

Although the ALR method has only been tested on a small sample of data, and it is intended to apply the technique to all of the RRL catchment data, it should be noted that the non-dimensional relationship shown in Fig. 18.5 holds for all circular pipes (with little variation depending on Θ). Thus, if the ALR method adequately approximates the RRL method for one catchment for which the uniform proportional depth assumption is valid, it should do so for all other such catchments.

Fig. 18.9 is taken from Watkins,[6] and demonstrates why the uniform proportional depth assumption was abandoned for areas such as Kensington. In the same way that the current RRL procedure routes the flow through a non-linear reservoir for each pipe, the ALR method can be modified to route through an 'equivalent' linear reservoir for each pipe and thus treat pipe systems which have little or no taper.

227

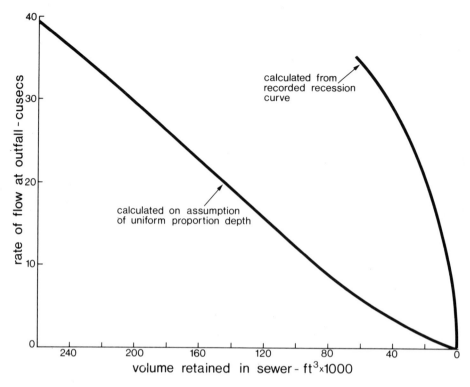

Fig. 18.9   Temporary retention in sewer system — Kensington

18.2.5   *The Chicago hydrograph method*

This method was presented by Tholin and Keifer [13] in 1959 and is a sophisticated model of the urban runoff process; the following steps were listed in the procedure:

1   Determination of the typical layout of the drainage areas.

2   Determination of chronological storm pattern or hyetograph of design storm.

3   The evaluation of the abstractions from rainfall.

4   The determination of runoff hydrographs at the lower end of elemental strips of both pervious and impervious ground surfaces and roofs.

5   Routing of the mixed flow from the elemental strips of pervious and impervious ground surfaces along the channel of the street gutter to the inlet or catch basin grating.

6   Routing of the sewer supply hydrographs from roofs and street inlets along a typical headwater lateral.

7   Routing of the lateral outflow hydrograph by a time-offset method

228

along the sub-mains and main outlet sewers to the point of discharge of the sewer system.

8   The production of a series of easy-to-use design charts.

In step 3 Horton's infiltration equation is used and an assumed relationship between the mean depth and overland flow supply rate to allow for depression storage. The overland flow calculation in step 4 is performed by using the continuity equation and a depth–discharge relationship due to Izzard. [14] In step 5 routing down the sewer is again calculated using the continuity equation, but using Manning's formula to relate discharge to depth. In steps 6 and 7 the flow is routed down the sewer pipes by a 'time-offset' method.

It should be observed that the overland and gutter flow calculations in the Chicago method are particular cases of kinematic wave theory described in the next section. Furthermore the 'time-offset' method, employed for the pipe flow, is equivalent to applying the area–time calculation to the inflow to the sewer system, which in turn is a particular case of kinematic wave theory.

18.2.6   *Kinematic wave theory*

Conservation of mass and momentum is fundamental to both overland flow and channel/pipe flow. The second of these balances is often represented by the so-called shallow-water equations, which may be approximated by neglecting the dynamic terms. This results in a balance between gravitational and frictional forces, the situation that would exist in steady, uniform flow – see, for example, Lighthill and Whitham. [15] This kinematic wave approximation results in the following governing equations:

$$\frac{\delta A}{\delta t} + \frac{\delta Q}{\delta x} = q_1 \qquad (18.15)$$

$$Q = f(A) \qquad (18.16)$$

where q_1 is the lateral inflow, x is distance in the flow direction, and the form of f depends on the friction law chosen. For example, using Manning's equation for overland flow $f(A) = \dfrac{1.49}{n} A^{4/3}$ for unit width of flow, the propagation speed of the so-called kinematic wave is given by

$$\frac{dQ}{dA} = f'(A) \qquad (18.17)$$

229

Chen and Shubinski [16] describe the FWQA model which is similar to the Chicago method in some aspects, but uses a constant depression storage which must be exceeded before overland flow commences. The FWQA model also uses Manning's equation in the kinematic wave approximation for overland, gutter and pipe flow; whereas the Chicago method uses Izzard's relation for overland flow, Manning's equation for gutter flow, and effectively a constant relation of the form (4) for the pipe flow (this being equivalent to the 'time-offset' approach).

The validity of the kinematic wave approximation depends on the value of the dimensionless parameter.

$$k = gS_0/(u_0 x_0) \qquad (18.18)$$

where g is the acceleration due to gravity, S_0 the slope, u_0 a typical velocity and x_0 a typical length. Woolhiser and Liggett [17] showed that for overland flow the approximation is valid for values of k greater than ten.

As a concept, kinematic wave theory is attractive because it embodies some of the important physical processes involved in urban runoff without being as intractable as solving the full momentum equation.

18.2.7 Conceptual models

A conceptual model may be defined as one which is not derived from physical laws or characteristics of the system, but emanates from broad concepts as to how the system operates.

For example, a single linear reservoir might be regarded as a conceptual model (with one parameter) of the urban runoff process. If the inflow to this reservoir is $q(t)$ and the time lag (which can be shown to be equal to the time delay between centroids of inflow and outlflow) is t_l, then the outflow is given by equation (18.14).

$$Q(t) = \frac{1}{t_l} \int_0^t q(\tau) \exp \left\{ (\tau - t)/t_l \right\} \, d\tau$$

The value of t_l may either be guessed, or chosen by fitting the model to observed data from the catchment. The adequacy of the model to describe the operation of the catchment can then be judged by using it to predict runoff from rainfall and comparing with observed results. To be able to apply the model to different catchments, the parameter t_l must be related to measurable catchment characteristics.

The same procedure can be generalised to much more complex models with many parameters, and the above example was given only as a simple illustration. Sarginson and Bourne [18] described a two-linear reservoir model which was applied to data from four urban catchments in the USA.[19] They subtracted an initial loss from the rainfall, constant for each catchment, and the infiltration rate for each storm was chosen so that the correct total flow (i.e. the observed value) was obtained. It was assumed that the time lag for one reservoir was proportional to the time lag for the other, and an optimum value of the ratio obtained by a random search. No indication of the general accuracy of the model fit was given but two hydrographs showed good agreement between model and observed values. Sarginson also attempted to relate the parameters to catchment characteristics with some success and hypothesised that the ratio of the time lag approaches unity as the catchment area increases.

It should be noted that the division between conceptual and physically based models is not clear cut: both the RRL method and the rational method could fall into either category.

18.2.8   *Limitations of prediction procedures*

The preceding list of methods for predicting urban runoff was not intended to be exhaustive but rather to give an indication of the range of techniques available. Similarly, the following limitations are not intended as criticism of the particular methods but more to demonstrate the type of problems which arise in the prediction of urban runoff.

One drawback of the first three methods (rational, area–time and RRL) is that they do not allow for different antecedent conditions, although if the rational method is considered in a statistical sense as by Schaake *et al.*,[5] the antecedent conditions have been averaged in some way. Although, when tested on catchment data, the RRL result was scaled by the runoff ratio, this could never be achieved in a design situation. Similarly, Sarginson's calculations require knowledge of the observed total runoff to calculate the infiltration rate for each storm: however, he attempts to relate the infiltration total to the total rainfall and catchment impermeability.

The Chicago hydrograph method requires a regular grid for the street and drainage layout, and so would be unsuitable for application to most urban areas in the UK. A difficulty which arises when applying kinematic wave theory to urban runoff is that two disparate time scales occur if flow down relatively short sections of pipe or surfaces is studied. The first is the time scale for the storm, and the second that for the flow down the pipe or surface: in practice the former may be many times the latter, resulting in very lengthy computations.

A general point is that techniques developed in the USA may not be

231

suitable for use in the UK. In the USA, rainfall intensities in storms are very much higher than in UK, where losses are consequently of greater importance.

18.3   Future work

One of the crucial requirements of any model for an urban runoff process is that the total flow be predicted correctly. There is no point whatsoever in having sophisticated routing procedures if for example the total flow can be in error by 100 per cent. Conversely, with the correct total flow it may be discovered that a very simple model will predict peak flow adequately. For example, Watkins[6] in comparing the RRL method and rational formula scaled both by the runoff ratio, and from Fig. 18.10 (which is derived from the data in Watkins[6]) it can be seen that the rational formula predicts the peak flow reasonably well.

A difficult problem in urban runoff research is to relate particular parts of a model to particular physical processes, and if the model is inadequate it is difficult to determine precisely where it fails to represent reality. To isolate each process and model it individually is the only effective solution: to this end one part of the Institute's research programme on urban hydrology is concerned with the measurement of rainfall and of runoff from short lengths of road, house roofs, etc. within Milton Keynes New City. Because of the short time scale involved, crystal clocks and magnetic tape recorders will be used to give time resolution down to 15 seconds. As urbanisation of the experimental area progresses, it will eventually be possible to model the entire urban area in detail. This will naturally be too complex to apply in anything but a research context and will be simplified – but still retaining the essential features – until a model sufficiently simple for design work is evolved. A second use of the very complex 'physical' model is that it may be employed to generate data for testing other (simpler) models.

The effect of storm movement over an area, which intuitively may significantly alter the peak flow, has received little attention (an exception being the work by Yen and Chow[20]). Also most design procedures and storms assume uniform rainfall over the catchment, which is unrealistic for summer thunderstorms over areas greater than a few hectares. Finally, having obtained a satisfactory method of translating rainfall into runoff for a given sewer system, it is still necessary to decide on a design storm, and secondly a methodology has also to be devised for adjusting the sewerage until it will cope with the chosen storm and consequent flow.

232

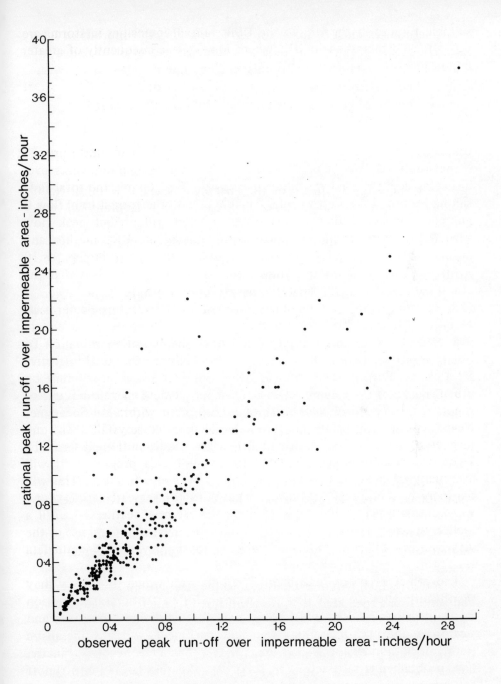

Fig. 18.10 Rational peak runoff over impermeable area and observed peak runoff over impermeable area

A final remark must be made concerning data. In the interests of future research it is important that data be conserved and made available in as simple a form as possible. To this end, a national data bank with a standardised system of storage would save a great deal of time and effort in the collection of existing urban rainfall—runoff data.

References

[1] Schaake, J.C., Synthesis of the inlet hydrograph (Technical Report Number 3, Storm Drainage Research Project, Johns Hopkins University 1965).

[2] Aitken, A.P., Hydraulic investigation and design in urban areas — a review (Australian Water Research Council, Technical Paper No. 5, Australian Government Publication Service 1973).

[3] Lloyd-Davies, D.E., The elimination of storm-water from sewerage systems (Proceedings of the Institution of Civil Engineers 64, Part II, 1905).

[4] Newton, S.G. and Painter, R.B., A mathematical examination of urban runoff prediction (Proceedings of the Institution of Civil Engineers 57, Part II, 1974).

[5] Schaake, J.C., Geyer, J.C. and Knapp, J.W., Experimental examination of the rational method (Proceedings of the American Society of Civil Engineers, Journal of the Hydraulics Division 93, No. HY6, 1967).

[6] Watkins, L.H., The design of urban sewer systems (Road Research Laboratory Technical Paper No. 55, HMSO 1962).

[7] Watkins, L.H., The relationship between rainfall and runoff on a small factory area at Kidbrooke, Kent (8½ acres) (Road Research Laboratory 1954).

[8] Watkins, L.H., An investigation into the relationship between the rainfall and runoff at a housing estate at Blackpool (11·9 acres) (Road Research Laboratory 1954).

[9] Watkins, L.H., An investigation into the relationship between rainfall and runoff on a road at Oxhey, Hertfordshire (1·12 acres) (Road Research Laboratory 1955).

[10] Watkins, L.H., Research on surface water drainage (Proceedings of the Institution of Civil Engineers 24, 1963).

[11] Watkins, L.H. and Young, C.P., Developments in urban hydrology in Great Britain (Road Research Laboratory 1965).

[12] Ackers, P., Tables for the hydraulic design of storm-drains, sewers and pipe-lines (Hydraulics Research Paper No. 4, HMSO 1969).

[13] Tholin, A.L. and Keifer, C.J., The hydrology or urban runoff (Proceedings of the American Society of Civil Engineers, Journal of the Sanitary Engineering Division 85 SA2, 1959).

[14] Izzard, C.F., Hydraulics of runoff from developed surfaces (Proceedings of the Highway Research Board 26, National Research Council 1946).

[15] Lighthill, N.J. and Whitham, G.B., On kinematic waves, Part I: Flood movement in long rivers (Proceedings of the Royal Society A 229, 1955).

[16] Chen, C.W. and Shubinski, R.P., Computer simulation of urban storm water runoff (Proceedings of the American Society of Civil Engineers 97, Hydraulics Division 1971).

[17] Woolhiser, D.A. and Liggett, J.A., Unsteady, one-dimensional flow over a plane — the rising hydrograph (Water Resource Research 3 No. 3, 1967).

[18] Sarginson, E.J. and Bourne, D.E., The analysis of urban rainfall, runoff and discharge (Journal of the Institution of Municipal Engineers 96, 1969).

[19] Sarginson, E.J., Relationship of rainfall and runoff in urban areas (Research, Colloquium of the Construction Industry Research and Information Association, 1973).

[20] Yen, B.C. and Chow, V.T., A laboratory study of surface runoff due to moving rainstorms (Water Resource Research 5, 1969).

19 Tropical Storm Characteristics in Relation to Urban Sewer Design (The East African Rainfall Project)

Dr Maureen E. JONES

19.1 Introduction

The East African Rainfall Project was established in 1964 by L.H. Watkins (Road Research Laboratory, Crowthorne), Professor F.K. Hare (Department of Geography, King's College London) and B.W. Thompson (East African Meteorological Department). The major objective of the Project is to obtain relationships between mean rate of rainfall, duration and frequency of occurrence for short-duration, intense tropical storms. With the variation of rate of rainfall with time, design storm profiles, for different frequencies of occurrence, can be deduced for the Road Research Laboratory Hydrograph for sewer design in East Africa. Additionally from the areal extent of storm rainfall, area–depth/duration–frequency curves can be extrapolated to provide estimates of intense rainfall over similar small areas.

The Road Research Laboratory Hydrograph method for the design of urban storm-water sewers is in general use in the United Kingdom. This design system employs the characteristics of heavy rainfall, the factors affecting the relationship between rates of rainfall and rates of runoff, and the hydraulics of sewer systems. In particular, the method requires a storm profile, the relationship between the mean rate of rainfall of a storm with its duration, for a given frequency of occurrence at each manhole. So the variability of rates of rainfall over an area during heavy storms is important. The basic data on rainfall characteristics in the United Kingdom were derived from Holland's investigation.[1]

The Road Research Laboratory Hydrograph method is universally applicable, but requisite data rarely exist. Hence, the Road Research Laboratory established several research projects to deduce design data for the hydrograph method under tropical conditions. The Laboratory has looked at the effects of unpaved areas on the relationship between rainfall and runoff rates, and has examined past rainfall records from conventional rain gauges for flood calculations. The East African Rainfall Project was set up to investigate the characteristics of storm rainfall.

19.2   Instrumentation and data processing

Three networks of rain gauges have been established in East Africa, in three of the four main urban areas; namely Kampala in Uganda, Nairobi in Kenya and Dar es Salaam in Tanzania. The original regular grid pattern proposed for the networks was abandoned in favour of secure sites with good exposure. Kampala (00° 20′ N, 32° 35′ E) has an annual rainfall of 1,000 mm. The city lies 30 km from Lake Victoria in a region of dissected ridges. The city covers several hills and valleys, and rain-gauge heights vary from 1,140 m in the south-east to 1,305 m in the north. There are 25 gauges, sited at a density of 1 gauge per $1·34$ km^2. Nairobi (01° 17′ S, 36° 50′ E) has 863 mm of rain per year. It is situated at an altitude of 1,670 m, between the Embakasi and Athi plains to the south and east and the broken landscape of the White Highlands to the north and west. In Nairobi there are 20 gauges, spaced at 1 gauge per 4 km^2. Dar es Salaam (06° 51′ S, 39° 18′ E) has an annual rainfall of 1,000 mm. The city is situated on the coast of the Indian Ocean, and is less than 40 m above sea level. The network consists of 25 gauges, with 1 gauge per $2·5$ km^2.

The basic rainfall data are derived from autographic records of Dines Tropical gauges, modified by a chart-drive of 6 in/h. Each chart runs for a week, time checks are made on the charts by observers at interim periods. The observers, from the East African Meteorological Department, maintain the rain gauges, change the charts and dispatch the charts to England for processing and analysis.

Rainfall amounts for each minute are extracted from chart co-ordinates with a D—Mac digitiser. The punched paper—tape output is edited, time corrections inserted, and lists of minute—rainfall for every gauge stored on magnetic tape. Initial data listings provide storm rainfall amounts and durations, maximum short-period falls and synchronous point-rainfall through every storm.

19.3   Storm analysis

The Kampala network of rain gauges was established in June 1967; in 1968 the Nairobi network was operational in June and the Dar es Salaam network started in November. The observation period was concluded in December 1972, so there are four years of synchronous data from the networks. The major part of the data processing has been completed. This paper will examine the large storms which occurred at the three networks, during the period January 1969 to December 1970.

The storms are defined as those rainfalls at any gauge which are greater than 10 mm over short periods, or greater than 25 mm over longer periods, or storms which occur with an intensity of at least 0·5 mm/min. In this period there were 40 large storms, with a total precipitation above 25 mm at Dar es Salaam, from 102 storms altogether. At Nairobi, 30 out of 80 storms were greater than 25 mm, and at Kampala there were 43 large storms from a total of 94 storms. The three most intense storms at each network are ranked in Table 19.1. Very tentative partial-recurrence curves suggest the most intense storms listed represent the storm which may occur once in 3 years at Kampala and at Nairobi, and once in 5 years at Dar es Salaam. Mass curves and a storm profile are given in Fig. 19.1 and 19.2. Maximum intensities occur in the first quartile of most storms. In very intense storms (1 April 1970) the more intense period is the second quartile. Long, less intense storms tend to maintain a more regular gradient in the mass curve. A design storm profile, representative of the Dar es Salaam area, is postulated in Fig. 19.3.

Table 19.1

Most intense storms over the Kampala, Nairobi and
Dar es Salaam networks — Jan. 1969 to
Dec. 1970

Network	Date (1970)	Total fall (mm)	Duration of storm (min)	Maximum hourly intensity (mm/hour)
Kampala	29 December	62·60	210	55·30
	8 January	55·44	75	55·33
	22 August	62·09	253	47·55
Nairobi	22 April	68·92	138	61·75
	3 April	59·49	162	43·86
	2 June	45·88	126	43·02
Dar es Salaam	1 April	115·02	194	89·67
	14 March	55·30	124	54·35
	15 December	47·84	82	46·89

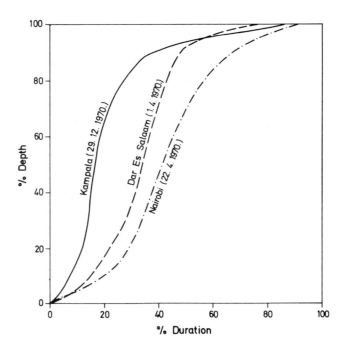

Fig. 19.1   Mass curves of rainfall

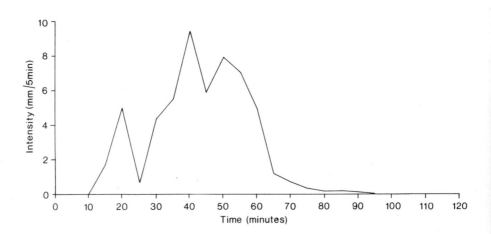

Fig. 19.2   Dar es Salaam: storm profile for 1 April 1970

240

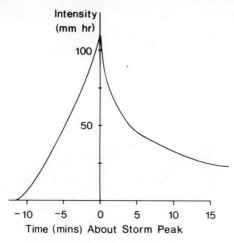

Fig. 19.3 Storm profile for Dar es Salaam

With 15 min isohyetal maps, conventional depth–area curves are derived for the storms; that is, the depth of rainfall equalled or exceeded over an area enclosed by an isohyet is plotted against the area enclosed. The depth of precipitation decays exponentially from the storm centre, approximately; the gradients of the curves reflect the intensity of precipitation (Fig. 19.4). The increasingly steeper curves found over larger areas in some storms appear to be associated with the movement of storm cells across the networks (Fig. 19.5).

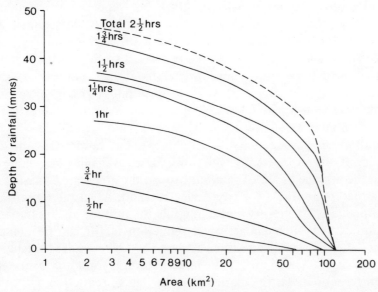

Fig. 19.4 Nairobi network: depth-area curve 3 April 1970

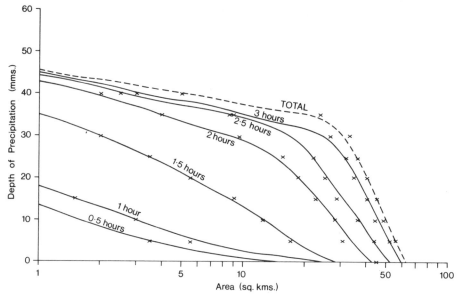

Fig. 19.5   Depth—area curves for storm on 28 October 1969 at Dar es Salaam

Depth—duration curves are plotted subsequently, which relate the depth of precipitation equalled or exceeded over any area with duration. A discontinuity is common in such curves[2]; this occurs between half an hour and 2 hours in Dar es Salaam curves, but generally at less than one hour in Kampala and Nairobi. A secondary discontinuity may appear as the storm decays, although this is not found with short storms, or rapidly moving storm cells (Fig. 19.6). In many cases, a single relationship can be postulated which is more appropriate to design curves, associating estimated rainfall (or intensity) with storm duration and areal coverage.[3] A possible relationship is $I \propto T^{-0.82}$, where I indicates intensity and T duration in hours.

Rainfall varies across a city or catchment, but rainfall at 'one gauge' ('point rainfall') is normally the only data available. A relationship between the average depth of rainfall through the area ('areal rainfall') and point rainfall is desirable for any design method. Areal reduction factors may be deduced to modify point rainfall to produce such estimates of areal rainfall. An approximate areal reduction factor can be computed from the largest storm. The ratio between the highest fall at a gauge, and the rainfall at that gauge during the largest storm is found for every gauge; the average ratio over the network is the areal reduction factor. The average areal reduction factors for the two years January 1969 to

December 1970 are 0·875 at Kampala, 0·92 at Nairobi and 0·86 at Dar es Salaam (i.e. 30 km^2, 80 km^2 and 60 km^2 respectively).

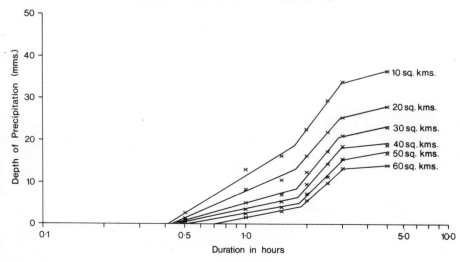

Fig. 19.6   Depth—duration curves for storm on 23 January 1971 at Dar es Salaam

The dense networks of rain gauges in these urban areas allow the examination of the movement of storms across the networks. The location of preferred storm paths is important in the estimation of areal reduction factors as well as to the understanding of the origin, movement and development, and decay of tropical storms.

The movement of a storm across Dar es Salaam is indicated in Fig. 19.7. Here, a single storm centre moved from the south-east to the north. Intensities were more than 20 mm/h over parts of the network for 2½ hours. Many storms give intense falls over part of the network only or are composed of several storm cells which are not easily discernible. The majority of storms do approach Dar es Salaam from the south-east, and rain gauges beside the coast have the heaviest falls. The gauges which most often collect the intense falls are alongside the harbour and to the north of the Msimbazi inlet.

Storms tend to move across Kampala from the south-east to the north-west, as indicated by the onset of rain displayed in Fig. 19.8. Some storms appear to move to the south and south-west, and several storms develop in situ. Storm centres are found most frequently in the north-west of Kampala though there is a secondary maximum occurrence in the east. Storm origin and movement is affected in the Kampala area with the lake-breeze convergence zone about Lake Victoria.[4]

243

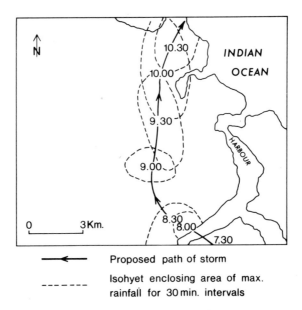

Fig. 19.7   Movement of storm on 28 October 1969 over Dar es Salaam

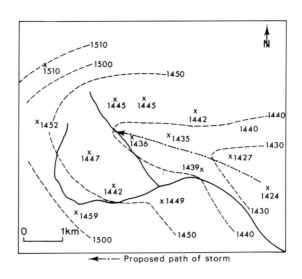

Fig. 19.8   Kampala – onset of rain on 26 August 1970

244

From the storm analysis to date, peak intensities are more common to the north-west of Nairobi. Most storms appear to move from the east to the west across the city, though some storms only affect parts of the city boundary, or grow and decay within the city with little movement. One storm which moved rapidly is shown in Fig. 19.9. On this occasion, one or possibly two cells originated to the south and south-east of the network and combined, to move across the city westward in 2 h.

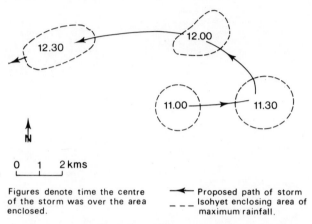

Fig. 19.9   Movement of storm over Nairobi on 1 May 1969

19.4   Conclusion

Rainfall rates vary with duration and location. At the coast, intensities decrease most rapidly over short periods. Individual design storms, dependent on intensity and storm origin, are required for each network. In these relatively small networks, areal reduction factors are high. Preferred storm paths will affect these factors.

References

[1] Holland, D.J., Rain intensity—frequency relationships in Britain (British Rainfall, HMSO 1961).

[2] Alexander, G.N., Heavy rainfall as a stochastic process (Reviews of the International Statistical Institute 38, 1970).

[3] McCallum, D., The relationship between maximum rainfall intensity and time (Memoirs of the East African Meteorological Department, 1959).

[4] Lumb, F.E., Topographic influences on thunderstorm activity near Lake Victoria (Weather 25, 1959).

20 Infra Red Linescan Imagery and Ground Temperatures

R. EVANS

20.1 Introduction

When studying evaporation from soil and crop surfaces it is necessary to know their temperatures, but measurements can often be taken only at a few sites within a small area. Warming of the soil in spring initiates germination of seed and temperature partially controls the growth of plants[1-4] and availability of plant nutrients.[5] Again, point measurements are often the only practical way of obtaining temperature data. Infra-red linescan imagery taken from an aircraft is a technique which appears capable of obtaining temperature measurements over a wide area.

Infra-red linescan imagery senses thermal emission from surfaces and the signal is proportional to the fourth power of the surface temperature and its emissivity ($W = E \sigma T^4$; where W is radiant energy, E is emissivity, σ is the Stefan-Bolzmann constant, and T is temperature in degrees Kelvin.[6] Emissivity is the ratio of the radiant energy emitted by an object at a certain temperature to that of a black body at the same temperature. Soil and vegetation have emissivities close to 1, but accurate data are not available.[7-9] The strength of signal at the airborne scanner depends upon path length and attenuation due to absorption and scattering by atmospheric particles; the greater the path length the greater the attenuation.[10-15] According to Carlon[16] atmospheric aerosols cannot be ignored as a significant source of emission in the $8-14 \mu m$ waveband.

The radiant energy from the ground is optically focused on to a cooled detector, which converts the radiant energy to electrical energy, recorded as a scan line on a cathode ray tube or on magnetic tape. The successive scan lines are photographed to build up an image of the distribution of thermal emission. Scan lines are transverse to the direction of flight.[17-22]

Imagery can be obtained through one of the two 'windows' in the atmosphere, between $3-5 \mu m$ and $8-14 \mu m$; outside these wavebands radiant energy is absorbed by water vapour and carbon dioxide[10]. At wavelengths shorter than $3 \mu m$ reflected radiation becomes important but accounts for less than 3-5 per cent of radiation between 3 and $5 \mu m$.[7] Some authors have noted that infra-red linescan imagery should only be obtained in the 8–14 μm waveband, as reflected solar radiation in the 3–5 μm waveband is sometimes a confusing addition.[6, 17, 23, 24] However, Stingelin [21] notes that imagery in both wavebands records surface temperatures, although he mentions that filtered longwave detectors should be used for daytime observations; the daytime infra-red linescan imagery he discusses was mainly taken in the 3–5 μm waveband. There are some technical advantages of the indium: antimonide detector in the 3–5 μm band. [21, 25] Studies of both 3–5 μm [21, 25–34] and 8–14 μm imagery [21, 35–40] are common. It will be shown in this paper that the 8–14 μm waveband is best for recording thermal emission.

Few studies correlate infra-red linescan imagery with temperature measured on the ground at the time imagery is obtained, [39, 41] although sea or lake surface temperatures have been correlated with infra-red linescan imagery or radiometer data. [42–45] In some instances there is no field data and information is derived from maps; [36, 37, 46] in others information was obtained at a later date, [28, 35, 47, 48] and even though ground temperatures were obtained [29, 40, 49] correlations can only be qualitative. In some studies ground radiometric and thermometric measurements were obtained and these give an insight into parameters which govern ground temperatures and allow a more realistic interpretation of the imagery. It is generally thought that infra-red imagery can only give qualitative information on the distribution of temperature. [35, 51]

20.2 Problems associated with infra-red linescan imagery

Once the technique has been proved and it has been shown that quantitative measurements can be obtained, imagery can be taken at any time or under variable weather conditions. Initially, however, it should be obtained under ideal conditions. There should be no wind, as this complicates the recording and interpretation of the imagery, [21, 23, 33] and the sky should be either cloud-free or completely covered by cloud so that uniform radiation characteristics prevail. The ground surface should not be wet, nor must imagery be taken when rain is falling as this will attenuate the signal and reduce ground temperature differences.

The time for taking imagery will depend on the reason for obtaining it. If objects are to be identified which are warmer than their surroundings imagery should be taken when adjacent temperatures are coldest; this will often be at dawn. This, possibly military viewpoint, has led to the suggestion that imagery is generally best taken during the hours of darkness, particularly early evening or just before dawn. Then differences

248

due to radiative cooling are greatest and the disturbing effects of insolation such as reflection of energy to the sensor, aspect, and elevation of the sun, are reduced. [23, 32, 35, 52] For the best separation of vegetation types, imagery should be taken at night if the water table is close to the surface, but for drier ground it should be taken in mid-afternoon when daily water stress is greatest. It is thought that as moisture stress increases, radiant emission from the stressed plant also increases.

For natural surfaces differences in emissivity are small and, as outgoing radiant energy is a function of temperature, thermal emission will decrease during the night. Thermometric measurements, and infra-red linescan imagery [21] show that temperature differences between natural surfaces decrease during the night to a minimum before dawn. To discriminate between natural surfaces, therefore, imagery should be taken when temperature and outgoing radiation are at a maximum, as then differences in emittance are greatest; this will be in the early afternoon on a clear day.

It is unlikely that equipment for non-military use will be stabilised on three axes, [52] and this can lead to serious distortions and scale variations of the image. Location of an instrumented site is then difficult, even where field boundaries provide what appears to be an adequate grid for fixing points. The angle of the line of scan to the ground becomes more oblique away from the centre line and for successful aerial coverage successive flights must overlap by 40 per cent. [61] Successive flights must be flown in the same direction.

The measurement of ground temperature poses problems. The infra-red linescan imagery is recording a surface of 'skin' temperature[8, 45] and this is difficult to measure, [53] even with sophisticated thermometric equipment, although adequate correlations of radiometer and thermometrically measured temperatures have been obtained. [41, 50] The fluctuation of temperature is greatest within ± 1 cm of the surface [53] and measurements taken outside these limits will not accurately reflect surface temperature movements. The soil surface is often very uneven, unless recently rolled and compacted after seed-bed preparation or after slaking by rainfall, and it is difficult ot measure temperature in this superficial cloddy zone. In this study, to overcome this problem thermometers and probes were covered by 5–10 mm of soil particles or small clods. The measurements need not be exactly those recorded by the infra-red linescan device, but if temperatures are recorded at the same shallow depth there should be a consistent relationship between ground and remotely sensed temperatures, if emissivities are similar. Even so, it was found that probes inserted fractionally deeper, because the surface clods were larger, recorded a cooler temperature during the day and were warmer at night than adjacent near-surface temperatures. This became apparent after receiving imagery when anomalous temperatures were noted, image tone being lighter (warmer) in relation to neighbouring sites than was indicated by ground measurements.

Soil temperatures vary over a lateral distance of a few centimetres, even when conditions appear exactly the same, and variations of 2–5°C were noted. The mean of these point measurements at a site is compared with linescan image density, a measure of the amount of light passing through the image. This is also a point measure, but because of scale factors actually represents an integrated mean temperature over a small area on the ground proportional to the scale of the image. The ground measurements need to be taken continuously or at very short time intervals so that the times of recording surface and image temperature will coincide.

20.3 Evaluation

Flights were made over (a) Breckland, Norfolk in July 1971; (b) the southern edge of the Fens in Huntingdonshire in April 1973; and (c) chalkland in southern Cambridgeshire in May 1973. Imagery in the 3·5–5·5 μm waveband was obtained over Breckland and in the 8–14 μm waveband over the other two localities. The 8–14 μm imagery is discussed first as the results are unequivocal. The ambiguous results from the earlier flight over the Breckland indicated that 8–14 μm imagery would record more successfully the spatial variation of temperature.

20.3.1 *Near Warboys, Huntingdonshire* (TL 5 337820)

Within a short distance very different soils occur on Fenland deposits and Oxford Clay, those on silted estuarine creeks [54] being very reflective in the visible wavelengths. Although these soils are mostly clayey, organic matter content and the proportion of silt, especially coarse silt, to clay varies widely (Table 20.1). Temperatures of bare soil in fields sown to barley and potatoes (five sites), grassland (three sites) and water (two sites) were monitored. Water temperatures were measured as these should be the coldest temperatures occurring within the locality.

Imagery in the 8–14 μm waveband was obtained from a height of 305 m between 1300 hours and 1330 hours (British Summer Time), 17 April 1973. Flights were from east to west. At altitudes of 300 m or less atmospheric absorption of radiation in the 8–14 μm waveband is

250

negligible under ordinary conditions.[55] The scale of the enlarged prints used for densitometry was about 1 : 4,000 along the flight line (east–west) and about 1 : 5,000 in the centre of the north–south scan.

Conditions were not ideal for obtaining imagery, cloud cover was generally complete but when there was a gap, heating of the surface was rapid. The northerly wind was strong, as was turbulence.

20.3.1 *Results and discussion*

The mean temperature of the probes in bare soil at site 1 is taken as representative, the range being $3°C$ (site $1^{(5-8)}$, Fig. 20.1); the coldest temperature recorded (the pond, Fig. 20.1) is equated with the highest density measured over a 10 m-wide drainage dyke 1 km to the east. An accurate measure of density cannot be made because of the very small area of the pond on the image. Mean temperatures of the thermometer positions on the potato ridges at sites 2, 3, 4 and 5, as shown in Fig. 20.1, were then plotted against density.

The temperatures at two sites (2 and 3) were lower than indicated by their image densities (Fig. 20.2). This was because they were taken at a greater depth from the air/clod interface as clods were of larger size due to their greater clay content. These values are not included in the regression analysis. Imagery in the $8-14 \, \mu m$ waveband accurately ($r = -0.97$) reflects surface temperatures, and emissivities of vegetation and soils are similar. The temperature and spatial resolution of this imagery is good, as at site 4 the darker tones of the cooler furrows ($c. 18.5°C$, Fig. 20.1), 75 cm apart, and the lighter-toned, warmer ridges ($c. 21.5°C$) are clearly recorded. Fields under pasture (site 7, Fig. 20.1), or carrying winter wheat or mustard with a closed canopy have the lowest temperatures. Within darker-toned fields variability of tone is due to differences in crop density, for instance denser growth in shallow valley floors or on slight depressions remaining after ploughing out medieval ridge and furrow. Highest temperatures occur in bare soil or in fields where emerging cereals (site $1^{(5-8)}$, Fig. 20.1), less than 10 cm high, cover less than 40–50 per cent of the ground surface. Elsewhere, differences in insolation are apparent; where thicker cloud has reduced incoming radiation temperatures are cooler and detail is lost within these dark-toned areas. Similarly, detail is lost in light-toned areas (over-exposed) where temperatures are very high because of direct insolation through a gap in the cloud. Minor contributors to the temperature pattern are differential heating of soil types, surface roughness, aspect and date of working.

Some creeks are dark toned, in contrast to their photo image, and are

Table 20.1

Description of sites near Warboys, Huntingdonshire

Size	Description	Analysis of plough layer soil (%)	
			Sand (54—2,000 μm)
1	Wicken series:* clay over Oxford clay; surface colour 10YR 3/3, dark brown; ridge above Fen, 2° slope, north facing; very little surface roughness after preparation of seed bed; probes 5—8 in bare soil; 1—15% emerging barley; probes 1 and 2 in pool in old pit, 3 and 4 in grass adjacent to pit		17·2
2	Chatteris series (Seale, in press): minor estuarine creek 10 m wide, humose silty clay loam over silty, calcareous deposits; surface colour 10YR 5/2, greyish brown; cloddy surface, 25—50 cm elevation above adjacent flat land; potato ridges from east to west c.25 cm deep, 70—75 cm wide; samples from top of ridge (R) and furrow (F)	Ridge Fen	6·5 6·9
3	Downholland series:** peaty loam over clayey, non-calcareous estuarine deposits; surface colour 10YR 3·5/3, dark brown; cloddy surface; potato ridges from east to west, c. 25 cm deep, 70—75 cm wide. Samples from top ridge (R) and furrow (F).	Ridge Fen	3·2 3·3
4	Adventurers' series:* peaty loam over peat over clayey estuarine deposits; surface colour 10YR 3/1·5, very dark grey to very dark greyish brown; potato ridges from east to west, c. 25 cm deep, 70—75 cm wide.	Ridge Fen	7·5 5·9
5	Chatteris series: major estuarine creek 100 m wide, humose calcareous silty clay loam over calcareous silty deposits; surface colour 10YR 4/2·5, dark greyish brown to dark brown; 1—15 m elevation above adjacent flat land; potato ridges from east to west, c. 25 cm deep, 70—75 cm wide	Ridge Fen	18·3 19·2
6	NNW—SSE trending dyke: 4 m wide, c. 1 m deep		
7	Wicken series (see 1): ridge above Fen, 1° slope, north-facing; pasture, 15—20 cm high, dense growth		
8	Wicken series (see 1): ridge above Fen, 1° slope, north-facing; site in 0·5 m deep depression; pasture 17—20 cm high, more vigorous, denser growth than site 7.		

* Hodge and Seale [63]
** Hall and Folland [62]

Coarse silt (20–53 μm)	Silt (2–19 μm)	Clay (<2μm)	Organic matter content	Soil moisture content at time of flight (per cent over dry weight)	Comments
8.9	21.3	52.6	3.7	6.5	Eight-channel automatic recorder; probes in water recording relatively changing temperatures
36.6	24.1	32.7	12.6	7.4	Mercury-in-glass thermometer placed at top ridge, in furrow, and half-way down on sun and shade side of ridge
29.5	31.2	32.4	–	11.2	
10.7	35.4	50.7	29.0	12.6	As for site 2
13.3	37.3	46.0	–	19.3	
21.2	30.0	41.3	32.0	22.2	Thermistor probes, in same position as sites 2 and 3
22.7	30.3	41.1	–	20.8	
42.3	16.4	23.0	14.3	5.6	As for site 4
43.5	14.4	22.9	–	7.6	
					Relatively slowly changing temperature of water
					Soil analysis similar to site 1; thermistor probe
					Soil analysis similar to site 1

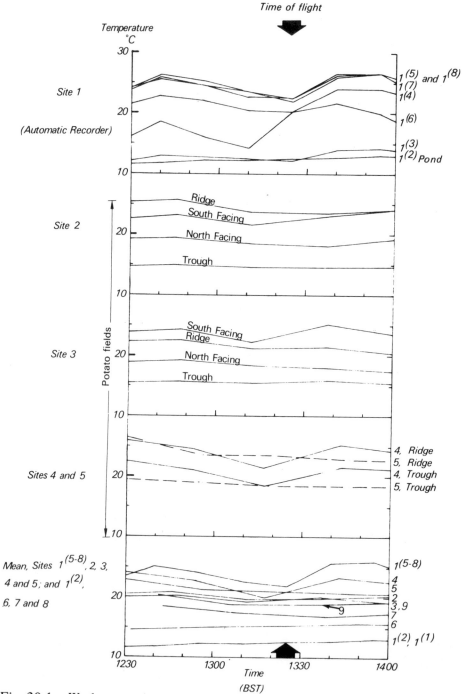

Fig. 20.1   Warboys – site temperatures

254

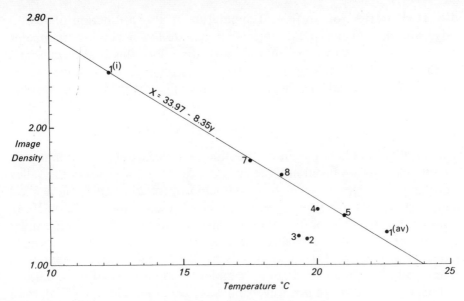

Fig. 20.2   Warboys — image density and temperature

cooler than the adjacent darker-coloured soils with more organic matter
and soil moisture; these darker-coloured soils absorb more radiant heat
and are warmer. However in the period in which imagery was obtained the
temperature relationships are reversed at sites 4 and 5, soils on creeks
being warmer (Fig. 20.1). In this locality the generally darker tones of the
image indicate a thicker cloud cover, reducing insolation and temperatures. As the dark-coloured soil is a better conductor it radiates heat
more rapidly than the creek soils and is cooler.

Fields down to potatoes (sites 2—5), the ridges being about 75 cm wide
and 25 cm high, are cooler than adjacent fields sown to spring barley (site
1), or of rolled bare soil; sugar beet was sown in these fields. It is the mean
temperature of the potato fields which is lower, as temperatures of the
top or south-facing sides of the ridges are similar to those of adjacent
smooth fields, for instance, site 1 (Fig. 20.1). The north-facing slope is
considerably warmer than the bottom of the furrow, which can be up to
10·7°C cooler than the top of the ridge, presumably because the air is
stagnant between the east—west ridges. On creek soils with lesser organic
matter and soil moisture (sites 2 and 5) than the adjacent soils (sites 3 and
4) the range of temperature between trough and ridge is greater. On soils with
a larger clay content (sites 4 and 5) the range of temperature is also greater.

Recently cultivated soils have cooler temperatures, i.e. are darker toned
on the imagery, as evaporation, causing cooling, is greater from a freshly

disturbed, wetter soil surface. Temperature is also a function of row or ridge aspect. In cereal fields, temperatures are lower because of shading where the cereal is sown in an east—west direction; this is also transverse to the wind. In a field carrying potatoes the temperature is lower where the ridges are aligned east—west than in the adjacent field where rows are north—south.

20.3.2a   *Near Balsham, Cambridgeshire* (TL 559514)

This locality is at the margin of the dissected chalk upland. Temperature measurements were taken in three adjacent fields, at two sites in the valley floor and on slopes adjacent to a south—north trending valley (nine sites) and, except for three sites in cereals, they were on bare soil (Table 20.2). Soils are on thin drift or directly on chalk, and surface textures are similar except for that of the chalky, light grey, reflective rendzina (Icknield series, sites 3, 5, 8, 11(i) and (ix), Table 20.2); soil moisture content is fractionally less for this soil but all samples are almost dry (Table 20.2).

Imagery in the $8-14$ μm waveband was taken on 16 May 1973 at 1555 hours (British Summer Time) and at 0610 hours (BST) the following day. At 1555 hours temperatures were falling slowly whereas they were just beginning to rise in the morning (Fig. 20.3). In the afternoon the sky was cloudless but there was a strong easterly wind, whereas in the morning there was about $^1/_{10}$ cover of thin stratus and a gentle south-easterly breeze.

Temperatures vary most widely around 1400 hours but were similar at dawn and began to rise 45 min to 1 h after sunrise (Fig. 20.3). The temperatures of soil under a cereal crop (sites 6B and 7B, Fig. 20.3) are lower during the day than temperatures of soil between crop rows (sites 6A and 7A, Fig. 20.3). Day temperatures 2—3 cm deep in the soil (site 8) and on the surface of light grey reflective soils (site 5) are also lower than those at the surfaces of darker-coloured soils (sites 1, 2 and 4). Air temperatures at 7 cm and 15 cm (sites 11(iv) and 11(v)) are cooler than surface temperatures (sites 11(i)–(vii)) and fluctuate more rapidly as cloud cuts off direct insolation.

20.3.2b   *Results and discussion*

(1)   *1555 hours*

The mean, highest and lowest temperatures at site 11 are plotted (Fig. 20.4) against mean, lowest and highest image densities. An accurate measure of density was not obtainable for sites 6A and 6B because of the variability of tonal values related to differences of temperature within a variable crop cover. The temperature at site 8 was recorded from too great a depth. The correlation of image tone and soil temperature is good ($r = -0.95$).

256

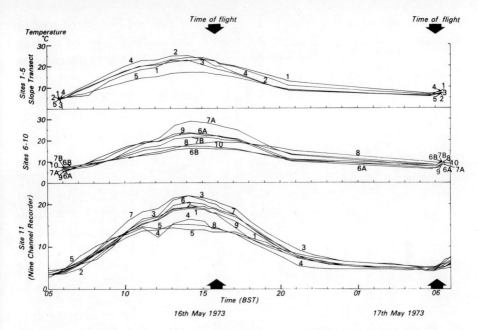

Fig. 20.3   Balsham — site temperatures: (a) slope transect; (b) other sites; (c) grouped sites

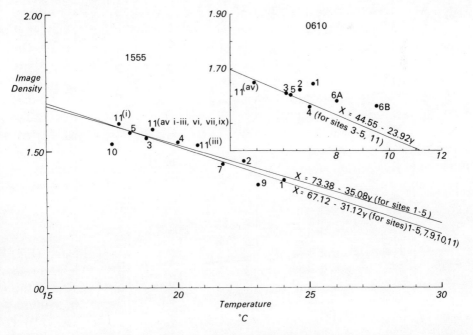

Fig. 20.4   Balsham — image density and temperature

Table 20.2

Description of sites near Balsham, Cambridgeshire

Site	Position and slope	Aspect	Soil	Comments
1	Valley floor (0°)	350°	Dullingham series;* sandy clay loam plough layer (53–2,000 μm 22·5; < 2 μm 20·4); surface colour 10YR 5/4, yellowish brown; surface stones – 3–5%; soil moisture (% oven dry wt.) – 4·1; organic matter content – 2·3%	Sites 1–5 along slope transect in field carrying sugar beet; two mercury-in-glass thermometers; about 1% cover – sugar beet up to 3 cm high in rows 44 cm apart
2	Concavity at margin valley floor (1°)	80°	Swaffham Prior series;* sandy clay loam chalk at 54 cm; surface colour 10YR 4/4, dark yellowish brown; surface stones – 3–5%; soil moisture – 4·2%	Two mercury-in-glass thermometers; intermediate between deeper soil in valley floor and rendzina over chalk; sugar beet is slightly taller and greener than at site 1
3	Valley side slope (4°)	100°	Icknield series; clay loam; highly calcareous plough layer (53–2,000 μm 36·8; 2–5 μm 36·0; < 2 μm 36·7); chalk at 30 cm; surface colour – 2·5Y 7/2, light grey; surface stones 15–20%; flint and chalk; soil moisture – 3·5%; organic matter – 1·7%	Two mercury-in-glass thermometers; highly reflective, chalky surface; beet is poor, up to 2 cm high, yellower, stunted
4	Convex slope (5°)	140°	Swaffham Prior series; sandy clay loam plough layer; chalk at 44 cm; surface colour – 10YR 5/4, yellowish brown; surface stones – 5–7%; soil moisture – 4·7%	Two mercury-in-glass thermometers; sugar beet is intermediate between sites 2 and 3
5	Near crest of spur (3°)	140°	Icknield series; loam to clay loam plough layer; chalk at 28 cm; surface colour – 10YR 7/2, light grey; surface stones – 20–25% chalk and flint, soil moisture – 2·1%	Two mercury-in-glass thermometers; stony, very chalky, highly reflective soil surface; rare sugar beet seedlings
6	Valley floor (1°)	25°	Dullingham series; loam plough layer; surface colour – 10YR 6/3, pale brown; surface stones – none; eroded material deposited in valley floor has cracked polygonally on drying	Thermistor probes in barley field, immediately south of beet field; 6A – surface temperature in clearing in barley; 6B – soil temperature within 30 cm high barley; 50–70% ground cover.

7	Valley side slope (4°)	270°	Shallow Swaffham Prior series; loam plough layer; chalk at 38 cm; surface colour – 10YR 6/3, pale brown; surface stones – 5%	Thermistor probes in barley field, immediately south of beet field; 7A – temperature of surface between barley rows; 17 cm gap; 7B – soil temperature within barley row, 23 cm high; 30–50% ground cover
8	Valley side slope (4°)	270°	Icknield series; chalky loam; chalk at 24 cm; surface colour – 10YR 7/2 – 2·5Y 6·5/2, light grey; surface stones 7–10%, flint and chalk	Same field as sites 1–5, opposing aspect; disturbed – thermistor probe to 3.0 cm; very thin, stunted sugar beet on very calcareous soil
9	Spur (4°)	325°	Shallow Swaffham Prior series; sandy clay loam (53–2,000 μm 50·09; 2–52 μm 21·6; < 2 μm 19·48); chalk at 30 cm; surface colour 10YR 5/3, brown; surface stones – 3–5%; organic matter – 1·0%	Bare soil; strip of recently ploughed soil to east of barley field and adjacent to wheat field (to east) containing site 10; thermistor probe
10	Spur convexity (3°)	280°	Shallow Swaffham Prior series; sandy clay loam; chalk at 32 cm; surface colour – 10YR 5·5/3, brown to pale brown; surface stones 7–10%	Thermistor probe in wheat field; soil temperature within wheat; 27 cm high; 50% cover
11	Tributary valley side (3°)	70°	(a) Deep Swaffham Prior series; sandy clay loam; chalk at 72 cm; surface colour – 10YR 5/6 and 5/8, yellowish brown; this merges to: (b) Icknield series; chalky loam, chalk at 21 cm; surface colour – 10YR 7/4, very pale brown; surface stones – 10%	At edge of strip of bare soil, recently ploughed, and bean field; to west barley field; nine-channel automatic recorder; 2–3 m meter between probes on 5 m diameter circle;

Comments
(i) in bean field; smooth, compact surface; surface colour – 10YR 7/4, pale brown;
(ii) In bean field; smooth, compact surface, surface colour – 10YR 6/4, light yellowish brown;
(iii) in bean field, smooth compact surface; surface colour – 10YR 5/4, yellowish brown;
(iv) plant/air temperature; probe inserted into stem 7 cm from surface;
(v) plant/air temperature; probe inserted into stem 15 cm from surface;
(vi) recently worked; rougher surface, up to 10 cm relief; surface colour – 10YR 5/5, yellowish brown;
(vii) recently worked; rougher surface, up to 10 cm relief; surface colour – 10YR 5/5, yellowish brown;
(viii) recently worked; probe inserted to 2 cm, edge micro-ridge; surface colour – 10YR 5/5, yellowish brown;
(ix) recently worked; rougher surface, up up 10 cm relief; surface colour – 10YR 6/3, pale brown

* Hodge and Seale[63]

Again temperatures are cooler within crops (Fig. 20.3), being coolest where cover is most dense (site 6B), generally on deeper, less calcareous darker soils. Fields carrying beans (sites 11(i)–(iii)) have temperatures similar to those of bare fields as cover is small and shading not important. Other factors governing distribution of temperature are aspect, insolation and soil colour. Highest temperatures, lightest tones on the image, are recorded in the early afternoon on west-facing 3–5° slopes on the east side of the valley and on the crest and gentle westerly slope of a minor spur and valley on the west side of the valley. Where the sun's rays are more oblique, as on the gently sloping watershed to the west, temperatures are cooler.

On the east–west transect dark-coloured soils are warmest, as chalky soils with an albedo of about 30 per cent reflect a higher proportion of radiant energy.[56,57] Ramdas[58] notes that adding chalk to a dark-coloured soil lowers the surface temperature. This is also true of site 11 where probes within a few metres record differences in temperature of 3°C between lighter and darker soils. Within the field carrying sugar beet two north–south trending darker-toned parallel lines are discernible, probably due to disturbance of the soil surface when thinning beet seedlings. The moisture content of these soils would be the same as of adjacent soils, only the top 1–2 cm being disturbed. Although the freshly exposed rougher surfaces may have been slightly damper than the adjacent dry surface, evaporation will not account for these lower temperatures, which were probably due to shading and lower conductivity and thermal capacity of the more porous disturbed soils.

(2) *0610 hours*

The imagery obtained on this flight is of moderate quality, of limited tonal contrast, and traversed by many parallel bands of darker and lighter tones attributable to a fault in the equipment. Fields of barley are slightly lighter in tone than adjacent bare fields and this correlates with a temperature difference of +1–2°C. The low tonal contrast, therefore, is associated with a small range of temperature. The most noteworthy features on the imagery are the warmer belt of trees to the east of the beet field, which is just catching the sun, and its shadow.

Because of instrument failure, imagery was not obtained of sites 7, 9 and 10. The mean temperature at site 11 is compared with density as the range of temperature is small (0.75°C). Points 3, 4, 5 and 11 lie close to a regression line ($r = 1.00$, Fig. 20.4) but points 1, 2, 6A and 6B, which are not included in the regression analysis, all appear colder on the image than is indicated by their measured temperatures. Sites 1 and 2 are within the shadow of the belt of trees, and surface temperatures of these darker soils are similar to that of the darker soil at site 4 and are higher than those of the chalky soils. This apparent anomaly may be due to evaporation of dew from the soil surface. The previous morning there was a heavy dew and at 0545 hours the soil surface was damp at sites 1 and 2 which were still in shade, but by 0619 hours, although site 1 was still in deep shade and site 2 in partial shade, the soil surface was dry. On the morning of the 17th dew was not heavy and was not noticed on the soil. Evaporation and cooling of the surface will not be registered by a thermometer 5–10 mm deep.

20.3.3a *Breckland*

Flights were made on 21 July 1971, between 0530–0630 hours (British Summer Time) and 1120–1220 hours (BST) at heights of 122 m and 762 m respectively. Imagery of the instrumented sites at Illington (Grid Reference TL 946900) was taken at 0547 hours and 1148 hours and the film was processed to provide a medium contrast. Image density measurements were made on enlarged prints of approximate scale of 1 : 16,500 (0547 hrs) and 1 : 8,500 (1148 hrs). Panchromatic air photo cover, at a scale of 1 : 8,500, was obtained on 13 July 1971.

20.3.3b *Site and temperature characteristics*

At seven sites soil and crop temperatures were measured and at one site (site 6), on unvegetated peat, only surface temperatures were recorded. Sites 1–5 were on a north-facing transect in a field of barley and sites 7 and 8 were within a sugar beet crop in the adjacent field to the east. These sites were on loamy sand, except for site 1, on peaty loam, and site 7, on chalky sandy loam. The barley was from 60 to 96 cm high and sunlight did not penetrate to the soil surface; the beet canopy was up to 47 cm high at site 8, but there were occasional gaps in the cover, as at site 7 where plants were sparse and soil was exposed to the sky. At sites 1 and 5 in barley, temperatures at different heights in the crop and at the top of the crop were recorded automatically every 15 min whilst four probes were placed in the soil beneath so that they were just covered. In the crop, probes were attached to the north side of white stakes and shaded by down-pointing cones of aluminium foil. At the remaining sites thermometers, calibrated with the temperature probes, were similarly attached to posts on a level with the top of the barley or beet.

During both flights cloud cover was complete, there was no breeze, and temperatures did not fluctuate although they were slowly rising at 0547 hours and falling at 1148 hours (Fig. 20.5). In the night, radiation cooling and the downslope flow of cold air created an inversion of temperature (Fig. 20.5a (inset)). At 0547 hours air temperatures at sites 1 and 5 were the same throughout the height of the crop and the soil surfaces at these, and sites 2–4 and 7 and 8, were 2°C to 3°C warmer (Fig. 20.5a). The temperature of the peat (site 6) was similar to soil temperatures at sites 3 to 5 in the barley and 7 and 8 in the beet (c. 14°C) but was higher than that of similar low-lying sites (1 and 2) under crop (Fig. 20.5a). There was an occasional light shower of rain in this period but soil and crop surfaces were mostly dry, an estimated 10 per cent of the ground and leaf surfaces being wetted at sites 7 and 8.

By 1148 hours, although temperatures had risen the temperature inversion had not dissipated and ground temperatures were now cooler than crop temperatures (Fig. 20.5). Crop and soil temperatures were within 1–2°C but at sites 7 and 8 the soil was warmer. The peat surface (site 6) was warmer than the other sites. At 1146 hours there was a heavy rain shower, and ground and crop surfaces were partially wetted, but between 30 per cent and 40 per cent of the soil surface at site 7 remained dry.

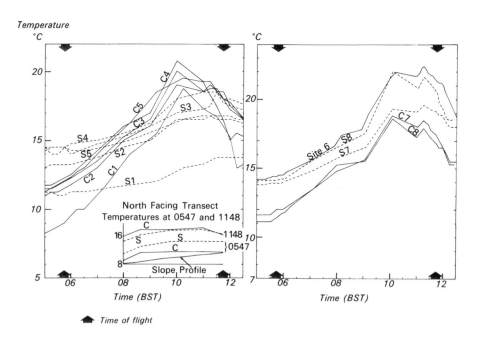

Fig. 20.5   Illington – site temperatures: (a) sites 1–5 barley; (b) sites 6–8 sugar beet

20.3.3c   *Results*

The resolution of the linescan equipment enabled temperatures to be recorded at site 6, a narrow strip of uncultivated peat. At site 7 the sugar beet crowns did not overlap between rows as growth was retarded on this very calcareous, light grey sandy loam and the signal recorded by the linescan device was a function of soil temperature. At the remaining sites it is debatable if the temperature sensed is that of the top of the crop or of the soil surface beneath. It is probably the latter, for as Penman and Long [59] note it is the soil surface, not the crop, which dominates the main energy exchange as leaf temperatures of wheat are generally less than the estimated air temperature at the same level.

Image density at each site was measured with a densitometer, but because of the narrowness of the uncultivated peat strip (site 6) relative to the width of the aperture (1 mm) of the densitometer, it was impossible to obtain a measure within this.

On the transect the correlation between image density and temperature is poor ($r = -0.31$ at 0547 hrs; and $r = -0.46$ at 1148 hrs, values not statistically significant). From site 4 to site 2, tonal densities change inversely to temperature (Fig. 20.6), as expected, but at site 1 the tonal value decreases (lighter in tone) whereas temperatures are lower.

Sugar beet growth was stunted at site 7 and the light grey (Munsell colour 10 YR 7/2) chalky soil exposed to the sky as only 60 per cent of the ground was shaded by leaves. At site 8 the dark green leaves formed a close canopy. If the response of linescan imagery is to soil temperature at site 7 and canopy temperature at site 8, the lower temperatures at 8 at 0547 hours and 1148 hours (Fig. 20.5*b*) correlate with darker image tones. However, the temperature difference between 7 and 8 is greatest at 0547 hours but then the density difference is least.

20.3.3.d   *Discussion*

Differences of temperature are recorded, for although no quantifiable measure of image density was obtained for site 6, the peat surface, which in the morning was about 3°C warmer than sites 1 and 2, gave an image slightly lighter in tone and which at midday, when it was about 7·5°C warmer than site 1, was much lighter in tone. Fields recently ploughed were much lighter in tone at midday than early in the morning and this may be due to their higher temperatures. Also, water in gravel pits gives images in light tones compared with its surroundings at 0530 hours and is darker toned at midday, indicating expected changes in thermal response. Similarly, at midday cold water being pumped from the underlying chalk into Larling Brook is clearly visible, the springs being 6·3°C and 6·0°C colder than the stream. However, a spring midway between these is not identifiable when the temperature difference is only 1·6°C. [60]

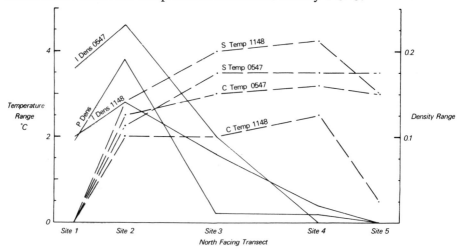

Fig. 20.6 Illington —images and photo-densities of the sites in barley, and their relationship to temperature

On the linescan images tonal changes along the transect in the barley are similar to those on the panchromatic air photograph especially for the early morning flight (Fig. 20.6). This suggests that reflected radiation is contributing to the signal received at the scanner. The darkest tones on the 0547 imagery correspond with dark tones on the photograph and are associated with crop lodging. There was no evidence of greater radiation cooling in these clearings; site 2 was at the southern edge of this lodged crop. Colour differences are due to different rates of maturing and lodging of the barley; in depressions adjacent to the valley floor, usually with humose or peaty soils, the crop was greener and often lodged. It is probable that the greater contrast between image tones at sites 7 and 8 at 1148 hours (not at 0547 hours when the temperature difference was greatest) is due to greater reflection of radiation at this time.

Davies [17] notes that reflected radiation is sometimes a confusing addition to infra-red linescan imagery, and reflection from dry silt loam in the 4 μm waveband accounts for 9 per cent of the total upward radiation.[7] Imagery in the 3—5 μm waveband, therefore, needs a filter to cut out reflected energy below 3·5—4 μm.[6] These findings are confirmed in this study and temperature differences smaller than about 3°C are not recorded. Other factors may be important, as at midday the signal may have been attenuated by rainfall [10] and transmissivity through the saturated air may have been reduced;[7] there is also a loss of resolving power at low temperatures.[25] Although soil and plants are almost black-body radiators,[8] their emissivities are not accurately known and a 10 per cent error may lead to an error of 6–10°C in sensing the earth's surface temperature.[41]

20.4   Conclusions

Infra-red linescan imagery in the 3–5 μm waveband records not only thermal emission but also, from surfaces with a high albedo, reflected radiation. Imagery in the 8–14 μm waveband solely records thermal emission and this can be correlated with ground temperature.

The main use of infra-red linescan imagery will be in showing spatial and temporal variations of temperature, not for identifying or discriminating between natural features. It is a technique which, with contemporaneous ground measurements, will aid in explaining the variability of surface temperature. Using a sophisticated densitometer, thermal maps could be produced or a more accurate mean ground temperature of an area could be obtained than that from a few point measurements. This may be important, for instance, when studying the energy balance of a locality, rather than of individual fields, especially under non-ideal cloudy and windy conditions. With the type of linescan equipment used in this study there may be 'drift' in readings because individual scan-line values depend on the mean of values of previous scan lines and slow changes in temperature over a distance will not be recorded. This could be overcome by placing temperature stations at wide intervals.

The good correlation of remotely sensed and thermometric measurements indicates that emissivities of soils and vegetation are similar. The distribution of temperature in daytime is controlled mainly by vegetation density and soil colour; the denser the vegetation the lower the temperature due to shading and evaporation from plant surfaces, and darker soil surfaces are warmer. Aspect is also important. Soils which absorb more radiant energy lose heat more quickly at night, and in daytime, too, if direct insolation is cut off. It is the properties of the soil surface which are most important in controlling surface temperatures; internal properties of the clod or soil profile such as thermal capacity or conductivity of heat from the surface into the clod are less important. Temperatures vary more at the surface than at depth and surface temperatures need not be a guide to those at depth.[61]

References

[1] Alberda, T., Responses of grasses to temperature and light in F.L. Milthorpe and J.D. Ivins (eds), The growth of cereals and grasses (Butterworths, London 1966).

[2] Friend, D.J.C., The effects of light and temperature on the growth of cereals in F.L. Milthorpe and J.D. Ivins (eds), op. cit.

[3] Monteith, J.L., Analysis of microclimate in cereals and grasses in F.L. Milthorpe and J.D. Ivins (eds), op. cit.

[4] Robson, M.J., The effect of temperature on growth of S.170 Tall Fescue (Festuca arundinaceae), Part II: independent variation of day and night temperatures (Journal of Applied Ecology 10 [1], 1973).

[5] Bailey, L.D. and Beauchamp, E.G., Effects of temperature on NO_3^- and NO_2^- reduction, nitrogenous gas production, and redox potential in a saturated soil (Journal of Canadian Soil Science 53, 1973).

[6] Morgan, J., Infra-red technology (Proceedings of the 1st Symposium on Remote Sensing of the Environment, University of Michigan 1962).

[7] Brooks, F.A., Atmospheric radiation and its reflection from the ground (Journal of Meteorology 9, 1952).

[8] Gates, D.M., Characteristics of soil and vegetated surfaces to reflected and emitted radiation (Proceedings of the 3rd Symposium on Remote Sensing of the Environment, University of Michigan 1965).

[9] Myers, V.I. and Allen, A.W., Electro-optical and remote sensing methods as non-destructive testing and measuring techniques in agriculture (Applied Optics 7, 1968).

[10] Hackforth, H.L., Infra-red radiation (McGraw-Hill, New York 1960).

[11] Hovis, W.A., Blaine, L.R. and Callahan, W.R., Infra-red aircraft spectra over desert terrain $8.5-16 \mu m$ (Applied Optics 7 [6], 1968).

[12] Kattawar, G.M. and Plass, G.N., Thermal emission from haze and clouds (Applied Optics 9 [2], 1970).

[13] Kondratiev, K.Y., Nicolsky, G.A., Radinov, I.Y. and Andreev, S.D., Direct solar radiation up to 30 km and stratification of attenuation components in the stratosphere (Applied Optics 6, 1967).

[14] Platt, C.M.R., Surface temperature measurements from satellites (Nature [Physical Science] 235 [54], 1972).

[15] Taylor, J.M. and Yates, M.W., Atmospheric transmission in the infra-red (Report NRL Progress, Washington 1956).

[16] Carlon, H.R., Infra-red emission by fine water aerosols and fogs (Applied Optics 9 [9], 1970).

[17] Davies, D.H., Electronic Sensors for Earth Resources Survey by Satellite (Royal Radar Establishment Memorandum 2594, 1970).

266

¹⁸ EMI Electronics Ltd., Handbook of Remote Sensing Techniques, (Prepared for the Department of Trade and Industry, Contract K46A/59, 1973).

¹⁹ de Loor, G.P., Uses of radar and thermal infra-red systems (Photogrammetria 24, 1969).

²⁰ Parker, D.C., Remote sensing for engineering of the investigation of terrain — infra-red systems (Proceedings of the 5th Symposium on Remote Sensing of the Environment, University of Michigan 1968).

²¹ Stingelin, R.W., Operational airborne thermal imagery surveys (Geophysics 34 [5], 1969).

²² Wolfe, W.L. (ed.), Handbook of military infra-red technology (Office of Naval Research, Department of the Navy, Washington D.C. 1965).

²³ Cantrell, J.L., Infra-red geology (Photogrammetric Engineering 30, 1964).

²⁴ Colwell, R.M. *et al.*, Basic matter and energy relationships involved in remote reconnaissance (Photogrammetric Engineering 29, 1963).

²⁵ Bastuscheck, C.P., Ground temperatures and thermal infra-red (Photogrammetric Engineering 36, 1970).

²⁶ Abdel-Hady, M., Abdel Hafez, M.A. and Karbs, H.M., Sub-surface drainage mapping by airborne infra-red imagery techniques (Proceedings of the Oklahoma Academy of Science 50, 1970).

²⁷ Blythe, R. and Kurath, E., Infra-red images of natural subjects (Applied Optics, 7, 1968).

²⁸ Chase, M.E., Airborne remote sensing for groundwater studies in a prairie environment (Canadian Journal of Earth Science 6, 1969).

²⁹ Fischer, W.A., Moxham, R.M., Polcyn, F. and Landis, G.M., Infra-red surveys of Hawaiian volcanoes (Science 146, 1964).

³⁰ Harris, E.D. and Woodbridge, C.J., Terrain mapping by use of infra-red radiation (Photogrammetric Engineering 30 [1], 1964).

³¹ Mattson, J.O., Infra-red thermography — a new technique in microclimatic investigations (Weather 24, 1967)

³² Stingelin, R.W., An application of infra-red remote sensing to ecological studies, Bear Meadows Bog, Pennsylvania (Proceedings of the 5th Symposium on Remote Sensing of the Environment, University of Michigan 1968).

³³ Vermeer, J., Interpretation of radar and infra-red images (De Ingenieur, JRG 82, NR 33, Technisch Wetenschappelijk Onderzoek 6, 1970 — in Dutch, English synopsis).

³⁴ Weaver, D.K., Butler, W.E. and Olson, C.E., Observations on interpretation of vegetation from infra-red imagery in P.L. Johnson (ed.), Remote Sensing in Ecology (University of Georgia Press 1969).

35 Myers, V.I. and Heilman, M.D., Thermal infra-red for soil temperature studies (Photogrammetric Engineering 35, 1969).

36 Rowan, L.C., Offield, T.W., Watson, K., Cannon, P.J. and Watson, R.D., Thermal infra-red investigations, Arbuckle Mountains, Oklahoma (Bulletin of the Geological Society of America 81, 1970).

37 Sabins, F.F., Thermal infra-red imagery and the application to structural maping in Southern California (Bulletin of the Geological Society of America 80 [3], 1969).

38 Waldrop, H.A., Thermal detection of glacial gravel. Yellowstone National Park, Wyoming (United States Geological Survey Professional Paper 750–B, 1971).

39 Weigand, C.L. et al., Detailed plant and soil thermal regimes in agronomy (proceedings of the 5th Symposium on Remote Sensing of the Environment, University of Michigan 1968).

40 Wolfe, E.W., Thermal infra-red for geology (Photogrammetric Engineering 37, 1971).

41 Marlatt, W.E., Remote and in situ temperature measurements of land and water surfaces (Journal of Applied Meteorology 6, 1967)

42 Lorenz, S., Temperature measurements of natural surfaces using infra-red radiometers (Applied Optics 7 [9], 1968).

43 McAlister, E.D. and McLeish, W., A radiometric system for airborne measurement of the total heat flow from the sea (Applied Optics 9 [12], 1970).

44 Platt, C.M.R. and Troup, A.J., A direct comparison of satellite and aircraft infra-red (10–12 μm) remote measurements of surface temperature (Proceedings of the 5th Symposium on Remote Sensing of the Environment 2 [4], 1973).

45 Wendland, W.M. and Bryson, R.A., Surface temperature patterns of Hudson Bay from aerial infra-red surveys in P.L. Johnson (ed.), Remote Sensing in Ecology (University of Georgia Press 1969).

46 Lattman, L.H., Geologic interpretation of airborne infra-red imagery (Photogrammetric Engineering 29, 1963).

47 Cooke, R.V. and Harris, D.R., Remote sensing of the terrestrial environment; principles and progress (Transactions of the Institute of British Geographers 50, 1970).

48 Schaber, G.C. and Gumerman, G.J., Infra-red scanning images: an archaeological application (Science 16, 1969).

49 Miller, L.D. and Cooper, C.F., Analyses of environmental and vegetative gradients in Yellowstone National Park from remote multispectral sensing in P.L. Johnson (ed.), Remote Sensing in Ecology (University of Georgia Press 1969).

268

⁵⁰ Lougeay, R., Patterns of surface temperature in the alpine/periglacial environment as determined by radiometric measurements in V.C. Bushnell and R.M. Rayle (eds), Iceland Ranges Research Project, Scientific Results, vol. 3 (American Geographical Society, New York, and Arctic Institute of North America, Montreal 1972).

⁵¹ England, G. and Morgan, J.C., Quantitative airborne infra-red mapping (Proceedings of the 3rd Symposium on Remote Sensing of the Environment, University of Michigan 1965).

⁵² Williams, R.S. and Ory, T.R., Infra-red imagery mosaics for geological investigations (Photogrammetric Engineering 33, 1967).

⁵³ Munn, R.E., Descriptive micrometeorology (Academic Press, New York and London 1966).

⁵⁴ Evans, R., Air photographs for soil survey in Lowland England: soil patterns (Photogrammetric Record 7 [39], 1972).

⁵⁵ Lenschow, D.H. and Dutton, J.A., Surface temperature variations measured from an airplane over several surface types (Journal of Applied Meteorology 3, 1964).

⁵⁶ Robinson, N., Solar Radiation (Elsevier, Amsterdam 1966).

⁵⁷ Wein, R.W. and West, N.E., Physical microclimates of erosion — control structures in a salt desert area (Journal of Applied Ecology 9 [3], 1972).

⁵⁸ Ramdas, L.A., Natural and artificial modification of microclimate (Weather 12, 1957).

⁵⁹ Penman, H.L. and Long, I.F., Weather in wheat: an essay in micrometeorology (Quarterly Journal of the Royal Meteorological Society 86, 1960).

⁶⁰ Downing, R.A., Remote Sensing Evaluation Flights, Thetford 1971 (Natural Environment Research Council 1974).

⁶¹ Taylor, J.A., Marling experiments to measure the modification of soil temperature regimes and relative productivity of Lancashire mosslands (Welsh Soils Discussion Group, Report No. 5, University College of Wales, Aberystwyth 1964).

⁶² Hall, B.R. and Folland, C.J., Soils of the South-West Lancashire Coastal Plain (ARC Memoirs of the Soil Survey of Great Britain, England and Wales, Harpenden 1967).

⁶³ Hodge, C.A.H. and Seale, R.S., The soils of the district around Cambridge (Sheet 188 of the ARC Memoirs of the Soil Survey of Great Britain, England and Wales, Harpenden 1966).

21 Some Observations on the Evaporation Rates from Different Crops in an Agricultural Catchment

G. RUSSELL

21.1 Introduction

In Britain it is only comparatively recently that people have begun to appreciate the importance of water as a resource. It is needed in industry as a solvent and for cooling purposes, in the home as an essential part of our diet and as a cleaning agent and in agriculture to nourish the crops we need for food. In our crowded island conflicts of water management exist. High flows of water in the rivers are needed for abstraction and dilution of effluent and low flows for flood control, and a solution requires knowledge of the components of the water balance. Although rainfall and river flow can be measured easily and records stretching back for decades exist for much of Britain, the estimation of evaporation presents problems. A major advance was the development by H.L. Penman[1] of an equation which used standard meteorological measurements to estimate the potential evaporation, or the evaporation which would take place from a short sward of grass freely supplied with water. This, however, does not give the actual evaporation, which will deviate from the calculated value because of effects of the type of crop and its stage of growth, the amount of water in the soil and the weather conditions. Neglect of these factors may cause serious errors in the evaporation estimates. Crop evaporation can be calculated from measurements of the gradients of water vapour and wind above the canopy. The gradient method is indispensable for finding the rate of evaporation over periods of hours, but the expense of the system, the need for maintenance and the errors induced in certain conditions limit its usefulness over longer time-periods. This paper presents and discusses estimates of evaporation made over a period of five years, by a different method, in fields subject to normal agricultural practice.

21.2   Method

For any period of time the water balance of an area can be represented by the following equation:

$$P - S = E + U + \Delta M$$

In this P represents precipitation including irrigation; S is the surface runoff, the water which is neither evaporated from the site nor absorbed by the soil; E is the amount of evaporation including transpiration, which is by far the major part of water use in summer; U is the amount of water lost by drainage or gained from a water table; M is the change in the amount of water stored in the soil. All these are expressed as mm of water.

Rainfall and the change in the soil water content were recorded throughout the study. The rainfall was measured at one place for each site but the variability of the soil necessitated the replication of the soil water measurements. The latter was determined at 10 cm increments down to a depth of 1·8 m using a neutron probe which allowed non-destructive measurements to be made quickly and easily. The surface runoff was considered to be insignificant for the sites under investigation, although it has possibly occurred on the barley plots after heavy rains before a soil water deficit has built up. Drainage however, was significant and prolonged and so ways had to be found to separate the change in water content due to drainage from that due to abstraction by the plant roots.

Two independent methods were used to achieve the separation. The original method, which was developed during the course of the work, was based upon graphical interpretation of the neutron probe data. Examination of the graphs of water content against time for any depth revealed that the gradual decrease in water content due to drainage would suddenly give place to a faster rate of loss. It was assumed that this meant that the drainage from that depth had ceased and was replaced by a more vigorous extraction of water by plant roots and the subsequent release to the atmosphere as transpiration. By finding this time and its corresponding water content for each depth, the zone from which water was removed by the plants was identified for the period of interest. It was assumed that any water gained from the soil outside this zone and any water which was lost from this zone as drainage would be small and tend to balance. Another method, which gave slightly different results, was used as a check and when it proved difficult to use the previous method. In the soil all water moves in response to gradients of hydraulic potential from areas of high to areas of low potential. The hydraulic potential was determined by the use of tensiometers and soil water release curves, and this allowed the direction of movement of the soil water to be deduced and the separation to be performed. These methods are further discussed by Williams[2] and McGowan.[3]

After this step it was easy to calculate the evaporation by adding the rainfall to the change of water content due to the plants. This method of estimating evaporation has been checked against micrometeorological estimates over short periods. Water content and rainfall were measured concurrently throughout the period of soil water deficit at intervals which were usually less than two weeks. Estimates of evaporation from barley and from pasture were made in the years 1969 to 1972 and of oilseed rape and pasture in 1973, the barley field having been sown with rape.

21.3   The experimental sites

The catchment area is situated about 20 km south-east of Nottingham and is approximately rectangular in shape, with the main stream, the Kingston Brook, following the line of the main axis westwards until it joins the River Soar. The relief is subdued, with low hills forming the watershed. The upper parts are covered in soils derived from Lias clays, the lower parts are mainly covered with a sandy drift overlying Keuper Marl. The average rainfall is about 600 mm and is distributed fairly evenly throughout the year. The most notable events were a dry period of three months in 1970, and in 1973 a dry start to the year was followed by torrential rainstorms in July so that the soil was wetter at that time than it had been during the winter.

Results from five sites are presented in this paper. Three of the sites are within one kilometre of each other and are on a sandy soil. Site A was sown to spring barley during the years 1969 to 1972 but the rotation was changed and oilseed rape was sown in 1973. Estimates of soil water were made at four places in the field. Site B contained three access tubes in a field of pasture in which the dominant species were ryegrass (*Lolium perenne*), clover (*Trifolium repens*) and Yorkshire Fog (*Holcus lanatus*). Although the soil of these two sites differed in certain respects, the amount of available water in the top 1·1 m was similar, being 104 mm for Site A and 108 mm for Site B. Site C was in a narrow belt of woodland containing Beech (*Fagus sylvatica*), Sweet Chestnut (*Castanea sativa*) and Sycamore (*Acer pseudoplatanus*).

Results are presented for sites D and E for 1970 and 1972 only. Site D was in a sandy field which was sown to barley in 1970 and 1972 while Site E consisted of a number of smaller plots scattered about in the clay part of the catchment and on which pasture similar to that of Site B was growing. There were six access tubes in Site D and ten in Site E.

21.4   Results

Tables 21.1, 21.2 and 21.3 give the monthly evaporation for each of the six months from May to October, which will be referred to as summer in this paper. Before they are discussed some more general observations can be made.

It has commonly been assumed that there is a certain value of soil water content — field capacity — to which the soil will drain in a few days after it has been wetted thoroughly and below which the rate of drainage will be slow. Unfortunately this does not hold true for the sandy soils of this study, which lose water steadily for weeks after wetting. For the purpose of calculating soil water deficit and available water, the value of field capacity chosen is the water content at which the roots begin to abstract water. These values are remarkably similar from year to year especially below a depth of 0·3 m. The available water for each site has been calculated by subtracting the amount of water held at a potential of −15 bars from the field capacity and summing these values to a depth of 1·1 m. On only a few occasions did the barley plants and the plants of the grass sward take water from depths greater than this and in wet years the reserves below 0·8 m might not be used at all. The maximum rooting depth was confirmed by excavating the sites at the end of the study. It was also shown that most of the roots occurred in the top 0·3 m, which corresponds to the plough layer in the barley field. The trees were found to take up water from much greater depths and there was evidence for an upward movement of water from a depth of 2·5 m.

To calculate the soil water deficit a base water content from which to reckon the difference is needed. This presented some difficulties because it was not easy to determine just when the plants began to remove water from the surface horizons. However, the errors are not thought likely to be large. Studies of the water content in winter have revealed that the soils may not be fully wetted up till spring. The hydrological year should begin towards the end of March when the soils are wet but the plants have not started to transpire.

21.4.1   *The evaporation from barley*

Some indication of the size and variability of the summer evaporation

274

from barley can be gained from the results taken in four consecutive years which are set out in Table 21.1. The data obtained in 1969 is, however, a little suspect as troubles were experienced with the neutron probe. Although the June evaporation of 102 mm seems high compared with other years it is certainly possible.

Table 21.1

Monthly evaporation from a field of barley (mm)

Site	Year	April	May	June	July	Aug.	Sept.	Total
A	1969	30*	55	102	81	37	34	339
A	1970	30	67	53	41	37	32	260
D	1970	30*	70	64	36	19	37	256
AA	1971	30	61	71	73	37	34*	306
A	1972	23	52	61	73	30	17	256
D	1972	33	66	72	65	26	22	284
Average		31	62	70	62	31	29	283

NB. Figures marked with an asterisk have been partly estimated.

Each year the crop was sown at the beginning of April, at which time the soil water deficit was zero, and was harvested towards the end of August. In April and early May the evaporation is low partly because the potential evaporation is low but mainly because the crop has not yet reached its maximum height or closed its canopy. In June and July maximum rates of evaporation are reached although there is a considerable degree of variation attributable to weather conditions. In late July and August, the crop has begun to ripen and the rate of evaporation falls. The amount of evaporation in August is also reduced because of the lower rate of evaporation after the crop has been harvested. The low September figures are for a field of stubble although they will have been slightly elevated by the presence of weeds.

Values of potential evaporation would have helped the interpretation of the results but are not yet available for the whole period, and so only qualitative conclusions can be drawn. From a consideration of the weather of each year it seemed probable that the highest monthly rates of potential evaporation occurred during May, June and July of 1970 when the solar radiation totals were high. This is reflected in the high figure for May. In spite of this, the June and July figures were well below average and the obvious explanation is that this depression was due to the dryness of the soil, which had been exacerbated by a rainfall in the three months of only 95 mm compared with the long-term average of 144 mm. By the end of June a deficit of 100 mm had been built up and remained near this value till the end of July when it reached 95 mm compared with 104 mm of available water. At this time the top 0·4 m of the soil was at or near the permanent wilting point (−15 bars). Because of this shortage of water, the amount of water evaporated in July was similar to the rainfall.

Although the effect of low soil water is pronounced on a monthly basis, it is less significant when the annual evaporation is considered. Allowing 70 mm of evaporation for the six months October to March, the annual totals range from 326 to 409 mm with a mean value of 353 mm.

21.4.2 *A comparison of evaporation from two fields of barley*

In 1970 and 1972 estimates of the evaporation from the barley growing on Site A could be compared with those for the barley of Site D. In 1970 there was little difference between the two estimates of summer evaporation, Site A losing 260 mm to Site B's 256 mm. This does disguise differences in the monthly totals especially in August when Site D was harvested after Site A. In 1972, however, the barley on Site A was sown approximately two weeks later than that on Site D, and even after this the rate of growth was slow and canopy closure was retarded. Consequently the evaporation was diminished in April, May and June compared with the better crop although the balance was partially redressed in the next two months. Thus although the maximum rate of evaporation was similar for both crops, the difference in management caused a large difference in the total amount of water evaporated: 256 mm compared with 284 mm.

21.4.3 *Evaporation from pasture*

The estimates of evaporation from the pasture sites are given in Table 21.2. From the five years of measurement of the evaporation from Site B an estimate of the long-term average can be obtained. This can be compared with the long-term average value of potential evaporation by expressing the average evaporation as a percentage of the potential. The value of this parameter rises from 55 per cent in April to 80 per cent in September, remaining near 70 per cent in June, July and August when it is presumably reduced by unfavourable soil conditions, considerable periods of stomatal closure, or both. Although the first signs of growth were noticed at the end of March, there is rarely much till the beginning of May, which coincides with the start of the high rates of evaporation. The maximum rate is attained in June and July when potential evaporation is high, but in a favourable September there can still be significantly more evaporation from this site than from bare soil.

Table 21.2

Monthly evaporation for a field of pasture (mm)

Site	Year	April	May	June	July	Aug.	Sept.	Total
B	1969	30*	55	80	81	61	44	351
B	1970	30*	58	61	50	44	37	280
E	1970	30*	43	61	46	50	39	269
B	1971	30*	59	63	67	61	43	323
B	1972	37	57	64	61	53	27	299
E	1972	34	54	61	63	46	34	292
B	1971	–	–	69	65*	53	40	–
Average		32	54	66	62	53	38	302
PE		57	84	93	91	75	47	447

NB. The figures for potential evaporation (PE) are long-term averages. Figures marked with an asterisk have been partly estimated.

As with the barley crop, 1970 is a year of special interest because of its long dry spell. The soil water deficit had reached 90 mm by the third week in June and gradually increased with minor fluctuations to 99 mm at the beginning of August. However, rain in this month reduced it to 70 mm, from which it climbed to 100 mm compared with an estimated available water of 108 mm. This large deficit is reflected in the lower evaporation in July and August although even under these extreme conditions, which are unusual in Britain, this depression is relatively small when taken over a month, being a maximum of 30 per cent below the potential.

The rate of evaporation from such a crop must be influenced by the nitrogen status of the soil which affects the growth and ageing of the crop and also by the intensity and duration of grazing. However, no information on this has been obtained here. The species of plant making up the sward may be of importance especially if they have different rooting patterns allowing them to utilise more of the water in the soil. There is a lot of untouched water at depths greater than 1·1 m.

21.4.4 *A comparison of evaporation from pasture on two different soil types*

In 1970 and 1972 estimates of evaporation from a sandy site (B) can be compared with those for a clay site (E). Although these two sites are situated about 10 km apart, the potential evaporation will be similar. Since the species composition and situation of the sites are not much different any difference in evaporation will be due to the soils. The soils appear to be quite different; the clay soils always have a higher absolute water content than the sandy soils. A very wet sandy soil holds about 30 per cent water by volume and a wet clay soil more than 50 per cent. Although the actual range of water contents encountered is similar, the sandy soil has a much greater proportion of large pores than the clay soil, so the water-release curve is a different shape.

In the dry summer of 1970, 280 mm was lost from the sandy site and 269 mm from the clay site. In the more normal year of 1972 the losses were 299 and 292 mm respectively. Although in both years more water was evaporated from the sandy site, the difference is not large when set against the intrinsic soil variability of each site, the errors in measuring rainfall and water content and the errors in correcting for drainage. These figures suggest that over a period of a month, evaporation from pasture is not significantly affected by the soil type. During 1970 the plants were certainly under stress for at times they wilted, evaporation was reduced and growth ceased temporarily. It may be that there were differences in the daily rates of evaporation, but data cannot test this. However, an explanation of this behaviour is that hydrologically the soils are similar. The available water in the clay sites was, in fact, found to be similar to that of the sandy site. In 1970 differences of soil type might have been expected to have caused differences in evaporation. As no significant differences were observed then and such long periods of drought are uncommon in this country, the annual pasture evaporation here is unlikely to be much affected by soil type.

21.4.5 *A comparison of the evaporation from barley and from pasture*

The comparison of the evaporation from barley and from pasture over a period of four years shows several important points. The absolute rate of evaporation is greater from the barley because of the lower resistance to vapour exchange above the taller crop. However, the barley ripens and is harvested in August so that the evaporation is greatly reduced, while the incoming solar energy is still great enough to cause high rates of evaporation from the pasture which is still active. The result of this is that over six months the evaporation from the pasture is about 7 per cent greater than that from barley. Although this is a consistent difference it is small when compared with the variability from year to year. An examination of the soil-water deficit shows a different picture. An extreme case of this is shown in 1970. While the deficit built up to nearly the same value in July at both sites, the reduced effectiveness of barley subsequently permitted the soil to wet up gradually while the soil of the pasture field remained drier till the beginning of September. This difference was pronounced in 1973, a year of heavy rains interspersed with periods of high potential evaporation, when the comparison was between oilseed rape and pasture. Once the rape had begun to lose its leaves the tensiometer readings showed that the rainwater penetrated further down under the rape and that it was removed much more quickly from the pasture site.

21.4.6 *Other crops*

Less information has been obtained about other types of ground cover (Table 21.3). The rate of evaporation from a strip of deciduous woodland was much higher than that for a barley or pasture field. This is to be expected, for not only is the turbulent exchange of water vapour greater above tall plants – and this is enhanced in this case by the greater exposure of a narrow strip of woodland – but also the tree roots extend through a greater volume of soil. This latter point is shown well in 1970 when the woodland is less affected by the drought than the barley and pasture, the evaporation hardly differing from the 1973 value. Nevertheless, this high rate of evaporation is not significant in relation to the water balance of the whole catchment because the woodland only occupies 2 per cent of the catchment area. Unfortunately it would be unjustified to extrapolate from this to consider what would happen if the whole catchment were tree- covered, because of the likely difference between large blocks and narrow strips of woodland.

Table 21.3

Monthly evaporation for other crops (mm)

Site	Year	April	May	June	July	Aug.	Sept.	Total
C	1970	51	48	84	90	72	58	403
C	1972	27	75	92	83	63	58	398
A	1973	–	–	80	–	38	–	–

Site C was a woodland site, site A was sown with oilseed rape.

The other crop investigated was oilseed rape. Because of the intense rain in 1973 it only proved possible to estimate evaporation in June and August. This crop differed from barley in two main ways: it was taller, suggesting a higher rate of evaporation, and its leaf area fell rapidly by the end of June as the leaves withered and died. By August the field consisted of stems supporting only pods — all the leaves having fallen off — and the evaporation would be expected to be low. In June the evaporation from the rape was 80 mm, considerably more than the 69 mm from the pasture, whereas the situation was reversed in August with the rape losing 38 mm to the pasture's 53 mm. This shows well how the duration of a crop is as important as its maximum rate of evaporation in setting the total evaporation.

21.5   Conclusions

Estimates of evaporation have been presented for a number of sites in several years and have shown certain similarities and certain differences. It is necessary, however, to consider how important the differences are. A statistical test of significance can be made but cannot take into account the many possible sources of error, and so it is of limited utility. The most important criterion for assessing differences depends on the practical use to which the results are to be put. The engineer who is interested in water resources needs to know the evaporation. These results show that the evaporation from barley as a representative of cereals and from pasture are similar, with the differences being less than the year-to-year variability. The farmer and the flood-control engineer are interested in soil-water deficits, in the amount of water left in the soil which the plants can abstract or in the amount of rainfall which can be absorbed. These results show that differences are liable to be important between pasture and cereals, especially in the latter part of the year after harvest when the pasture soils are usually much drier than those under barley.

Also shown is the large variability in evaporation from one type of crop due to difference in management and growth. This is much more important than a differences in soil type, the effect of which seems to be insignificant, at least for the soils studied. Finally, these figures show the overriding influence of weather on evaporation.

References

[1] Penman, H.L., Natural evaporation from open water, bare soil and grass (Proceedings of the Royal Society A193, 1948).

[2] Williams, J.B., The water balance of an agricultural catchment, PhD thesis, University of Nottingham 1971.

[3] McGowan, M., Depths of water extraction by roots (Proceedings of the Vienna Symposium (IAEA) on Isotope and Radiation Techniques in Soil Physics and Irrigation Studies 1973).

22 Soil Water Budgets and the Suitability of Marginal Areas in Uganda for Crops

Dr L.W. HANNA

22.1 Introduction

Water availability is the most important single factor in limiting the growth of agricultural crops in Uganda. The detailed relationships between dry-matter production or economic yield and environmental factors are difficult to determine without long-term trials. Experience with most commercial crops has been restricted until very recently to the densely settled and most favoured climatic areas. Fluctuations in yields of these crops at a few sites largely reflect the variations in soil-water conditions, since at each site soil fertility and farming practice have remained fairly constant. Radiation and temperature in Uganda vary little from year to year at any one site so that the dominant meteorological factor affecting growth is the highly variable rainfall. It has been possible to find close relationships between final yields of tea and sugar cane and soil-water parameters for the humid areas of southern and western Uganda, but the validity of these results in other areas of Uganda with very different climates can only be tested by field experiments and pilot planting schemes.[1, 2]

Food crops are more widespread and experimental data are now available from agricultural research stations which are scattered throughout Uganda and represent a very wide range of environmental conditions. The problem then is comparability of yield data and one would expect the relationship between yield and soil-water parameters to be partly masked by other environmental variables such as soil fertility, temperature or disease which may be difficult to measure yet contribute significantly to the yield variation. Nevertheless, the use of a single variable which leaves some unexplained variation in yield is useful in testing the suitability of areas of agricultural expansion since some of the data on which it is based was derived from marginal areas of crop-growing. This has the merit of being more realistic than long-term experiments at a single site, controlled to eliminate as many variables as possible. Maize, because of its increasing popularity as a food crop in East Africa and the adaptability of its hybrid varieties to different rainfall regimes, provides a useful example of the agro-climatological problems of establishing annual food crops in areas with little or no experience of the crop.

22.2 The maize crop in Uganda

Maize was recently introduced into Uganda following the adoption of successful hybrids in the Kenya highlands in the first two decades of this century. An estimated 100,000 ha equivalent of maize in pure stand is cultivated fairly widely in Uganda, though its demands for reliable water have contained its importance to the south-east and southern parts of the country, though even here it represents less than 30 per cent of the cultivated land. It is generally planted to take advantage of the first rains in southern and eastern Uganda, while the cash crop cotton is planted at the end of the first rains, usually in the period May to July. In northern Uganda it is restricted to the single rainy season and so competes with the cash crops. The planting of maize in the north depends on the length of this rainy season and, especially where this is inadequate or erratic, millet is the dominant food crop.

The introduction of maize into new areas is dependent on its chances of success under the variable rainfall of Uganda. Some water stress is inevitable even in the most humid areas, and it is important to assess the degree of stress which can be tolerated by the plant. Through the development of different varieties the plant is able to cover a wide range of climatic conditions. For example, some recent hybrids introduced to the semi-arid areas of Kenya experience much less water stress than the traditional varieties. Dagg[3] has shown that under the conditions at Muguga, Nairobi, the critical period of growth when the plant is silking will have reduced water stress if shorter-term varieties are grown. The limits to the growth of maize throughout East Africa have been suggested as the length of the rainfall period and altitude;[4] however, no attempt has been made to delimit these precisely.

Maize is one of the least demanding crops as far as water is concerned when compared with perennial crops such as tea or the 2-year crops of sugar cane which make high water demands throughout most of the cycle. It is on the basis of a maize crop that a threshold of 750 mm (30 in) annual rainfall (Fig. 22.1) was considered the limit of agricultural settlement.[5] However, annual totals do not give information on the rainfall distribution within the year and the problem is essentially one of matching the cycle length with known water demands with the period of water availability. Varieties have been developed for Kenya to utilise two 80-day wet periods, two 90- to 100-day wet periods or a single 150- to 180-day wet season. The success of this versatile crop can only be assessed in terms of its economic yield. Since water needs and growth rates vary with variety, relationships between water availability and crop yields for one variety cannot be applied to all maize crops with equal confidence.

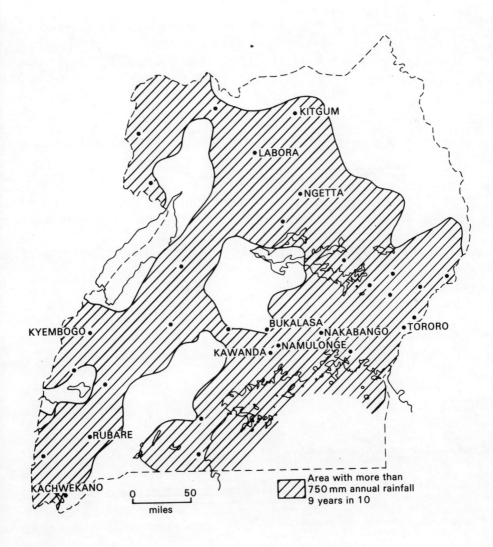

Fig. 22.1   Agricultural research stations — Uganda.

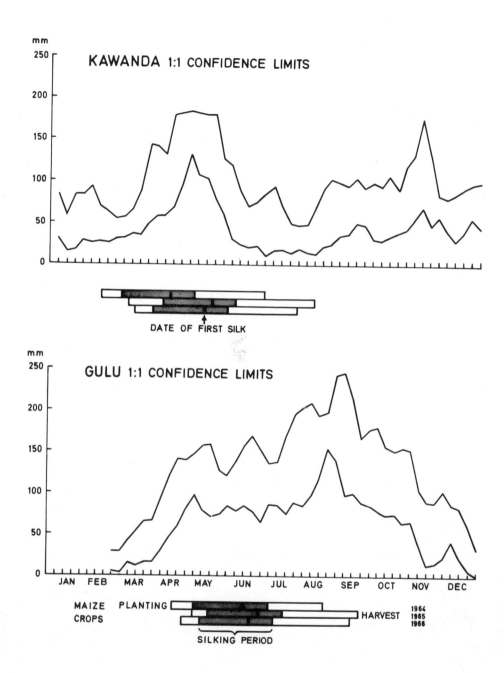

Fig. 22.2 Phenological periods for maize crops and the pattern of rainfall

286

22.3   Yield data and water budgets at experimental sites

In the years 1964, 1965 and 1966 variety trials at a number of research stations in Uganda provided yield data for a total of 79 crops of the maize plant 5314 RRM/58, which could be compared with estimated soil-water conditions. Because of the short run of years at each site it was necessary to group the data from all the trials into one sample for regression analysis. While daily rainfall was available for most of the sites, the meteorological data necessary for estimating potential evapotranspiration, Penman E_0, was only available at or near nine of the trial sites while two other sites had US Weather Bureau Class A evaporation pans which could be corrected for excessive advection in the dry periods to give estimates comparable to Penman E_0. Only seven of the eleven stations had complete records of maize crops for each of the three years so that in all twenty-seven crops during the period 1964–66 could be analysed on the basis of accurate soil-water estimates. It would be difficult to increase the sample without introducing serious errors in the water balance through inaccurate estimates of potential evapotranspiration.

As yet no lysimeter studies have been made for maize in Uganda. Water balances for maize in Kenya have been based on an E_t/E_0 curve derived from studies in the United States[3] and subsequent lysimeter studies at Mwea, Kenya confirm the general shape of the curve of E_t/E_0 ratios, though the maximum reached 1·6 for one crop in 1967 but in the following year it was nearer to the 1·0 maximum in the US study.[6] The E_t/E_0 ratios were taken as 0·45 after planting, rising to 1·0 in July and falling more steeply to 0·45 again at harvest. The Kenya crops had 209-day cycles and the short-term varieties 184-day cycles and it was necessary to fit these curves to the generally shorter cycles in Uganda, averaging 140 days but ranging from only 115 days for a cycle at Lira to 177 days at Kachwekano near Kabale. These theoretical E_t/E_0 curves were applied to smoothed daily E_0 values to derive daily E_t throughout each plant cycle.

The availability of soil water is a function of rainfall, E_t and soil-water storage. In East Africa it has been demonstrated that crops can transpire at a uniform rate from field capacity to permanent wilting point and thus E_t was not reduced according to the fraction of available soil water in the root zone. Planting usually follows a dry season, so that soil-water storage is low, and in the more arid areas is frequently zero at the beginning of the cycle. However, to avoid errors due to rainfall arriving before the planting period or the complete absence of a dry season, which can happen in southern Uganda, daily water balances were calculated for the month

287

preceding planting. The low demand for water early in the plant's life ensures a rapid filling of the soil profile though in some cases the complete root range does not reach field capacity until after silking (Fig. 22.3). In the drier areas of northern Uganda a single rainy season does not completely fill the profile. When the rainfall is less than E_t water is assumed to be extracted from the surface downwards, and this process is only arrested when precipitation is in excess of the water requirements and the surface layer is recharged. Using this procedure it is possible to estimate the position of available soil water throughout the root range and this is demonstrated diagrammatically in Fig. 22.3. In these diagrams available soil water (A.W.) is shown within the column from 0 mm A.W. on the surface to 200 mm A.W. at the extremity of the root range. The assumption of an available soil-water capacity within the root range of 200 mm is based on the normal rooting depth of 150 cm and an average of 127 mm A.W. m^{-1} soil. Water content of Uganda soils varies considerably and depends on texture and organic content.[7]

For soils with poor retention or which have the root zone confined by water tables or rock the available water capacity is much less. If it is 100 mm A.W. instead of 200 mm A.W., wilting point in this profile will be much earlier. However, the pattern of water availability will not differ from the 200 mm A.W. regime demonstrated in Fig. 22.3 except that it will be truncated at the 100 mm level. The question of the capacity of the root range becomes critical only if the plant is sensitive to the presence or absence of soil water in the deepest layers of the soil.

22.4 The relations between water and maize yields

The performance of maize has been related to water using a variety of indices. Studies in North America have used soil-water deficits or the difference between field capacity and available soil water,[8] and Dale and Shaw[9] developed the concept of moisture stress for the maize crop. Baier and Robertson[10] calculated soil-water budgets based on meteorological data and demonstrated the value of subdividing the surface 10 mm A.W. into six layers. It has been suggested that the response of the maize plant in East Africa is different,[4] but this can only be resolved by a careful analysis of yield and soil-water conditions.

A general relationship has been developed between rainfall and maize yields in Western Kenya[11] suggesting an optimum of 750 mm during the maize cycle, April–August, with yields decreasing with lower rainfall and also with rainfall in excess of the optimum. Glover has explained the

Fig. 22.3   Soil water for the three cycles of maize

depression in yields with excessive rainfall by the effect of increased cloudiness and therefore reduced energy for growth. Seasonal rainfall is a coarse guide to soil-water conditions, for severe stress in the young stage does not affect final yield so severely and the young plant is drought-resistant. [12] The period of silking is critical and during this period of maximum demand stomatal damage caused by wilting can have disproportionate effects on final yield and if prolonged can lead to crop failure. Dale and Shaw[9] defined the critical period as six weeks before and three weeks after silking, and this nine-week period they considered most sensitive to soil-moisture stress. Excessive rainfall is detrimental largely due to nutrient leaching, and in the early stages waterlogging can cause roots to die back, and with shallow roots the plant is more susceptible to drought later in its life cycle.

22.5   Maize yields and soil-water availability in Uganda

An assessment of water stress for the maize crops at each of the experimental sites was derived from the soil-water budgets already described. For this study the silking period defined by Dale and Shaw was adopted and for this period the absence of available soil water estimated on a daily basis for depths equivalent to the ranges 0–25 mm, 0–50 mm and 0–100 mm A.W. There were very few days at some stations where drying proceeded throughout the root range to the maximum 200 mm A.W. If the soil profile is dried throughout the range 0–100 mm A.W. the shallower layers will also be dried out, though some days with dried-out surface layers could retain water at greater depths. Each of the ranges was used, though intercorrelated, to find the most sensitive layer for soil-water availability.

Since previous work on the maize plant has suggested that excessive water is more detrimental than drought in the early growth period, an estimate of waterlogging in the surface layer during the period preceding silking was attempted. This was done by accumulating the number of days that the soil profile was at field capacity or that rainfall exceeded daily E_t and the profile was filling.

Using these soil-water variables a stepwise regression with final yield as the dependent variable was calculated. The most significant variable was the number of days that the layer of soil equivalent to 0–50 mm A.W. was completely dry (Fig. 22.4):

$$Y = 1902.88 - 44.45\,X_1 \qquad (r = 00.68) \qquad (22.1)$$

where Y = yield of maize in lb/acre, X_1 = days with no available soil water in the range 0–50 mm A.W.

Using the test of Ezekiel and Fox [13] this regression was found to have a true correlation coefficient not less than 0·45 at the 95 per cent level. The number of days with no soil water in the ranges 0–100 mm A.W. and 0–25 mm A.W. were closely correlated with X_1 so that the regression coefficients could not be identified with any certainty and provided little further explanation. The variable for the pre-silking period, that is the number of days with field capacity in the surface layer, was also not significant (Fig. 22.4) and showed a high correlation with X_1.

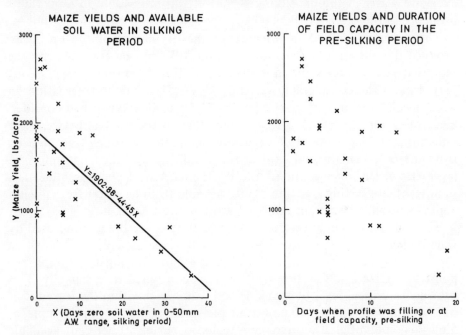

Fig. 22.4 Maize yields and available soil water in silking period and duration of field capacity in the pre-silking period.

While a single soil-water variable is desirable for purposes of testing the suitability of marginal areas for the maize crop it is worth considering why this provides the most significant linear regression and explains 47 per cent of the yield variability. In all trials used in this analysis the maize was planted near the beginning of a rainy season, but since the date of arrival of the rains and their intensity can vary considerably from year to year the water balance of cycles was not consistent. If the rains arrive early then the heaviest rainfall can occur during the early life of the maize plant, which will produce conditions of field capacity during a large proportion of the pre-silking period. Also, the rain will tail off and finish earlier so that stress will coincide with the silking period. Both conditions will be effective in reducing yields. If on the other hand the rainy season arrives later than usual, the pre-silking period will be dry, encouraging root extension with drought-resistant seedlings, and the heavy rain will coincide with the period of maximum water demands during silking. The farmer's difficulty in fitting a plant cycle to a fairly short and variable wet season can explain the correlation between duration of field capacity at the beginning of the cycle and the duration of water stress during silking. Thus despite the sound physiological reason for the importance of excessive water in the pre-silking period, it was impossible to separate its influence in this analysis.

The apparent lack of significance of the drying-out of the profile to produce deficits of the order of 100 mm A.W. can be explained by the fact that many cycles did not experience this condition for very long periods, and the considerable variation in yield was due to fluctuations in water availability in surface-soil layers. These shallow layers had considerable soil-water changes due to the fact that in the interval between the rainstorms the layer could be dried out completely through transpiration from the crop. This would explain the significance of the 0–5 mm A.W. layer. However, drying out of the 0–25 mm A.W. layer was much less significant, suggesting that the plant was able to draw water from greater depths without any serious effect on growth rates.

The availability of soil water was also estimated by the method used by Dale and Shaw[9] in the United States. Using some experimental work on the maize plant these workers devised a graph showing the turgor loss point for maize as a function of evapotranspiration at field capacity. This provided a critical level of available soil water held within the top foot of soil with approximately 50 mm available water capacity. For example, at 5 mm/day potential E_t, turgor loss would occur at 50 per cent available water capacity. Non-stress days were counted for the silking period of each cycle and correlated with yield.

$$Y = 33.10 \, X_2 - 29.12 \quad (r = + 0.66) \tag{22.2}$$

where Y = yield of maize in lb/acre, X_2 = non-stress days.

This does not improve the level of explanation provided by regression (22.1), and since it involves much more complicated analysis of the daily water balance it is less attractive for agricultural users.

There are many other factors influencing yield besides soil-water conditions. Crop density should affect the yield per acre, though under dry conditions lower crop densities would be partly offset by reduced water demands so that available soil water would be under-estimated in those calculations. Also cycle lengths could affect growth and weight of grain harvested. Their importance was tested by including both cycle and stand with the soil-water parameter in a multiple regression on yield, but neither proved significant. While water has been accepted as the major limiting factor to crop growth in this study the effect of incoming radiation on photosynthesis and total dry-matter production is obviously of importance when considering contrasting areas within Uganda. The contrasts in radiation climates between northern Uganda and the southern lake-shore zone may have similar effects on the rate of dry-matter production to those found in the rain forest and savanna environments of Nigeria. [14] The effects would be much less evident with rain-grown crops than if water control were introduced by irrigation.

22.6 Marginal areas

This study suggests that the economic yield of the maize plant in Uganda is correlated with soil-water conditions in a depth of soil equivalent to 50 mm available water capacity during the 9-week silking period. The performance of the crop can be predicted from a relatively simple soil-water budget based on daily precipitation and estimated E_t.

In dealing with marginal areas with little or no experience with the crop the problem is twofold: (a) to attempt to fit the plant cycle into the soil-water regime, and (b) to predict the level of expected yields. The first problem can be partly solved by the use of rainfall confidence limits developed by Manning [15] for the cotton crop examples of which are shown in Fig. 22.2. Griffiths developed the concept of a rainy pentade which was the central 5—day period in 15 days with a total rainfall over 1·5 in (38 mm) and attempted to define rainy seasons in East Africa as the period with 50 per cent chance of getting rainy pentades. While this provides a quantitative assessment of rainy seasons it does not give a soil-water statistic to allow prediction of crop yields. This problem is more difficult for the critical 9—week silking period which cannot be isolated in computation from a continuous soil-water regime. Daily soil-water budgets derived from meteorological data and a theoretical maize crop cycle can be simulated by computer and the planting date adjusted to find the optimum period of growth for each season. In reality it is more difficult to find the optimum planting time, and a difference of a few weeks could have a very great effect on the soil-water conditions for the crop. Assuming the planting is only attempted after sufficient rain has fallen to allow germination and the growth of seedlings, computation of soil-water budgets for theoretical maize cycles could provide seasonal estimates of yield from which confidence limits of expected yield could be derived. Estimates of crop yields have been made for tea and for sugar cane in Uganda, though in these cases the problem is less complex in that the crops' water demands vary little throughout the year. [17] For these crops it was possible to simplify the water balance and use monthly rainfall and evapotranspiration, which facilitated the analysis of long runs of meteorological data. With the maize crop, because of the short cycle one can expect a considerable variation in the yields in any one season, brought about by differences in the dates of planting and harvest, and any yield prediction at any one site must make allowances for this fact.

22.7 Conclusion

The present study highlights the major problem in agro-climatology, namely the unique pattern of water demands made by a crop. It is impossible to analyse meteorological data or to devise a soil-water statistic of value without considering the type of crop. Different patterns would be developed for other crops, and since economic yield is an important consideration it would be necessary to derive different environmental parameters from experimental work. For this reason this study has concentrated on the maize crop, which demonstrates the problem associated with a short-term crop which can be planted and harvested in a single wet season. In the more marginal rainfall areas the timing of the planting becomes critical, so that the plant can avoid serious water stress during its most demanding growth period. The relationships between soil-water parameters and final yield developed at a number of sites in Uganda provide a measure of the economic significance of the rainfall pattern. The soil-water budgets take into account daily fluctuations, and any useful prediction must be based on a continuous water balance over a number of years.

References

[1] Hanna, L.W., The effects of water availability on tea yields in Uganda (Journal of Applied Ecology 8, 1971).
[2] Hanna, L.W., Climatic influence on yields of sugar cane in Uganda (Transactions of the Institute of British Geographers 52, 1971).

[3] Dagg, M., A rational approach to the selection of crops for areas of marginal rainfall in East Africa (East African Agricultural and Forestry Journal XXX [3], 1965).

[4] Brown, L.H. and Cocheme, J., A study of the agroclimatology of the Highlands of Eastern Africa (FAO/UNESCO/WMO Technical Note No. 125, 1973).

[5] East African Royal Commission, Report 1953—55, Cmd. 9475 (London 1955).

[6] Wangati, F.J., The water use of maize and beans; results obtained with hydraulic weighing lysimeters, Mwea irrigation scheme (4th Specialist Meeting on Applied Meteorology, Nairobi 1968).

[7] Pidgeon, J.D., The measurement and prediction of available water capacity of ferrallitic soils in Uganda (Journal of Soil Science 4, 1972).

[8] Munn, R.E., Biometeorological Methods (1970).

[9] Dale, R.F. and Shaw, R.H., The climatology of soil moisture, atmospheric demand and resulting moisture stress days for corn at Ames, Iowa (Journal of Applied Meteorology 4, 1965).

[10] Baier, W. and Robertson, G.W., A new versatile soil moisture budget (Canberra Journal of Plant Science 46, 1966).

[11] Glover, J., The relationship between total seasonal rainfall and yield of maize in the Kenya Highlands (Journal of Agricultural Science 49 [3], 1957).

[12] Glover, J., Water demands by maize and sorghum (East African Agricultural and Forestry Journal XIII [3], 1948).

[13] Ezekiel M. and Fox, K.A., Methods of correlation regression analysis (1959).

[14] Kassam, A.H. and Kowal, J.M., Productivity of crops in the Savanna and rain forest zones in Nigeria (Savanna, vol. 2, 1, 1973).

[15] Manning, H.L., Cotton crop potential and rainfall expectation in Uganda in D.J. Bargman (ed.), Tropical Meteorology in Africa, Munitalp, Nairobi 1960).

[16] Griffiths, J.F., Bioclimatology and the meteorological services in D.J. Bargman, op. cit.

[17] Hanna, L.W., Bioclimatology and land evaluation in Uganda in B.S. Hoyle (ed.), Spatial aspects of Development (1974).

List of contributors

Professor Lord Zuckerman, OM, KCB, FRS

Dr J.P. Barkham, School of Environmental Sciences, University of East Anglia
Mr R.A. Barnes, Department of Geography, University College, London
Mr D.I. Brotherton, Countryside Commission, Cheltenham
Mr F.G. Charlton, Hydraulics Research Station, Wallingford
Dr R.A. Cox, Atomic Energy Research Establishment, Harwell
Dr S.J. Craig-Smith, School of Environmental Sciences, University of East Anglia
Dr T.D. Davies, School of Environmental Sciences, University of East Anglia
Dr A.M.C. Edwards, Yorkshire Water Authority, Leeds
Mr R. Evans, Soil Survey of England and Wales, Cambridge
Dr J.A. Garland, Atomic Energy Research Establishment, Harwell
Mr F.W.H. Green, Department of Agricultural Science, Oxford University
Dr L.W. Hanna, Department of Geography, Newcastle University
Dr Sylvia Haslam, Department of Botany, Cambridge University
Dr R.D. Hey, School of Environmental Sciences, University of East Anglia
Dr D.G. Jamieson, Water Resources Board, Reading
Dr Maureen E. Jones, Department of Geography, Kings College, London
Dr S.G. Newton, Institute of Hydrology, Wallingford
Dr P.E. O'Connell, Department of Civil Engineering, Imperial College, London
Dr R.B. Painter, Institute of Hydrology, Wallingford
Dr P.H. Phillips, Department of Geography, Massey University, New Zealand
Mr G. Russell, School of Agriculture, Nottingham University
Mr B.G. Wales-Smith, Meteorological Office, Bracknell

The Authors

Richard Hey took a first degree in Geography at the University of Bristol and completed his doctorate at the University of Cambridge in 1972. Since 1968 he has lectured at the School of Environmental Sciences, University of East Anglia. He is also a consultant river engineer and hydrologist.

Trevor Davies has a first degree and a doctorate from the University of Sheffield. Since 1970 he has been lecturer in Meteorology at the University of East Anglia.

Date Due

MAY 1 1 1997

APR 2 4 1987

NOV 1 8 2000

NOV 0 9 2001